Revisiting the Jewish Question

Revisiting the Jewish Question

Élisabeth Roudinesco

Translated by Andrew Brown

polity

First published in French as *Retour sur la question juive* © Éditions Albin Michel, 2009

This English edition © Polity Press, 2013

INSTITUT
FRANÇAIS
ROYAUME-UNI

This book is supported by the Institut français (Royaume-Uni) as part of the Burgess programme (www.frenchbooknews.com).

Polity Press
65 Bridge Street
Cambridge CB2 1UR, UK

Polity Press
350 Main Street
Malden, MA 02148, USA

ISBN-13: 978-0-7456-5219-1
ISBN-13: 978-0-7456-5220-7 (pb)

A catalogue record for this book is available from the British Library.

Typeset in 10.5 on 12 pt Sabon
by Toppan Best-set Premedia Limited
Printed and bound in Great Britain by Clays Ltd, St Ives PLC

The publisher has used its best endeavours to ensure that the URLs for external websites referred to in this book are correct and active at the time of going to press. However, the publisher has no responsibility for the websites and can make no guarantee that a site will remain live or that the content is or will remain appropriate.

Every effort has been made to trace all copyright holders, but if any have been inadvertently overlooked the publisher will be pleased to include any necessary credits in any subsequent reprint or edition.

For further information on Polity, visit our website: www.politybooks.com

Contents

Acknowledgements

My thanks go to all those who have helped me, in one way or another, to write this book: Laure Adler, Jacques-Martin Berne, Stephane Bou, Mireille Chauveinc, Raphaël Enthoven, Liliane Kandel, Guido Liebermann, Arno Mayer, Maurice Olender, Benoît Peeters, and Michel Rotfus.

Thanks to Dominique Bourel for reading the proofs.

And thanks, of course, to Olivier Bétourné for all his support.

Things have been said about the Jews that are infinitely exaggerated and often contradictory to history. How can the persecutions they have suffered at the hands of different peoples be held against them? These on the contrary are national crimes that we ought to expiate by granting the Jews imprescriptible human rights which no human power could ever take from them. Faults are still imputed to them, prejudices, a sectarian spirit and selfish interests. [. . .] But to what can we really impute these faults but our own injustices? After having excluded them from every honour, even from the rights to public esteem, we have left them with nothing but lucrative speculations. Let us deliver them to happiness, to the homeland, to virtue, by granting them the dignity of men and citizens; let us hope that it can never be a policy, whatever people say, to condemn to degradation and oppression a multitude of men who live among us.

Maximilien de Robespierre, 23 December 1789

That Céline was a writer given to delirium is not what makes me dislike him. Rather it is the fact that this delirium expressed itself as anti-Semitism; the delirium here can excuse nothing. All anti-Semitism is finally a delirium, and anti-Semitism, be it delirious, remains *the capital error*.

Maurice Blanchot, 1966

Introduction

'Nazis, that's what you are! You drive the Jews out of their homes – you're worse than the Arabs.'[1]

This accusation was uttered in December 2008 by some young fundamentalist Jews settled in Hebron, in the West Bank, who had never experienced genocide: it was aimed at other Jews, soldiers of the Israeli Army (Tzahal) who had been given orders to evacuate their compatriots, and who had also never experienced genocide.

'Nazis worse than Arabs': these words symbolize the passion that has been spreading unstoppably across the planet ever since the Israeli–Palestinian conflict became the main issue in every intellectual and political debate on the international scene.

At the heart of these debates – and against a background of killings, massacres, and insults – we find extremist Jews reviling other Jews by calling them 'worse than Arabs'. This shows how much they hate the Arabs, and not just the Palestinians, but *all Arabs* – in other words, the Arab-Islamic world as a whole, and even those who are not Arabs but who claim a stake in Islam in all its varieties:[2] Jordanians, Syrians, Pakistanis, Egyptians, Iranians, inhabitants of the Maghreb, etc. So they are racist Jews: in these words, they are comparing what they call Arabs – i.e., both Muslims and Islamists – with Nazis, *except that the Arabs are not so bad*. But the same Jews identify other Jews with people *worse than Arabs*, i.e., with the worst assassins in history, those genocidal killers responsible for what, in Hebrew, they call the Shoah, the catastrophe – the extermination of the Jews of Europe – that was such a decisive factor in the foundation of the State of Israel.[3]

If you cross the walls, the barbed wire, the borders, you will inevitably encounter the same passion, kindled by extremists who, though they may not represent public opinion as a whole, are just as influential. From Lebanon to Iran, and from Algeria to Egypt, the Jews are often, in one place or another, called Nazis, or seen as the exterminators of the Palestinian people. And the more Jews as a whole are here viewed as perpetrators of post-colonial genocide, as followers of American imperialism, or as Islamophobes,[4] the more people find inspiration in a literature that has sprung from the tradition of European anti-Semitism: 'The Jews', they say, 'are the descendants of monkeys and pigs.' And: 'America has been corrupted by the Jews; the brains of America have been mutilated by those of the Jews. Homosexuality has been spread by the Jew Jean-Paul Sartre. The calamities that befall the world, the bestial tendencies, the lust and the abominable intercourse with animals come from the Jew Freud, just as the propagation of atheism comes from the Jew Marx.'[5]

In that world, people eagerly read *Mein Kampf, The Protocols of the Elders of Zion*, or *The Mythical Foundations of Israeli Policy*;[6] they deny the existence of the gas chambers and denounce alleged Jewish plans to take over the world. It's all thrown into the brew: the Jacobins, the supporters of liberal capitalism, communists, freemasons – all are presented as agents of the Jews, witness for example the Twenty-Second Article of the Charter of Hamas, which marks a real step backwards compared with that of the PLO:[7]

> The enemies [the Jews] have been scheming for a long time, and they have consolidated their schemes, in order to achieve what they have achieved. [. . .] [Their] wealth [permitted them to] take over control of the world media such as news agencies, the press, publication houses, broadcasting and the like. [. . .] They stood behind the French and the Communist Revolutions and behind most of the revolutions we hear about here and there. They also used the money to establish clandestine organizations which are spreading around the world, in order to destroy societies and carry out Zionist interests. Such organizations are: the Freemasons, Rotary Clubs, Lions Clubs, B'nai B'rith and the like. [. . .] They also used the money to take over control of the Imperialist states and made them colonize many countries in order to exploit the wealth of those countries and spread their corruption therein.[8]

If we turn now to the heart of Europe, especially to France, we see that the same insults erupt with equal vehemence. Many essayists, writers, philosophers, sociologists, and journalists support the Israeli cause while heaping insults on the defenders of the Palestinian cause, while the latter insult them back – and both sides endlessly call each other 'Nazis', 'Holocaust deniers', 'anti-Semites', and 'racists'. On the one side are the sworn opponents of the 'Shoah business' or 'Holocaust industry', the 'genocidal Zionist state', 'national-secularism', 'collaborators' 'Judaeolaters' and 'Ziojews' (Zionist Jews). On the other, we have the fierce critics of 'collabo-leftist-Islamo-fascist-Nazis'.[9]

In short, the Israeli–Palestinian conflict – experienced as a structural split tearing the Jews and the Arab-Islamic world apart, but also as a rift within the Jewishness of the Jews or as a break between the Western world and the world of its former colonies – now lies at the centre of all debates between intellectuals, whether they are aware of it or not.

And it is easy to understand why. Ever since the extermination of the Jews by the Nazis – a tragic event underlying a new organization of the world from which sprang the Universal Declaration of Human Rights and the State of Israel in Palestine – the notions of genocide and crime against humanity have become applicable to every country in the world. As a consequence, and gradually, the so-called Western discourse of universalism has been seriously undermined. Since the most civilized nations in Europe had given birth to the greatest of barbarities – to Auschwitz – it was now possible for all the peoples humiliated by colonialism or the various forms of capitalist exploitation, as well as for all minorities oppressed on grounds of their sex, the colour of their skin, or their identity, to criticize so-called universal values of freedom and equality. After all, in the name of these values, Western states had committed the worst crimes and continued to rule the world while perpetrating crimes and misdemeanours that went completely against the principles of the Declaration of Rights that they themselves had enacted.

What we are thus witnessing is a new quarrel over universals. Whether we take an interest in anti-globalization, in the history of colonialism and post-colonialism, of so-called ethnic minorities and minorities of 'identity'; whether we focus on the construction or deconstruction of definitions of gender or sex (homosexuality, heterosexuality); whether we highlight the need to study the phenomenon of religion or the desacralization of the world; or whether we take the side of history as memory or 'memorial history' [*l'histoire mémorielle*] versus scholarly history [*l'histoire savante*], we always start with reference to the question of the extermination of the Jews, insofar as it is a foundational moment in all possible thinking about conflicts over identity. Hence the exacerbation of anti-Semitism and racism we are witnessing, accompanied by a new type of thinking about being Jewish.

As a result of the secular structures of its institutions, France for a long time seemed to be exempt from this type of conflict, to such an extent that Ashkenazi Jews living in Germany, Russia, or Eastern Europe used to dream of it: happy as God in France, they said. If God did actually live there, he would not be disturbed by prayers, rituals, blessings, and requests to interpret delicate questions of diet. Surrounded by unbelievers, God too would be able to relax when evening fell, just like thousands of Parisians in their favourite cafés. There are few things more agreeable, more civilized, than a tranquil café table outside at dusk.

But times have changed: the French model of secularism has been questioned, the Israeli–Palestinian conflict has become a major issue in civil society, and – with the appearance of claims relating to identity and religion – the French Republic has encountered new difficulties in assimilating immigrants from its former colonies. It even seems to have fallen prey, recently, to the mania for evaluating things by their origins – a mania which, in spite of politics, encourages human beings to be categorized in accordance with so-called ethnic and sexual criteria, or on the basis of the 'community' to which they 'belong'. This mania for gauging people is, in the last analysis, perhaps just a return of the repressed, since the country in which human rights were born, and the first country to have emancipated the Jews (in 1791), was also the origin, around 1850, of the first anti-Semitic theories and, in 1940, betrayed its own ideal with the establishment of the Vichy regime.

Revisiting the Jewish question, then, means reviewing the different ways of being Jewish in the modern world ever since, at the end of the nineteenth century, anti-Semitism triggered a revolution in Jewish consciousness. But this will be a historical, critical, dispassionate review, in the spirit of the Enlightenment. It will aim at giving a final answer to this question: who is anti-Semitic and who is not? How can we contribute serenely to freeing the intellectual debate from the follies, hatreds, and insults that are voiced around these questions?

In the first chapter, 'Our First Parents', a clear distinction is drawn between mediaeval (persecuting) anti-Judaism and the anti-Judaism of the Enlightenment (emancipatory and hostile to religious obscurantism): some people today would seek to identify the second form with the first in order to discredit it more definitively – they are all anti-Semitic, it is claimed, from Voltaire to Hitler. In the second chapter, 'The Shadow of the Camps and the Smoke of the Ovens', I examine the stages in the formation of European anti-Semitism, which took a political form in France (from Ernest Renan to Édouard Drumont) and a racial form in Germany with Ernst Haeckel. 'Promised Land, Conquered Land' then takes the reader to Vienna where the Zionist idea was born, conceived by its founders (Theodor Herzl and Max Nordau) as a self-decolonization, by the Arab world as a colonialist plan, and by the Jews of the diaspora as a new factor of division: one idea, three reactions, each of them as legitimate as the others.

In 'Universal Jew, Territorial Jew', this conflict over legitimacy is embodied in a celebrated debate between Sigmund Freud and Carl Gustav Jung. 'Genocide between Memory and Negation' examines the conditions in which 1948 saw the establishment of a State *of* Jews (Israel) in Palestine. The foundation of Israel responded to the need both to set up a Jewish memory of the Shoah and to judge Adolf Eichmann in Jerusalem. Over his trial, two great figures of modern Jewishness [*judéité*] (Hannah Arendt and Gershom Scholem) clashed, while in Europe the idea started to spread, beneath the surface, that the genocide was an invention of the Jews. En route, I analyse the positions adopted by various intellectuals on the question of life after Auschwitz, from Jean-Paul Sartre to Maurice Blanchot, via Theodor Adorno, Pierre Vidal-Naquet, and Jacques Lacan: what should be said, done, and thought, how can Jewish identity be redefined?

'A great and destructive madness': this is how I present Holocaust denial, a 'logical' discourse constructed as the utterance of an insane truth that falsifies the (real) truth and to which Noam Chomsky, the linguist of meaningless structures, gave his weighty authority. The last chapter, 'Inquisitorial Figures', focuses on the trials for anti-Semitism brought by certain revisionists of history with the sole aim of muddying the waters and reducing the debate on the Jewish question to a conflict over legitimacy, mapped onto an axis of good and evil.

1

Our First Parents

As Hannah Arendt eloquently points out, we must avoid confusing anti-Semitism, the racist ideology that spread from the end of the nineteenth century onwards, with anti-Judaism, which developed in the West once Christianity had become the state religion under Emperor Theodosius at the end of the fourth century. It was in this period – in other words, over forty years after the Council of Nicaea (summoned in 325 by Emperor Constantine) – that Christianity finally transformed itself into an official religion imposed by the secular power: Jesus had announced the Kingdom, and what arrived was the Church. The pagans, who had previously been the persecutors of the first Christians, were now persecuted in their turn, just as survivals of Graeco-Latin culture were eradicated: the Olympic Games were banned, and homosexuals were put to death – at that time they were labelled 'sodomites' and were already regarded as perverts because they represented an attack on the laws of procreation.

The Christian anti-Judaism which then spread throughout Europe – until the age of the Enlightenment – rested on the same principles, with one difference: for Christian monarchs, Judaism was far from being a form of paganism. So the Jew was neither the enemy from outside, nor the barbarian from beyond the frontiers, nor the infidel (the Muslim), nor the heretic (the Albigensian, the Cathar), nor the *other*, foreign to himself. He was the enemy within, placed at the heart of a genealogy – the first parent, according to the Christian tradition – since he gave birth to Christianity: the founder of the new religion was Jewish.

The Jew as bearer of Judaism was thus all the more hateful as he was simultaneously *inside* and *outside*. He was inside because he existed within the Christian world, but outside because he did not recognize the true faith and lived in a different community from that of the Christians. If Christianity was to become the only universal monotheistic religion – and Christ to cease being a bearer of the Jewish name – it still needed to be rid of its Jewish origin, which was now deemed insidious. The sexual theme of the treacherous, perverse Jew, with unnatural morals (it was claimed that Jewish women slept with goats), was ubiquitous in the anti-Jewish persecutions of the mediaeval period, and this is why the figure of the Jew was often associated with that of the sodomite and the committer of incest.

Evidence for this can be found in the astonishing legend of the Jewish curse, repeated by Jacobus de Voragine around 1260, which turned Judas into an equivalent of Oedipus, destroying the *genos* (dynasty) of the Labdacids and thus the family order too, and combining incest with parricide. Here is the story in outline: Ciborea, pregnant with Reuben, dreamt that she would give birth to an accursed child, sullied by vice, who would bring about the ruin of the Jewish people. After the birth of this son, called Judas, she got rid of him, putting him into a basket on the open seas. But the frail vessel was shipwrecked on an island whose queen was barren: she adopted the child. When he grew up and learned that he was not the son of his parents, Judas fled to Jerusalem and entered the service of Pilate. One day, the latter came to taste the apples in a neighbouring garden: Judas hurried across and quarrelled with the owner, unaware that it was Reuben. He killed him, and Pilate bequeathed on him Reuben's wife and his belongings. When he discovered that he had killed his father and married his mother, Judas went over to Jesus and became his disciple. But he later betrayed him and hanged himself.[1]

In short, throughout the long history of the mediaeval world, the Jew was simultaneously devil and sorcerer, his father's murderer and his mother's husband; but he was also both sexes in one. Furthermore, he was often described as an animal, embodying a highly particular duality of male and female: he was a union of male scorpion and female sow. In the order of humankind, he abolished the difference of the sexes and the generations, being incestuous and double-sexed (masculine/feminine), and, in the order of animal existence, he disregarded the barrier between different species, indulging in unnatural copulation. A master of poisons, of usury and knowledge, lustful and gluttonous, he was thus the incarnation of absolute horror.

The Jews were denounced as deicides until the Council of Trent:[2] in Europe they formed a 'community' that was assigned to no particular territory: a community at once visible and invisible, a wandering community. Confined to practising trades from which Christians were debarred, the Jews were accused of all sorts of repellent activities linked to their status as transgressors of sexual difference and the separation between species: bestiality, ritual murder, incest, child stealing, profanation of the host, consumption of human blood, polluting the waters, exploiting lepers for their own purposes, spreading the plague, laying all sorts of plots. But especially, and for the same reason, they were regarded as holding the three great powers proper to humanity as such: the power of finance, the power of intellect, and a perverse power over sexuality. So it then became necessary, in order to reduce the power attributed to them, to force them either to convert or to accept a continual humiliation: 'Talmud-burning', wearing elbow caps, yellow hats, or badges of infamy, and confinement within Jewish ghettoes – or 'jewries' ['*juiveries*'] – under strict surveillance.[3]

This anti-Judaism – which aimed not to exterminate the Jews but to convert them, to persecute them, or to expel them – was not a form of anti-Semitism in the modern sense, since it occurred at a time in human history when it was God – not human beings – who governed the world.

The Christian anti-Judaism of the mediaeval period actually presupposed the principle of divine sovereignty – of a single God (monotheism) – while anti-Semitism, which saw the Jew as the specimen of a 'race', and no longer as a partner in a divine covenant (even one that was decried), rested on a transformation of the religious Jew into a Jew-by-identity, the bearer of a stigma – in other words, a 'remainder': Jewishness.

Embodied up to the eighteenth century by divine right monarchs as supported by the Roman Catholic Church,[4] the God of the Christians decided the future of the world, while the God of the Jews, invisible and unrepresentable, continued to promise his people the coming of a Messiah and a return to the Promised Land. For as long as the West remained Christian, Jews and Christians had one and the same God, even though the relationship between the two groups and this one God was not identical.

For while Christianity is a religion of individual and collective faith, represented by a Church – and even more by the Roman Catholic Church – Judaism is a religion of belonging, accompanied by a cult of memory, of a thinking comprised by glosses and commentaries and obedience to ancestral rites affecting clothing, the body (circumcision), food (*kashrut*), and behaviour (Sabbath). It is based on the primacy of an original and endlessly renewed alliance (or testament) between God and his chosen people.

In other words, the Jewish religion is different from the two monotheisms to which it has given birth. Ever since they have existed, the Jews have designated themselves not simply as Jewish – in other words, as observing a religion called Judaism – but as a mythical people and a nation, springing from the Kingdom of Israel and then Judaea (Zion), with Jerusalem as its holy city. Consequently, according to the Jewish law (Halakha), every Jew remains a member of his people, even when he has ceased to practise his Judaism and even when he rejects his Jewishness by converting. And when a non-Jew converts to Judaism he becomes Jewish for all eternity, whether he wants this or not.

To be Jewish, then, is not like being a Christian since, even when he abandons his religion, a Jew continues to be part of the Jewish people and thus the history of his people: such is his Jewishness, his identity as a godless Jew, as opposed to the Jewishness of those who remain religious. This idea was never taken up by any other religion: according to Jewish law, you remain Jewish (in the sense of Jewishness) even when you have stopped being Jewish (in the sense of Judaism). And you are a Jew once and for all, without any possibility of changing, either by descent through the mother or by conversion.

The German satirist and journalist Ludwig Börne, who converted to Lutheranism in 1818 and then settled in France, the native land of human rights and the emancipation of the Jews, summed up the principle of this always suspect and forever fraught identity: 'Some reproach me with being a Jew, some praise me because of it, some pardon me for it, but all think of it.'[5]

And this people, ever since its mythic origins, has been characterized by the cult of its own memory. It never stops remembering catastrophes (Shoah) that have always been visited upon it by God, each time condemning it to exile and scattering (diaspora or *galut*), and thus the loss of its territory and its holy places: Nebuchadnezzar destroyed the First Temple built by Solomon, the Jews were taken off into captivity in Babylon, they returned from captivity, they rebuilt the Second Temple that was then destroyed by Titus – and of which only a wall of cries and lamentations (the Wailing Wall) would remain – and they were persecuted by the Romans, who renamed Judaea *Palaestina*,[6] and then by the Christians.

The history of the Jewish people is the history of eternal suffering, of profound misfortune, and of boundless lamentation that finds expression, throughout the expulsions and the massacres, in the dream – which can never be realized without some catastrophe – of a return to the Promised Land: 'The Everlasting will scatter you among all the peoples from one end of the earth to another. He will make your heart restless, your eyes languishing, your soul suffering.' Until the rise of Zionism, a result of the desacralization of the European world, the Jewish people would remain the people of memory, of looking back, perpetually awaiting an entry into history.

And when the new religion (Christianity) was proclaimed, a religion to which Judaism had given birth and which in a sense subsumed it, the Jews then had to fix the oral Law (Torah), in Jerusalem and in Babylon, in texts and commentaries (Mishnah and Gemara), so that Judaism would become an orthodox corpus of unified rules (the Talmud). Remember the land that is always promised (Eretz Israel) by Yahweh to the ancient Hebrews, the people of the Bible, wandering and nomadic; remember the land that is always lost and regained; remember the Everlasting and his uniqueness; remember Noah, the father of the ark and the covenant, Abraham, the common ancestor of the three monotheisms,[7] and Moses, the founder of the law; remember what remains of the Jew when the Jewish people is scattered and when the Jew is no longer altogether Jewish. 'Next year in Jerusalem': such is the complex fate of the Jews.

In this regard, Jewish mysticism has always borne a certain messianism of return and withdrawal, since the redemption promised by God can come about only in two ways: either by a spiritual regeneration leading to internal exile or by a concrete and collective break that finds expression in departing for the Holy Land, a land that can be granted by God only through the voice of a new Messiah.

This indeed was the choice made by Sabbatai Zevi, who, under the Ottoman Empire in the middle of the seventeenth century, proclaimed himself to be the Messiah. After inflicting severe mortifications on himself, and having swung several times from a state of melancholia to a state of exultation, he defied Jewish law and was subjected to a *herem*.[8] With the help of his disciple Nathan of Gaza, abandoning the attempt to imbue himself spiritually with God's intimate presence, he so roused the Jewish communities of the East that he convinced them to work towards the rebirth of the ancient Kingdom of Israel. He was imprisoned, and agreed to convert to Islam before being exiled to Dulcigno in 1676, abandoned by the faithful.[9]

At the end of a magnificent study of the main currents in Jewish mysticism, Gershom Scholem describes how, in its final phase, Hasidism, which had followed Sabbateanism, eventually transformed its theoretical search, and indeed its mystical quest, into an inexhaustible source of narratives: everything has become history, he says – in other words, history as memory. And he relates this anecdote, borrowed from a Hebrew storyteller (Maggid):

> When the Baal Shem had a difficult task before him, he would go to a certain place in the woods, light a fire and meditate in prayer – and what he had set out to perform was done. When a generation later the 'Maggid' of Meseritz was faced with the same task he would go to the same place in the woods and say: We can no longer light the fire, but we can still speak the prayers – and what he wanted done became reality. Again a generation later Moshe Leib of Sassov had to perform this task. And he too went into the woods and said: We can no longer light a fire, nor do we know the secret meditations belonging to the prayer, but we do know the place in the woods to which it all belongs – and that must be sufficient; and sufficient it was. But when another generation had passed, and Rabbi Israel of Rishin was called upon to perform the task, he sat down on his golden chair in his castle and said: We cannot light the fire, we cannot speak the prayers, we do not know the place, but we can tell the story of how it was done. And, the story-teller adds, the story which he told had the same effect as the actions of the other three.[10]

Even beyond the world of Hasidism, this anecdote bears witness to the sense of belonging and identity experienced by the Jews and defined as a 'remainder' and as a 'remember!', making the return to the Holy Land at once possible and impossible.

Jacques Le Goff relates how Louis IX, in the middle of the thirteenth century, behaved towards the enemies of the faith: heretics, infidels, and Jews. He regarded the first group as the worst since they had practised the faith and then denied it, thereby becoming traitors, felons, and apostates, 'infected by the stain of perversity'. He advised burning them or expelling them from his kingdom. He viewed the second group as enemies 'full of filth', but they did have a soul as they belonged to a religion. As for the Jews, 'hateful and filled with venom', he proposed that they be enslaved forever, turned into pariahs and outsiders 'subjected to the yoke of slavery'.

However, from this point of view, the Jewish religion was regarded neither as a heresy (Albigensian or Cathar) nor as the religion of the external enemy (the Saracens). It was recognized and familiar since it had given rise to the Christian religion. So the Jews needed to be protected as well as controlled. And if only they accepted conversion, they would be reincorporated within Christianity. 'How are we to describe Saint Louis's attitude towards the Jews?' asks Jacques Le Goff.

We currently have two terms at our disposal: anti-Judaism and anti-Semitism. The first concerns religion exclusively and, whatever the importance of religion in Jewish society and Saint Louis's behaviour towards it, it is inadequate. The set of problems concerned by this behaviour goes beyond the strictly religious context and activates feelings of hatred and a desire to exclude that go beyond hostility to the Jewish religion. But 'anti-Semitism' is inadequate and anachronistic. There is nothing racial about Saint Louis's attitude and ideas. Not before the nineteenth century did pseudo-scientific racial theories foster racist and anti-Semitic mentalities and sensibilities. The only term I can think of to describe Saint Louis's behaviour is 'anti-Jewish'. But this anti-Jewish conception, practice and policy paved the way for later anti-Semitism. Saint Louis is a stage on the path of Christian, western and French anti-Semitism.[11]

This is an excellent lesson in method. There are actually two ways of discussing the Jewish question. The first consists in accumulating facts and events and smoothing over differences, while the second emphasizes changing paradigms and breaks, and prevents us from projecting our own beliefs onto the past and interpreting utterances in an opportunistic way. The conclusion should never precede the evidence.

In other words, in order to discuss the Jewish question, we should favour neither the fiction of a Jewish historiography that presents an apologetic vision of victims persecuted since the dawn of time by murderous villains who always remain the same, nor the fiction of an anti-Jewish historiography resting on the claim that there is a Jewish plot whose conspirators aim to take over the world. Rather, we need to show – so as to go beyond them – how these two representations fuel each other, whenever new debates on Jewishness and anti-Semitism arise.

In virtue of this method, in which I will forebear from inventing a genealogy of the plot *against* the Jews (the symmetrical opposite of the mythology of the plot ascribed *to* the Jews), I will be claiming that, while the persecution of the Jews is ancient and proven, it has varied from one period to the next, just as the Jews have not remained self-identical throughout their history.

In this spirit, I will also suggest that we can call the history of the persecution of the Jews a 'history of anti-Semitism', though only on condition that the word 'anti-Semitism', as defined at the moment of its coining in 1879 and its massive spread as a racial ideology and a political movement, cannot be retrospectively applied to Christian anti-Judaism, and even less – as we shall see – to the anti-Judaism of the Enlightenment period.

In other words, the term 'anti-Judaism' comes with several para-digmatic variants that change with the period under study. Thus, Saint Louis's policy went beyond mere mediaeval anti-Judaism and targeted the Jew behind the Jew, without this being made explicit, and without this anti-Jewish policy being a form of anti-Semitism. The anti-Judaism of the Enlightenment, on the other hand, did not rise from any anti-Jewish policy but from a desire, shared by both Jews and non-Jews, to reform the status of Judaism as well as the status of the life of Jews in society.

Conversely, I will be claiming that, these days, the language of anti-Semitism also finds utterance, *to various degrees* and sometimes unconsciously, in almost all discourses of Christian, Islamic, or atheist anti-Judaism. This stems from the fact that anti-Semitism eventually incorporated, in its very definition, the main signifiers of hatred of the Jews. This is why the word can be kept as a generic term that enables us to designate every form of anti-Jewish discourse.

One episode of the history of Christian anti-Judaism – that of *limpieza de sangre* – shows that, at the end of the fifteenth century, which to some extent marks the end of the Middle Ages, the theme of race was present in Spain in the designation of certain people who were deemed to be repellent: these included converts, whether Jews or Muslims (Marranos and Moriscos respectively), and the descend-ants of lepers. Encouraged to convert, the Jews of the Iberian penin-sula, or Sephardim, were actually suspected of secretly continuing with their former practices while making a show of their new faith. In this way they were, as heretics, subject to punishment by the Inquisition. And, as they were powerful in society, the 'old Chris-tians', said to be 'of pure stock', labelled them as impure, or as 'pigs' (*marranos*).

Hence the appearance of 'statutes on purity of blood' that author-ized converts, by means of various documents – certificates of baptism, production of proof that one's parents were converts, etc. – to become Christians. Of course, reference to purity of blood, in *ancien régime* societies, was based on lineage and heredity, and not on biological race in the sense of the nineteenth century. But ultimately, the idea that an identity could be based on a definite stigma, even after a spiritual commitment that might have made it possible to escape from distinctive signs (yellow hat or elbow cap), was a clear indication that the status of the convert was itself suspect: a declaration of faith was not enough to turn a Jew – or indeed a Muslim – into a real Christian. Whatever the degree of their sincerity or lack of it, new Christians were definitely, in the eyes of other Christians, nothing but imposters or apostates. Hence the discriminatory laws that would be laid down over two centuries.[12] These did not prevent the great expulsion of 1492: the Alhambra Decree drove 150,000 Sephardic Jews into exile – in other countries in Europe, North Africa, and the Ottoman Empire – while 50,000 others became Christians without ever managing to ensure for themselves full and entire membership of the Catholic community.

The Marranos were in a dreadful situation. As converted Jews, they were both new Christians and new Jews. In Spain and Portugal, forced to convert, they secretly practised their faith. But, if they emigrated, they had to convert (back) to Judaism, while other Jews continued to suspect them of still being ex-Christians, culturally speaking. In this respect, Marranism can be defined structurally as a passing or transition between two existences.[13] The Marrano subject was forever a convert, and everywhere an outsider, divided against himself and a prisoner of his past as well as of his future: he was a Jew to the Christians and a Christian to the Jews. This proved a real opportunity either for fomenting rebellious ideas about faith, religion, and dogma or else for turning out real dogma-driven fanatics.

It was in Amsterdam, that unique melting pot of the mid-seventeenth century, that Spinozan deism, later to turn into atheism, gained a foothold. Baruch de Spinoza was born a Jew and never converted: he was the product of the Marrano community which had fled the Iberian peninsula in order to escape the Inquisition. In 1656, though he had not as yet published anything, he argued against the immortality of the soul and the divine status of the scriptures, thereby denying the fundamental principles of the Jewish and Christian faiths. Indeed, he was almost killed by a fanatic. To avoid scandal, the *parnassim*[14] offered him all sorts of compromise positions: 'If Spinoza had so wished', writes Henry Méchoulan, 'he could have retired to some nearby village, with a small pension granted by the community, or he might even have been able to continue the outward practice of a faith he had now lost. But Spinoza refused all compromise. By breaking away from the religion of his fathers, Spinoza was endeavouring to act on behalf of universality.'[15]

Because he refused to countenance any pretence, Spinoza was himself enacting a break that would lead him to Spinozism. In other words, he was ratifying his own exclusion (*herem*), marking this as a precondition for the future development of his doctrine. This is why his *herem* implied a deliberate non-return (*shamatta*), on both sides in the dispute. On the judges' side, this *herem* was garnished with violent curses that are found in the formulation of no other *herem* of that period:

After the judgement of the Angels, and with that of the Saints, we excommunicate, expel and curse and damn Baruch d'Espinoza [. . .] with the consent of this holy congregation [. . .] in front of the holy scrolls [. . .]. Cursed be he by day, and cursed be he by night; cursed be he when he lies down, and cursed be he when he rises up [. . .]. The Lord will not pardon him [. . .] the Lord will destroy his name from under the heavens [. . .] We order that nobody should communicate with him orally or in writing, or show him any favor, or stay with him under the same roof, or come within four ells of him, or read anything composed or written by him.[16]

It thus becomes clear why Spinoza later, in his philosophical works, attacked the Jewish religion so violently, emphasizing the way the universal hatred which the Jews aroused stemmed partly from the way they distinguished themselves from other peoples by their attachment to rites aimed at their own preservation. In so doing, he was criticizing nothing other than the intolerance and hatred which the Jews demonstrated in their 'execration' of those who dared to question their dogmas.

And, through this judgement, Spinoza was ultimately denouncing the forms of religious intolerance proper to theocratic states, also showing that the sons of Israel (the Hebrews) had invented an authentic democracy which had then decayed. Taking a new look at the argument of complaint, lamentation, and catastrophe – as Voltaire, Marx, Freud, and many others would do after him – he drew the conclusion that, as a result of their scattering and their characteristic way of living apart from other people, the Jews had brought down the hatred of other nations on their own heads – which, indeed, had enabled them to survive as a people. And, as Rousseau would do, he conjectured that the Jews might one day return to Israel: 'If the foundations of their religion have not emasculated their minds they may even, if occasion offers, so changeable are human affairs, raise up their empire afresh, and [that] God may a second time elect them.'[17]

In short, contrary to what is claimed these days by certain inquisitorial spirits hostile to the Enlightenment, Spinoza was very far from anti-Semitic – after all, David Ben Gurion proposed, in the middle of the 1950s, that the State of Israel solemnly annul his excommunication.[18] But his suggestion was not followed up.

As everyone knows, the spirit of the Enlightenment emerged with the Renaissance when the old representation of a cosmos dominated by divine power collapsed. Once, in the wake of Galileo, the heliocentric system had succeeded the geocentric system, God could no longer wield the same power over men. Human beings were thus condemned to thinking of themselves as responsible for their own destinies and for ruling their fellows. This marked the beginning of the critique of religious obscurantism in Europe, from Spinoza to Voltaire, via Kant, Montesquieu, Diderot, and d'Holbach. From now on, the point was to enlighten the world rather than helping to make it darker, to turn man into a creature of reason able to use his judgement freely in order to reject belief and false knowledge.

In the eighteenth century, as the *philosophes* continued to question religious obscurantism, enforced conversion also, of course, ceased to be perceived as a solution to the integration of the Jews. Only emancipation and then the voluntary membership of another order of the world – that of human, secular citizenship – now appeared as a possible way for the Jews to emerge from the confinement and victimization that had made them the obstinate enemies of the child to which they had given birth.

Hence the growth, especially in Germany, the home of the Lutheran reform, of a great movement, the Haskalah, which aimed to reform Judaism and make it more of a humanism, based on the use of reason (*Aufklärung*) and not just on submission and exclusion. That way, the Jews could, as Moses Mendelssohn, founding father of the Jewish Enlightenment, proclaimed, be both 'Jews *and* Germans' – and not 'Jews in private and Germans outside'.[19] They would not live as members of two mutually exclusive communities but would have two clearly defined and positive identities, one based on a more internalized faith void of any external signs (dietary rituals, various restrictions) and the other on the land where they were born: 'Conform yourselves to the morals and conditions of the land in which you have been placed, but hold steadfastly to the religion of your fathers. Bear both burdens as best you can.'[20]

In France, in order for the Enlightenment programme to be realized, people strove to go a step further and emerge from the 'burden of two identities': all that counted was human beings as subjects of law [*sujets de droit*] in their universality, freed from the grip of religion and community and thus authorized to worship as they saw fit.[21]

By the same token, the genealogy characteristic of the former monarchical order needed to be overthrown, and Christianity viewed no longer as the fulfilment of an emancipatory messianism able to overcome Judaism – by conversion, persecution, or expulsion – but, on the contrary, as an expression of the highest degree of intolerance towards all other forms of thought and thus towards *the other religion*, the 'mother religion', that of the 'first parent'. 'Judaism and Christianity', Diderot would say, 'are two enemy religions; the one labours to build itself on the ruins of the other; it is impossible to sing the eloquent praises of any religion that works towards the destruction of the religion one believes and professes.'[22] This reversal obviously meant it was possible to criticize the obscurantism of the first religion as much as that of the second. Diderot immediately added:

> We must not expect to find among the Jews any correctness in their ideas, any exactness in their arguments, or any precision in their style, in a word any of what must characterize a healthy philosophy. On the contrary, what we find among them is a chaotic mixture of principles of reason and of revelation, an affected and often impenetrable obscurity, principles which lead to fanaticism, a blind respect for the authority of the learned and for antiquity – in a word, all the defects that indicate an ignorant and superstitious nation.[23]

While emancipation led in Germany to the creation of a 'Judaeo-German' humanism,[24] in France it entailed the invention of a secular humanism, universalist in scope: the subject of human rights would be a subject – i.e., a citizen – only by being de-Judaized if he were Jewish, and de-Christianized if Christian. But he could just as much be Jewish, Christian, or whatever he wanted, so long as this was in private.

There were several tendencies running through the French Enlightenment, but overall the *philosophes* agreed on one point. They all thought, to different degrees, that the Jews would cease to be attached to a religion of tyranny and superstition when the persecution to which they were prey came to an end, and when religions – always mutually hostile – no longer governed the world and were finally subjected to the rule of reason. No more bloody wars between Protestants and Catholics, no more St Bartholomew's Day massacres, no more deaths at the stake or witchcraft trials, no more heretics or infidels: whether or not God was accessible, whether he really existed or was a human invention, he must no longer be used to divide them from one another.

Some targeted the Bible, and denounced the ancient Hebrews rather than the Jews of their own age; others, however, outlined a new future for the Jews.

Among those who embarked on the first path, d'Holbach was the most violent – and the most atheistic. He described the God of the Hebrews as a barbarian and his followers as superstitious priests, brigands, thieves, and murderers.[25] Voltaire was the most ironic, but also the most blasphemous, resorting as he did to the tones of the satirical pamphleteer: 'We find in them only an ignorant and

barbarous people, who have long united the most sordid avarice with
the most detestable superstition and the most invincible hatred for
every people by whom they are tolerated and enriched. Still, we ought
not to burn them.'[26]

Voltaire did, then, lambast the Jews for submitting to the mother
religion, but he claimed to love the Jewish people and to feel compassion for the Jews because they had suffered persecution. Thus, after
blaspheming the Hebrew religion, he attacked not merely what he
regarded as so many sects – Papists, Calvinists, Nominalists, Thom-
ists, Molinists, and Jansenists – but Christianity in particular, the
'most absurd and bloody' religion. And, making a rather sly joke, he
recommended to everyone the religion of Muhammad, as 'simpler,
without a clergy, without any mystery. In this religion, they did not
worship a Jew who loathed Jews; they did not succumb to the raving
blasphemy of saying that three gods make one god; finally, they did
not eat the one they worshipped and they did not turn their creator
into excrement.'

Among those who adopted the second perspective, Jean-Jacques
Rousseau was the most visionary about the possible destiny of the
Jews, and Montesquieu the most rigorous in his treatment of the
relation between persecutors and persecuted.

Unlike his contemporaries, Rousseau thought that emancipation
and equality, even though necessary, were not sufficient to solve
the question of the singular status of the Jewish people. They would
need, he said, to have a state of their own: 'I shall never believe that
I have seriously heard the arguments of the Jews until they have a
free state, schools, and universities, where they can speak and dispute
without risk. Only then will we be able to know what they have to
say.'[27]

As for Montesquieu, he claimed that there was a Jewish problem
only because those who persecuted the Jews had a problem with the
mother religion:

> Among Christians, just as happens among us, they display for their
> religion an invincible, obstinate loyalty which borders on fanaticism.
> The Jewish religion is an ancient tree, from which have sprung two
> branches that cover the whole earth: Mohammedanism and Christian-
> ity; or rather, it is a mother who bore two daughters who have wounded
> her in a thousand places: for in matters of religion, those who are
> closest are the bitterest enemies. But whatever cruel treatment the
> Jewish religion may have received from its progeny, it does not cease
> to take pride in having brought them into the world; it uses both of
> them to embrace the whole world, while at the same time embracing
> all the ages by virtue of its venerable life-span.[28]

In November 1791, after vehement debates that had occupied the Constituent Assembly since September 1789, French Jews of every tendency became citizens, free to worship in their own way and to enjoy every other liberty.

Rabaud Saint-Etienne launched the first salvo: 'I demand liberty for all those peoples who are still proscribed, wandering and homeless, across the face of the earth, those peoples doomed to humiliation: the Jews.'

The same proposal was supported by Abbé Grégoire, then by the Comte de Clermont-Tonnerre, and then by Mirabeau, Robespierre, and Barnave, while the more reactionary deputies protested. Several members of the Constituent Assembly went on to propose that Turks, Muslims, and men from all 'sects' should be given the same rights. Later still, another deputy, Regnault, requested that anyone speaking against the Jews should be given an official reprimand: such an action would comprise an attack on the Constitution itself.

On 13 November 1791, Louis XVI, who had been favourable to the emancipation of the Jews, ratified the law declaring them to be French citizens. The Enlightenment had led to this significant decision.

Given all this, it is clearly wrong-headed to describe the anti-Judaism of the Enlightenment as anti-Semitism when the former, unlike its equivalent in the *ancien régime*, never aimed to eliminate, exclude, or persecute the Jews, but rather to denounce the misdemeanours committed by the three monotheistic religions – Judaism, Christianity, Islam ('Mohammedanism')[29] – as well the archaic and hateful way of life of those who practised them.[30] In regard to the Jews, the great slogan of the new age was their possible 'regeneration'. This demand would be taken up by the founders of Zionism: invent a new Jew, freed from prayers, rituals, circumcision, and dietary constraints. No longer hate the Jews, but love the Jews, sometimes in spite of the Jews themselves – love them so much that you wished for them a better destiny than that of victims caught up in a spiral of rejection, persecution, and stigmatization.

To love the Jews, then, meant wishing them to be men before being Jews: free men, and no longer subjects alienated by their traditions. And this wish was one to which the Jews themselves would subscribe, so as no longer to arouse hatred or, in return, to be haunted by the catastrophe of being Jewish: 'The people of Israel', as Theodor Lessing was to say in 1930, 'is the first, perhaps the only one, to have sought within itself for the guilty origin of its sorrows. In the depths of every Jewish soul lies hidden this same tendency to conceive all misfortune as a punishment.'[31]

Certain French thinkers – philosophers and historians – convinced themselves, at the beginning of the 1970s, that the Enlightenment, in Germany and France, had merely been the original melting pot of the two totalitarianisms, Nazi and Stalinist. Since then, it has become commonplace to turn Marx, like Spinoza, Voltaire, and Hegel before him, into one of the founding fathers of anti-Semitism.[32] And, by the same token, it is claimed that the Revolution of 1789, despite having emancipated the Jews, was simply all the more odious as it led to all later bloodbaths: the Terror, the Napoleonic epic, Bolshevism, Stalinism, the 'Final Solution', and, finally, Islamist terrorism. As a result, all the subversive or radical thinkers of the latter half of the twentieth century who dared to write on the works of Nietzsche, Marx, or Freud have been criticized for supporting this abominable heritage. No one can be surprised, of course, that within such a context the bicentenary of this same revolution, deemed to be so hateful, was in 1989 celebrated under the sign of counter-revolution: Joseph de Maistre rather than Robespierre.[33]

While it is perfectly legitimate to show, for example, that the spirit of emancipation is quite able to turn into its opposite, and while it is consistent to point to the contradictions within the ideals of democracy and the Rights of Man and bring out their dark sides,[34] it is difficult to accept without demur the idea that the Gulag and genocide were already lurking in Marx and thus in Robespierre, and thus in Voltaire and Rousseau, and thus in Spinoza – in short, that anti-Semitism is to be found where, in fact, it is not.

And yet it is in virtue of this logic that a short forty-page article published in 1843 in response to two others by Bruno Bauer, and devoted to the question of Jewish emancipation in Germany, has become a sort of racialist manifesto harbouring genocidal designs. It has even been claimed, in the name of psychoanalysis, that Marx was merely a 'latent homosexual', 'anti-Marxist', and 'criminal', with a desire to eliminate the Jews so as to cope better with the failing of a father guilty of having converted to Protestantism in order to exercise the profession of a lawyer.[35] This, it must be admitted, is a fascinating way of claiming to be more Marxist than Marx while at the same time stigmatizing homosexuality.

It is known that Karl Marx's father, Heschel Levy, son of the rabbi Marx Levy, had been baptized in Trier in 1824, under the name Heinrich Marx, six years after the birth of his son. A Prussian patriot, an admirer of Voltaire and d'Holbach, he had not found it difficult to renounce his Jewishness since he considered his conversion as a step towards civilization and a liberation from all Jewish prejudice. As for the son, who was a complete atheist, his dream was to rid mankind of all religion, that 'opium of the people'.

Some writers, such as Pierre-André Taguieff, have unhesitatingly drawn on the private correspondence of the founder of communism to make him seem even more criminal and to misread the true meaning of his hostility to Judaism. And they have found what they were looking for. Marx, as fond of the art of the virulent pamphlet as Voltaire, mocked friends and enemies alike: a 'backward' Russian, an 'idiotic' Pole, a 'brainless' Frenchman, etc. As for the Jews, his co-religionists, he was inclined to attach the most malicious nicknames and adjectives to them: 'stock-exchange Jew', 'Jew Süss of Egypt', 'cursed Jew', Jewish pig', 'windbag of a Jew', 'greasy Jew', 'Slavonic Jew', 'nigger Jew', etc. And, when it came to Ferdinand Lassalle, his companion, he indulged in a hail of invective. But Lassalle made no bones about his hatred for the people of the Bible – his own people. And he lambasted the Jews in the same way that Marx did, and as Karl Kraus, the great Viennese journalist, would later do.[36]

It is all perfectly clear: the refusal to be Jewish, the dislike for the biblical narrative (so full of stories of murder), the rejection of rituals deemed to be grotesque and alienating: these were the main components in a 'Jewish self-hatred' through which, in the nineteenth century – and in Vienna far more than elsewhere[37] – the biting humour of the de-Judaized Jews was displayed, as they turned against themselves the hatred which they aroused among others. And for the German-speaking Jews, the Ashkenazi heirs of the Haskalah who no longer believed in the chosen people, or in Judaism, or in any promised land, this self-execration was the last stage in the catastrophe: 'I hate Jews', said Lassalle, 'and I hate journalists. Unfortunately I'm both.'[38]

In 1842, the question of Jewish emancipation was making its presence urgently felt in Germany. The country was composed of an agglomerate of autonomous states, all different from one another, in which Jews did not enjoy civil rights, as they would in 1871, after German unity was achieved.

It was within the context of the promotion of liberal ideas that Bruno Bauer, who belonged to the circle of Young Hegelians, endeavoured to demonstrate to the Jews that they should renounce their religion. As long as the Jews remained Jewish, he basically said, they were unripe for any emancipation. So they needed to renounce the perpetuation of their rites before laying claim to any secularization of the state. Unlike the Christians, whose religion had become universal, the Jews, as a result of their attachment to the Law of Moses, were thus in Bauer's view particularists unable to gain access to human rights.

Against this argument, the young Marx retorted that the Jews could perfectly well be emancipated without having to abandon

Judaism, but that they would be well advised to realize that obtaining civil rights would remain a pure illusion as long as the state itself rested on a theological foundation. Only a non-religious state was in a position, he thought, to guarantee the freedom of each citizen, including freedom of worship. Therefore, the question of Jewish emancipation was just a particular case of the question of human emancipation.

In this sense, Marx favoured the French model, and, at the request of the president of the consistory of Cologne, he was more than willing to draw up a petition to the Diet in favour of the Prussian Jews: 'However much I dislike the Jewish faith, Bauer's view seems to me too abstract. The thing is to make as many breaches as possible in the Christian state and to smuggle in as much as we can of what is rational. At least, it must be attempted – and the embitterment grows with every petition that is rejected with protestations.'[39]

In the second part of his article, the shortest and most controversial section, Marx maintained that the 'everyday Jews', the 'real Jews', were conditioned no longer by their membership of Judaism but by practices of life imposed on them by their persecutors that had turned them into 'money Jews' who willingly accepted the iron law of capitalism: 'The god of the Jews has become secularized and has become the god of the world. The bill of exchange is the real god of the Jew. His god is only an illusory bill of exchange.' As a result, only religious emancipation – and thus emancipation from any theologico-political state – could allow the Jews to emancipate themselves socially: 'The *social* emancipation of the Jew is the *emancipation of society from Judaism*.'[40]

So Marx was not in the slightest anti-Semitic, and his correspondence cannot be used to support such a thesis, even when it sometimes makes for painful reading. As for the pejorative mention of the Jew as a worshipper of the God of money – a common feature in the texts of traditional anti-Semitism – it did not in his case spring from any such position, but rather from a conflict which in the nineteenth century, especially in Germany, set the 'money Jews' against the 'intellectual Jews'. What Marx criticized was not the Jew as such but the Jew as he had become in the bourgeois world. So he attacked the principles of a society based on the worship of money – in which real Jews now played a full part, after initially being persecuted – but he does not see the God of money as the emanation of some Jewish essence that has corrupted mankind. In his view, it is bourgeois society that needs to be abolished and not the Jew, who, once Judaism has been abolished, will finally be able to enter history and renounce his status as a Jew in the abstract to become a historical Jew.

The mature Marx, the Marx of *Capital*, would refer to the dialectic of domination and exploitation when he remembered this internal split within his own Jewishness, that of a Judaism-hating Jew. Commodities, he said then, were 'inwardly circumcised Jews', 'a wonderful means to make money'.[41] And he contrasted this invisibility of the Jew circumcised within and transformed into a commodity with the suffering visibility of the body of the factory worker, the new chosen people alienated under Capital, as the Jews had been under Jehovah.

Finally Marx, needing to prepare the advent of communism and the proletariat, remained (perhaps unwittingly) attached not to the Jewish religion as such, but to the history of his people who, by inventing Judaism, had given birth to its enemy, Christianity. By the same process, Judaism converted to Capital was – in his view – giving birth to a new chosen people destined to subvert it.[42]

The representatives of the French Enlightenment insisted on the need to link the particular with the universal and to free the individual from any form of sovereignty – religious, monarchical, territorial, etc. – so as to turn him into a free subject, able to think for himself and thus achieve the highest dignity. In this sense, in accordance with the ideals of 1789, the people would be incorporated into a nation – in other words, a social collective defined not by borders or roots but by reference to a state of law whose responsibility it was to represent this same people.

From this point of view, the term 'nation' was akin to that of 'native land' [*patrie*], designating simultaneously one's homeland and the chosen land – the land which the citizen of human rights chose *freely* to serve and defend with his life. Thus the new hero of the Enlightenment, like the ancient Greeks, could identify with a nation that had nothing nationalist about it and a native land whose ideal he served without retreating into the shell of ethnic identity.

This was the creed of the French Enlightenment, and it was taken up throughout the revolutionary epic: to unite the people (the nation) with the elite (the free subject) so as to serve the native land – in other words, the Revolution, the Republic, the equality of men with one another – and thus the human race. We owe to Montesquieu the most strenuous formulation of this thought of the abstract universal that sought, while respecting differences, to free human beings from any particularism of identity, religion, or sexuality: 'If I knew something that was of use to me', said Montesquieu, 'and harmful to my family, I would cast it out of my mind. If I knew something of use to my family, but not to my native land, I would seek to forget it. If

I knew something that was of use to my native land, and harmful to
Europe, or useful to Europe and harmful to the human race, I would
regard this thing as a crime.'[43]

In virtue of this principle, revolutionary France was the first
country in Europe to emancipate the Jews, which meant that the
Jewish religion was to be treated the same way as other religions.
However, whatever their nationality, the Jews of the nineteenth
century found themselves faced with a dilemma: that of having to
choose between human universality and Jewish particularity.

Judaism, it has been said, is in fact the only religion to state that
you remain Jewish (in the sense of a member of the Jewish people)
when you have ceased to be Jewish (in the sense of a practitioner of
Judaism). Irrespective of any religious membership, the Jews – unlike
the Christians – are thus a people and form a nation, even if this does
not come with any territory. How, in these conditions, can they fail
to be Jewish? Mendelssohn had clearly seen the dilemma when he
recommended to his co-religionists that they should be at the same
time 'Jewish *and* Germans'.

In fact, in Germany as in France, the Jews who were inclined
towards Enlightenment humanism usually opted for conversion. For
German Jews, this was the only way they could gain civil rights; for
the French Jews, it was a patriotic choice – but also a way of escaping
from the hatred they aroused within civil society. On both sides, the
conversions and name changes gave rise to a real assimilation and
thus to a renunciation of Jewishness. But, by the same token, though
they became less visible, they did not stop being accused – the minute
a social or economic crisis blew up – of disguising themselves, or of
fomenting plots against the nation that had emancipated or tolerated
them. The civil society that had integrated them so thoroughly was
thus capable, as soon as it felt vulnerable, to designate the Jews as
an accursed share, stigmatizing them as financial speculators, a people
within the people, a nation within the nation.

And since the assimilated Jews did eventually become well and
truly invisible within civil society, it became necessary, if they were
again to be subjected to opprobrium, to replace this invisibility
acquired by assimilation with a new visibility. But how could a Jew
be distinguished from a non-Jew, now that no sign of religious
membership or separate clothing made it possible for them to be
identified? This would be the great question that spurred the
anti-Semites.

It was in France, the native land of human rights and the emancipation of the Jews, that the anti-Semitic idea was born, in the middle
of the nineteenth century, even before the term was invented, twenty

years later, in the Germanic world. And anti-Semitism would be all the more powerful in France as it was the consequence of radical emancipation.

But, in order for it to make its appearance, a radical paradigm shift would be necessary.

2

The Shadow of the Camps and the Smoke of the Ovens

The word 'nation' initially expressed all the aspirations of the peoples of Europe to be self-determining, but it turned into its opposite when the patriotic ideal inspired by the Enlightenment spirit became transformed into a communitarian project based on attachment to the soil. This was how the term 'nationalism', derived from 'nation' and invented in 1797 by the Abbé Augustin de Barruel, a sworn enemy of the Jacobins, as a way of referring pejoratively to the patriotic ideal seen as a 'masonic plot',[1] eventually became – forty years later – a doctrine based on chauvinism, the exclusion of otherness, and the primacy of the collective over individuality.

And yet, the aspiration to become a free nation had been, throughout the whole of Europe until 1850, an ideal of progress and freedom – witness the great revolutionary movement of 1848: the springtime of the peoples, the springtime of revolutions, the springtime of liberalism, the springtime of socialism, and the dawn of communism. Everywhere, Europeans called for the abolition of the monarchical *anciens régimes* that had been restored, after 1830, in every country where the Napoleonic Wars had contributed to spreading the ideals of 1789: 'A spectre is haunting Europe – the spectre of communism. All the powers of old Europe have entered into a holy alliance to exorcise this spectre', wrote Marx and Engels in 1848.[2] These revolutions were, of course, severely put down, and the aspiration for peoples to gain self-determination changed into a desire to unify not men with other men, Europeans with non-Europeans, but individual nations which would then stand opposed to one another.

From then on, every nation, now turned in on itself, could be identified with the sum of its particularisms. Thus, nationalism became a doctrine that ran counter to the original ideal of which it had been the bearer. 'The Constitution of 1795', de Maistre wrote in 1796, 'like its predecessors, was made for man. But there is no such thing as man in the world. In my lifetime I have seen Frenchmen, Italians, Russians, etc. [. . .] But as for *man*, I declare that I have never in my life met him; if he exists, he is unknown to me.'[3]

In the bourgeois France of the second half of the nineteenth century, which now scorned socialism, Valmy, and the uprisings of the starving, the term thus assumed a new significance. Far from serving to designate the union of the people and their native land, it was used around 1850 to define a community bonded by a collective soul, by resemblance and by genealogical identity. And this entity, characterized by a certain historical given, was given the name 'race'. Later on, with the development of Darwinism, a biological twist was added to this new notion, fostering the shift from a historicist or morphopsychological conception of the origin of peoples (and races) to an organicist conception. A designation based on culture or identity would no longer be sufficient: physical anthropology supplied further specifications: skin colour and the shape of the skull, ears, nose, and feet.

Against the Enlightenment spirit, German and French historicist scholars sought to rid themselves simultaneously of universalism and of the question of the origin of religions by claiming to discover a way of secularizing theology via the study of languages. Leaving behind God, faith, and myths, they set out to imagine how civilizations had begun, drawing on a science of languages – philology – whose task it was to express the national soul of different peoples and the organic body of different nations. In this way, they invented the infernal couple of Aryans and Semites, convinced that each of these two imaginary peoples was the bearer of a secret identity whose values had been transmitted since the dawn of time, so that every European nation could find its origins in them.[4] In this way, they reinvented the ancestral myth of race war – and thus of the dialectic of the conquest and enslavement of one race by another.[5]

From this point of view, the Semites, i.e., the Hebrews (and thus the Jews) had the privilege of inventing monotheism but, remaining nomadic, were incapable of creation, knowledge, progress, and culture. On the other hand, the polytheistic Aryans – confused with the Indo-Europeans – were seen as having all the virtues of dynamism, reason, science, and politics. Only Christianity then showed itself able to bring about a harmonious synthesis between Jewish monotheism, saved by Jesus, and the Aryan dynamism that had such future potential.[6]

It is easy to see how the infernal couple operated structurally, and how it later gave rise to anti-Semitism. While the Jews were, of all the Semites, the first people, people of the first religion, they became uncreative nomads, harmful, wandering, and useless, once the Christians had taken from them their most sublime possession: monotheism. So they were viewed as inferior to the so-called Aryans, who were defined as alone being able to fuse the qualities of monotheism, imported by Christianity, with the (intrinsic) qualities of an Indo-European tradition rebaptized as Aryanism – hence their superiority.

Whatever the variations on this theme – Aryanizing Christianity, Semitizing Aryanism, inventing intermediate stages between them – the proponents of this approach were consistently intent on demonstrating that Christianity was superior to Judaism, not as a religion but as a civilization; that language was an affair of race; and that Judaism, as a cultural identity, did not find itself continued in Christianity but in Islam, a culture pronounced to be just as Semitic as the culture of the Jews. Seen this way, the Muslims were of course scorned, insofar as they belonged to the Semitic camp, but the Jews were scorned even more, as they had given birth to Islam. The thesis of the 'first parent' was here immortalized while being both secularized and then 'racialized'. There was thus a shift from anti-Judaism to anti-Semitism and then to racism: the Jews were viewed no longer as followers of a religion but as Semites – and, of all Semites, as the worst – in other words, as part of a race that was historically inferior to all others.

This train of thought reveals the deep reasons why racism is bred in the womb of anti-Semitism – why, to put it another way, all racism is first and foremost the expression of a form of anti-Semitism. Let us note, first, that, while racism and anti-Semitism are two distinct manifestations – one has to do with an obvious otherness and the other with an otherness without any apparent stigma – they both converge, always, however tortuous the routes they have followed. But anti-Semitism comes first and racism second. Since Judaism was the first monotheistic and Abrahamic religion, and gave rise to the two others, when the Jews were designated as a so-called Semitic race, around 1850, they remained the first parents, no longer just because they had produced the other monotheisms, but because they had become the original basis for all primary racial projections.

Furthermore, what we find is that the shift from anti-Judaism to anti-Semitism has as its historical corollary the invention of racism,[7] itself popularized by colonialism. I will be returning to this.

Around 1848, fascinated by the infernal couple of Aryan and Semite, Ernest Renan set out to produce a great philological thesis, without knowing that it would make him one of the founding fathers of anti-Semitism. He was an *agrégé* in philosophy, fascinated by the Orient and heavily influenced by the work of Johann Gottfried Herder and Franz Bopp. He became one of the greatest Hebrew scholars of his age, a remarkable expert in ancient languages and archaic cultures, which – he claimed – revealed the secret of the way modern societies functioned. And he then conceived the crazy plan of turning philology into the exact science of mental productions and thus of the human race. It was within this context, once he had freed himself from the yoke of religion, that in 1855 he published his major study on the question: *Histoire générale et système comparé des langues sémitiques* [*General history and comparative system of Semitic languages*].[8]

When we read the five hundred pages of this work devoted to the origin of languages and mankind, when we leaf through the great saga that leads us from the study of the Bible to that of the Semitic and Indo-European peoples, we are struck by the rigour of the demonstration, and by the passion that the author brings to reconstructing an amazing mythology which, he thinks, must open the way to a science of the foundations of human nature. At the heart of this monument of erudition, saturated with bibliographical references and Greek, Hebrew, and Arabic terms, we watch the great fable of the Semite and the Aryan unfold – between '[the] sublime and [the] odious'.[9] We learn about the lives of, for example, the Hebrews, the Aramaeans, the Hevites, the Hethites, the Pherezites, the Gergezites, and the Jebusites, and we are dumbfounded to discover how much this newly promoted science may act as the basis for a web of legends that apparently demonstrate that languages are nothing other than the product of human consciousness, that all theory of language resides in its history, and that, finally, languages are nothing but an illustration of the existence of a natural inequality between the different components of the human species. Not the least rhetoric, not the least emotion, not the least romanticism, not the least renunciation of reason: this is Renan's manner – a cold passion.

And so, four years before Darwin's publication of *The Origin of Species*, this great scholar, a fervent humanist, serenely proclaimed that mankind, ever since its origins, has been composed of three types of race:[10] the inferior, those of the archaic epoch, now vanished; the Chinese and Asiatic races, materialistic, attracted to business, incapable of any artistic feeling and possessing an underdeveloped religious instinct; and, finally, the noble races, composed of two branches: the Semites and the Aryans. The former, who invented monotheism, then succumbed to the greatest decline, giving birth to Islam, which 'simplifies the human mind', while the latter, superior in every way, had become – after incorporating monotheism – the lords of the human race, alone able to ensure the forward march of the world: 'If the Indo-European race had not appeared in the world', writes Renan, 'it is clear that the highest degree of human development would have been something analogous to Arab or Jewish society, a society without philosophy, without thought, without politics.'[11]

To judge from appearances alone, some would say that the anti-Judaic imprecations of the men of the Enlightenment – from Voltaire to Marx – make for much more painful reading today than Renan's scholarly language, smooth and elegant, always careful to respect the truth of different peoples and their history. And yet, let us not be fooled. The verbal excesses of the former are merely the expression of a desire to emancipate mankind, to free it from religion, while the historicizing elegance of the latter foreshadows the coming of a doctrine of extermination. In this sense, it joins hands, despite the differences, with the tradition of persecution in Christian anti-Judaism. It will come as no surprise that Renan was the first person in France to incorporate Christian anti-Judaism within an apparent science of the historical inequality of the Semites. Though he moved away from religion – so much so that he was treated as a blasphemer by the Catholic Church for having historicized the life of Jesus – he still continued to hold to its main prejudice. He replaced the 'perfidious Jew' with the degenerate Semite, thereby making the idea of this degeneracy – and thus of this inferiority – acceptable. 'French anti-Semitism's debt to Renan is undeniable', writes Zeev Sternhell: 'it is difficult to imagine Drumont's success and his influence up to the race laws of 1940 without the respectability that – thanks to Renan – the idea of the inferiority of the Semites had acquired.'[12]

And when, in 1882, Renan spoke out for the rights of different peoples to self-determination, this was – yet again – simply so as to combat the spirit of the Enlightenment. For what he called 'nation' was not the native land of the constituent members but, rather, the kernel of nationalism, that nation which presupposed that each man was duty-bound to belong to an organic and hierarchical collective body. And Renan hated Germany. So he supported French democracy out of French nationalism.[13]

This was quite different from Nietzsche's revolt against the French Enlightenment. Keenly interested in philology, the German philosophy never succumbed to the passion of anti-Semitism, despite the claims of those who make him out to be a precursor of Nazism.[14] Nietzsche did not like Christianity (a 'slave religion'), or socialism, or democracy, or the masses, or nationalism, or even the Jewish religion in the strict sense. But, if he criticized the Enlightenment, this was only to light new lamps, darker and at the same time more dazzling. So he hoped that transcending the Enlightenment by a new Enlightenment might give rise to a 'fusion of nations' capable of producing a new European man.

This is why, in 1878, just as German anti-Semitism was becoming established, Nietzsche condemned the persecution of the Jews as one of the most hideous faces of nationalism, consisting as it does in 'leading the Jews to the sacrificial slaughter as scapegoats for every possible or private misfortune. As soon as it is no longer a question of the conserving of nations but of the production of the strongest possible European mixed race, the Jew will be just as useable and desirable as an ingredient of it as any other national residue.' And, after singing the extravagant praises of Spinoza and hailing the genius of freethinking Jews, he added, taking a position diametrically opposed to that of Renan and the followers of the infernal couple,

> it is thanks not least to their efforts that a more natural, rational and in any event unmythical elucidation of the world could at last again obtain victory and the ring of culture that now unites us with the enlightenment of Graeco-Roman antiquity remain unbroken. If Christianity has done everything to orientalize the occident, Judaism has always played an essential part in occidentalizing it: which in a certain sense means making of Europe's mission and history a *continuation of the Greek*.[15]

Finally, in 1887, in a letter to Theodor Fritsch, whom he viewed as an idiot, he attacked anti-Semitism in the proper sense of the term:

> Believe me: this abominable 'wanting to have a say' of noisy dilettantes about the value of people and races, this subjection to 'authorities' who are utterly rejected with cold contempt by every sensible mind (e.g., E. Dühring, R. Wagner, Ebrard, Wahrmund, P. de Lagarde – who among these in questions of morality and history is the most unqualified, the most unjust?), these constant, absurd falsifications and rationalizations of vague concepts 'germanic,' 'semitic,' 'aryan,' 'christian,' 'German' – all of that could in the long run cause me to lose my temper and bring me out of the ironic benevolence with which I have hitherto observed the virtuous velleities and pharisaisms of modern Germans. – And finally, how do you think I feel when the name Zarathustra is mouthed by anti-Semites?[16]

The same year as Renan gave his lecture, Count Arthur de Gobineau, a mediocre writer and failed diplomat heavily influenced by romanticism and haunted by a fatalism typical of anti-Enlightenment thinkers, published his notorious *Essay on the Inequality of the Human Races*, which, at that time, met with little success. Instead of taking as the foundation of this alleged inequality the infernal couple of the Aryan and the Semite, he sang the praises of the Jews – 'a free, strong people which had provided the world with as many doctors as merchants'[17] – so that he could lambast all the more effectively what he called the inferior races, in the morpho-psychological or physiognomic and not the biological sense. So he postulated the existence, at the origin of human history, of an archetypal race – the Arians or Aryans – a real aristocratic caste or 'pure race' that, he claimed, had given birth to the most civilized peoples in the world. And he also stated that the mixing of races – or interbreeding – had always led to the decay of civilizations.

At the pinnacle of the pyramid he set the white race, superior in all respects, in beauty, intelligence, and powers of resistance. Then, at the bottom of the scale, came the black race, savage and abject. In the middle, he placed the obese and apathetic yellow race, always in thrall to material pleasures and sensual impulses. But, as a good Catholic, he preserved the idea of an original unity of the human race, emphasizing that even in the most repellent cannibal there could still be found a spark of the divine fire. No people can evolve because race determines the human condition: so no progress is possible, and, as a corollary of this, any colonization is futile.

In fact, Gobineau was not concerned – as was Renan – to provide his arguments with any rational content. He systematized them simply in order to apply them to an analysis of the post-industrial society that he loathed. So he attacked socialists as well as liberals, both followers of the Declaration of the Rights of Man. And he compared them on occasion with people of the yellow race, who were good only at satisfying their natural wants. He thus created a skilful amalgam of race with social class. At the bottom of the scale, he said, was the 'peat', as in a bog – peasants and workers, similar to the blacks; in the middle, the industrious bourgeois – the yellows; at the pinnacle, the nobility, or white race, which alone was capable of any grandeur, but was dying out.

It will come as no surprise that Gobineau's ideas, venerated by the Nazis and collaborationists (as were those of Edmond Drumont), were rehabilitated in the 1980s, not only by supporters of the new right, but also by those who attacked the so-called anti-Semitism of the Enlightenment. Since the count was an apologist for the Jews, they basically said, his doctrine of inequality matters little: it is simply an affirmation of the structural diversity of cultures, and is conceivable even in the terms of modern anthropology. And, in support of this claim, they used a quotation from Lévi-Strauss, though first taking care to decontextualize it.[18] In *Race and history*, Lévi-Strauss does emphasize that Gobineau thought of the inequality of races in a qualitative, not quantitative way, which might have been a positive feature of his thought. But Lévi-Strauss immediately adds that Gobineau had made the mistake of confusing race and culture: he had thus become trapped in the infernal circle of an 'unwitting legitimation of all attempts at discrimination and exploitation'.[19] In the rest of his text, Lévi-Strauss dissolves the notions of race and inequality, showing that the existence of a diversity of cultures is one of the main principles behind the notion of mankind. This is the complete opposite of Gobineau's ideas.

In reality, Gobineau's work successfully gave credence to the inegalitarian idea that became one of the main components of anti-Semitism. It added to Renan's ideas the element that they lacked, without which the notion of race (in the biological sense) could not have been used to complement the old morpho-psychological formulation. It then became of little importance if the Jews did not appear in it as such. For the later development of Social Darwinism, and then eugenicism, a doctrine based on the prospect of an alleged improvement in the human race, was sufficient basis for the birth of political anti-Semitism, founded on an anti-modern, anti-democratic, anti-liberal, and nationalist vision of the world. Sophisticated discussions that had hitherto been the province of dapper orientalists, keen to preserve the lofty authority of the Bible and carefully determine the origins of our first parent, were transformed, in some fifteen years or so, against a backdrop of social and ethnic crises, into the realistic, dangerous, and populist expression of a mass anti-Semitism: the 'socialism of imbeciles', as August Bebel called it.[20]

In Germany, after the failure of the 1848 revolution, the middle classes aspired to a profound reform of culture and society. While several radicals from the extreme left, hostile to liberalism, moved towards a pan-Germanic ideal, the liberals, who had gone over to Bismarck and his policy of unification based on the Prussian model, embraced the nationalist cause for reasons of economic efficiency, but also because they supported the disillusioned realism that succeeded the optimism of the springtime of the peoples.[21] Thus, in 1870, a wave of anti-modern pessimism swept across Germany just as France suffered a humiliating defeat, which soon led to a nationalist and Germanophobe reaction.

It was at this juncture that, on both sides of the new borders drawn by the peace treaty between the two countries, the Jews were made responsible for all the misfortunes that seemed to have befallen both nations. In a Germany that was now powerful and unified, but reduced to a *Kleindeutschland* dominated by Prussia, and mainly Protestant in character, the Jews were accused of having contributed to a social and cultural modernization that went against the old imperial ideal of *Grossdeutschland*, with its Catholic majority (with Austria) and its romantic and Goethean tradition.

In Austria, however, the Jews – coming as they did from all the communities spread across the central empires – had been integrated into the liberal bourgeoisie by adopting German language and culture. Between 1857 and 1910, Vienna became the great Jewish metropolis of *Mitteleuropa*.[22] But this was just the problem: in this new context, the integration of the Jews within Viennese society fostered the rise not only of anti-Semitism but also – and much more than elsewhere – of the notorious Jewish self-hatred (*jüdischer Selbsthass*) found especially among intellectuals such as Karl Kraus, Otto Weininger, and many others: 'This characteristically Austrian form of ego rejection, this Jewish doubt, this passionate instinct of self-denial', wrote Arnold Zweig, 'first appears when the life of non-Jewish society produces or reflects a real, coloured, magical attraction, and a humane humanity.'[23]

From 1873, after the financial crisis, the urbanized Viennese Jews were faced with violent rejection and accused of being responsible not just for the destabilization of the markets but also for the decline of patriarchy. In other words, yet again, they were held responsible for the process of social transformation that would logically lead to an evolution in their lifestyle and a new family organization. Had not the Jewish people always been a wandering people, without native land or borders, always inclined to practise ritual murder, to favour perverse sexual practices, to be drawn by the lure of gain?[24]

In fact, the repercussions of the political disintegration of the Austro-Hungarian Empire turned Vienna, at the end of the nineteenth century, into one of the 'most fertile melting pots for an ahistorical culture' of the period, as Carl Schorske has shown.[25] As a result, the children of the Jewish bourgeoisie, faced with the onslaught of anti-Semitism and the rise of pan-Germanic nationalism, rejected the liberal illusions of their fathers and expressed other aspirations: Freud was fascinated by death and timelessness; Theodor Herzl and Max Nordau dreamt of a promised land.

In France, a country that had been defeated, and then weakened by civil war, the Jews were marked out as plotters who had worked for the defeat of the nation with the complicity of the Germanic enemy. Nationalists of every stripe then saw anti-Semitism as 'the common denominator able to act as the platform for a mass move-ment',[26] as Zeev Sternhell put it. These nationalists ranged themselves against liberal democracy and bourgeois society (in the case of certain socialists and anarchists who suffered the repression imposed by the Versailles government) and against the spectre of the Revolution of 1789 and internationalist German Marxism (in the case of the radical anti-universalist right, hostile to the Communards and devoted to the ideas of the old monarchical France).

The adjective 'anti-Semitic' made its first appearance in Germany in 1860, in a piece of writing produced by Moritz Steinschneider, an eminent orientalist Jew from Bohemia, who used this term to desig-nate the expression of a prejudice hostile to the Jews (*antisemitisches Vorurteil*). And it was in connection with an article on Renan's work by another Jewish philologist (Heymann Steinthal) that Steinschnei-der criticized the so-called anti-Semitic thesis which claimed that Semitic peoples laboured under cultural and racial defects.[27]

Nineteen years later, in 1879, the word had migrated from the sphere of scholarly debate to constitute, in the writings of Wilhelm Marr, the kernel of a new vision of the world: *Antisemitismus*. A mediocre publicist and a product of the extreme Left, Marr moved towards anarchism and atheism before founding a league that saw it as its task to expel the Jews of Germany to Palestine, and above all to stigmatize them as belonging to a class that spelled danger for the purity of the Germanic race.

In a few years, up until the First World War, anti-Semitism spread throughout Europe in several variant forms: biological, hygienist, and racialist in Germany, nationalist and Catholic in France.

Its proponents set up leagues everywhere and founded a press specializing in denunciation and insult, aiming at a broad public in search of scapegoats. They published several pamphlets against the Enlightenment spirit and absorbed, to different degrees, the main components of Christian anti-Judaism, so as to integrate them into a political programme that was oppositional, anti-liberal, monar-chist, anti-Marxist, populist, xenophobic, anti-universalist, anti-modern, anti-emancipatory, and anti-progressive. Now, when the word 'anti-Semitism' was used, it targeted exclusively the Jews – and not the other Semites, the Arabs in particular, who had previously been associated with the Jews. By adding to Renan's ideas those of Gobineau and his heirs, this meant they could describe the Jews as representatives of an inferior race, identifiable by the stigmas it bore and, since the dawn of time, hell-bent – through the alleged intensity of its three instinctual powers (perverse sex, money, and intellect) – on devouring the civilized 'Aryan' peoples.

In France, in Germany, and then throughout Europe, anti-Semitic leagues spread, stigmatizing the so-called Jewish race, of which other peoples needed to rid themselves at all costs. The age of assimilation and integration, which had torn the European Jews so violently apart – especially the German Jews – finally led to the advent of a great project of eradication. Hatred of the Jew was replaced by the premises of a policy of extermination that would be put into practice fifty years later.

It was Édouard Drumont, a Catholic and monarchist journalist, inspired by the writings of Hippolyte Taine and hating the liberal bourgeoisie as much as he did the heritage of the Enlightenment and the 1789 Revolution, who produced the most abject book ever written against the Jews. *La France juive (Jewish France)* was a veritable manual and founded a tradition of consummate anti-Semitism: published in 1886,[28] it set out to trace objectively, in six parts, a truth that had been permanently hidden: the history of the destruction by the Jews of the civilized peoples of Europe. And, to provide the world with the proof of his ideas, Drumont adopted the entire conspiracy theory of Christian anti-Judaism: the Jews spread the plague, they committed ritual crimes, cut children into pieces, and so on. But he incorporated the history of these alleged plots into the long epic of the fight to the death that had been waged over the centuries between Semites and Aryans. And he drew the conclusion that the greatest victory won by the Aryans against the Semitic scourge was the expulsion of the Jews in 1394. Between this date and the outbreak of the 1789 Revolution, he said, France, 'thanks to the expulsion of this vermin, had finally become a great European nation'.[29] After which, he explained, France had started to decline.

Drumont describes the Semite as a vile, grasping, cunning, feminine being, the slave of his instincts, and a nomad, while the Aryan is a veritable hero, the son of heaven, death-defying, and driven by a chivalrous ideal. He contradicts Renan's view that the Semites invented monotheism, and explains that the true Semite is no longer the Saracen (who was at least capable of heroism) but the barbarous Jew recognizable from the stench he gives off – a result of his 'immoderate taste for the flesh of goats and geese.'[30]

So the Semite is the Jew and nothing but the Jew, a person who belongs to a 'race' before he practises a religion.[31] As for the Aryan, he gave birth to the Christian, who invented monotheism. The anti-Semitic discourse founded by Drumont thus drives a decisive wedge between, on the one hand, Judaism and Christianity and, on the other, Judaism and 'Mohammedanism'. As for Protestantism,

Drumont equates it with a 'semi-Judaism': 'Protestantism acted as a bridge over which the Jews could enter the ranks, not of society, but of mankind. The Bible [i.e., the Hebrew Bible], relegated to secondary status in the Middle Ages, took its place closer to the Gospels. The Old Testament was set beside the New. Behind the Bible appeared the Talmud.'[32]

From this point of view, negroes or 'Mohammedan' Arabs are indeed inferior peoples, but they are less dangerous for Aryan, i.e., Christian, civilization than are Jews: and so, while the former group need to be enslaved, the others – the 'Semitic race' – must be eliminated. Since they have no territory of their own, the Semites are assimilated only in order to destroy the peoples who have taken them in. In other words, contrary to Gobineau (whom he does not quote), Drumont is less racist than anti-Semitic, which confirms the hypothesis that anti-Semitism was the matrix of the modern racism to which it led.

Although he sought to be European in his crusade against the Jews, Drumont labelled everything that was not 'French' as 'Jewish'. So immigrants were Jews. But that was not enough. For a non-Jew to be equated with a Jew, he still needed to be either a freemason, or an atheist, or a republican, or a Protestant, or a Jacobin. So Cambacérès was designated as a Jew since he was defined as a freemason, and so was Léon Gambetta, since he was a republican of Italian origins. Thanks to this line of argument, France has been 'turned Jewish' on every level ever since the Jews had acquired all powers thanks to their emancipation – and this was the fault of Voltaire and the Abbé Grégoire, the first because he was anti-Christian and the second because he was an apostate. In this respect, Drumont was not in the least bothered by the anti-Judaism of the Enlightenment, having understood that this anti-Judaism was aimed at freeing the Jews from the burden of religion.

Popularizing the ideas of Barruel and a considerable number of anti-Enlightenment thinkers, Drumont stated that 'Semitism' was born in the eighteenth century, which meant that the Revolution was, in his view, nothing other than a Jewish plot against the real France, which was Christian and Aryan.[33] But since he also claimed to be inspired by the rebellious people of 'French stock' who opposed the now Jewish-influenced liberals, and by Christian France against the cosmopolitan socialists who were also *enjuivés*, he accused the conservative French (the supporters of the Versailles government) of crushing the 1871 Commune, and the socialists of hijacking the revolt of the Communards, so as to benefit the reactionaries. As a result of all this, the destruction of the Commune had been brought about by the Jews: 'So the Commune had two faces. The one was unreasonable, unthinking, but brave: the French face. The other was mercantile, grasping, and thieving: the Jewish face. The French *fédérés* fought well and were killed. The Jewish communards stole, murdered, and petrolled (*sic*) [i.e., used petrol bombs] to conceal their thefts.'[34]

Not only were the Jews, in Drumont's eyes, cosmopolitan creatures, dirty, lustful, and stinking, but he described them as affected by all sorts of physical and mental illnesses that were indicative of corruption of blood and soul: scurvy, mange, scrofula, neurosis: 'Examine the specimen that is dominant in Paris: political pimps, stock exchange speculators, journalists – you will find them consumed by anaemia. Their eyes roll feverishly, their pupils are the colour of toasted bread, which denotes hepatitis: and the Jew has in his liver a secretion produced by a hatred that has lasted for eighteen hundred years.'[35]

Not content with revising history by explaining that the victims were the persecutors and the murderers were victims,[36] Drumont invented a style, a vocabulary, and a syntax based on insult and incrimination. He thereby created the new mode of journalistic expression to which I referred above, and which would be the special brand, as it were, of *La libre parole* [*Free Speech*], his newspaper, and also prevalent during the Dreyfus Affair, before re-emerging, in an even more virulent form, in the interwar period and up until 1945 – with the pamphlets of Louis-Ferdinand Céline and Robert Brasillach's incitements to murder. Drumont drew up lists, named names, passed on rumours, and painted portraits of the anti-France: Rothschild, Fould, Crémieux, Kahn, Halévy, the valets of Marx, Heine, and Disraeli. In a word, he founded the language of anti-Semitism, which would subsequently be repeated indefinitely, like a structure, giving rise to a discourse that always remained the same, and has indeed become almost unvarying, in spite of its many metamorphoses.

And, going the whole hog, Drumont dragooned into his services the most popular writer of the nineteenth century, thereby playing the romantic card against classicism: Victor Hugo against Voltaire. Ventriloquizing through the dead, he explained that the great poet, who had, one year earlier, been given a state funeral, was a real anti-Semite and defender of Christian values. Hugo, he says, systematically stuffed his texts with the adjective 'filthy' [*immonde*] whenever he mentioned Jews. Furthermore, Hugo was apparently himself the victim of a Jew who wormed his way into his house and assassinated him after preventing him from 'returning to Christ'.[37]

The choice of Hugo was loaded. By turning the Jews into regicides (1793), murderers of the people (1871), and the assassins of the most famous writer of the nineteenth century, an awakener of consciousness and freedom, Drumont attempted to bring together – so as to fight more effectively against them – the ideals that lay behind the founding of two Frances: mediaeval France on the one side, embodied by Joan of Arc and Christianity, and the people's France on the other, the France of the oppressed, wretched, and rebellious. Now Hugo, as everyone knows, was the true symbol of *both* those Frances. He was so in his life, since he had been a monarchist in his youth, liberal during his maturity, and republican as he entered old age; and he was so in his work, since he had never stopped narrating France's heroic metamorphoses while suffering from his inability to solve the ancestral struggle between Judaism and Christianity. By exposing the hatred that the Jews aroused, Hugo had really been stating that he 'could not quietly let men be Jews, in other words, persecuted'.

To stir up the entire French people against the Jews in this way, Drumont summoned Hugo to his side. But he neglected to say that, if Hugo sometimes – in his comments on the Bible, or when he reinvented the legend of the 'ritual crime' – uncritically indicated that the Christians viewed the Jews as a deceitful and deicide people ('I love so I hate'), he had nonetheless stated that they should be blessed after being cursed, and that the curse that weighed down on them was a tragedy: 'There is a curse on the Jews; there is a mystery in the gypsies. The Jews are caught up in a tragedy, the gypsies in a drama.'[38]

And, of course, the author of *La France juive* also ignored the poet's appeal, in 1882, on behalf of persecuted Russian Jews,[39] and the celebrated letter written in 1843 to the director of the Israelite Archives, after a performance of Hugo's play *Les Burgraves*, which the director had severely criticized for its representation of the Jews: 'The thirteenth century', he said,

> was a twilit age. It was filled with thick shadows, little light, much violence and crime [. . .]. The Jews were barbarous, so were the Christians, the Christians were the oppressors, the Jews were the oppressed, the Jews reacted [. . .]. We need to depict historical periods as they were. Does this mean that, in our own time, the Jews murder little children and eat them? Monsieur, in our day, Jews such as yourself are full of knowledge and light, and Christians such as myself are full of esteem and consideration for Jews such as you. So declare an amnesty on *Les Burgraves*, Monsieur, and allow me to shake you by the hand.[40]

Drumont concluded his work with a summons to France to find for itself, at long last, a 'chief dispenser of justice' capable of wiping out the 'Jews who are rolling in wealth'. 'Have I prepared the way for our renaissance? I do not know. I have, in any case, done my duty, by responding with insults to the countless insults that the Jewish press pours down on Christians.'[41]

The fact that Drumont needed to turn the situation upside down in this way, converting hatred against the Jews into a hatred emanating from the Jews, clearly shows that anti-Semitic discourse, in its deepest structure, proceeds to a perverse or delirious revision of history that, in its very excessiveness, is always transformed into a denial of reality. The facts are replaced by a fable of memory. From this denial, once the genocide of the Jews had been accomplished, would spring Holocaust denial.

But in 1886, at the age of forty-two, as anti-Semitism spread across Europe as a political movement, Drumont really was the man of the hour.

Poor, déclassé, filled with thoughts of revenge and with hatred of the rich and the educated, he never stopped blaming society – and thus the Jews – for the manic-depressive madness of his father, who was interned in the asylum at Charenton in 1862, and the insignificance of his practically half-witted mother, of whom he was ashamed. Brought up amid stupidity and deprived of any emotion, he suffered from his ugliness, his squalor, his myopia, a puny body – and therefore projected onto the Jews all the vices from which he himself suffered.

And when he was accused – he, the Christian visionary – of being nothing but the valet of the Jesuits, he would then appeal to the shades of his republican father, a follower of Voltaire, even though he felt nothing but contempt for him. And when he was challenged to a duel by Arthur Meyer, a journalist whom he had insulted, he drew from the scratch he received an additional glory: 'The finest day in my life', he called it. Reduced for years to a poverty-stricken existence, thanks to his sloth and his inability to live off his wits, he was also forever seeking consolation from ugly women from modest backgrounds so that he could more easily mistreat them. When he eventually grew rich from his writings, he simply became even stingier than before.

Such was the man who claimed to be the redeemer of the French nation, supported by an important fringe of the press and the intellectual right: by Alphonse Daudet, who untiringly sang his praises, then by Alphonse's son Léon, the harsh critic of Freud's theories, then by Edmond de Goncourt, and finally by the cohort of anti-Dreyfusards: Maurice Barrès, Charles Maurras, Paul Bourget, etc.

As for Georges Bernanos, he regarded *La France juive* as a literary masterpiece, an event in the history of the French people, a people who had shown their ability to express themselves in words finally liberated from the yoke of the Republic: '*La France juive* struck home, hit the regime at the very spring of life, right in the artery.' And he added, in the purest Drumontesque style: 'Clemenceau was not deceived. From the depths of his study, in the midst of his ridiculous Chinese knick-knacks, that cruel and magical fellow, an expert in poisons, consumed by contempt, fixed his eyes, the eyes of a Mongol murderer, on the anguish of the accomplices, and gazed on that spurt of golden blood, quivering with hatred and pleasure.'[42]

In 1939, accusing Louis-Ferdinand Céline of being in the pay of Germany and spreading 'hideous anti-Semitic propaganda' on their behalf, Bernanos stated that the Jews, on their side, were racists. In this way he made his own the anti-Semitic idea that, by considering themselves to be the chosen people, the Jews had invented racism: 'We must neither hate nor scorn the Jews. Nonetheless, Jewish racism is a Jewish fact. It is the Jews who are racists, and not us.'[43]

Apart from Zola's *J'accuse*, which, after 1898, put an end to Drumont's career and that of the other anti-Dreyfusards, only one thing really disturbed Drumont. It was a weapon he had not thought of: humour, the genius of Jewish humour. And it was by resorting to this humour that his enemies managed to lash out at him, spreading far and wide the legend that this ugly customer with his curved nose and brachycephalic cranium was none other than . . . a 'renegade Jew', a 'Semite in disguise', the descendant of an illustrious family of opticians from Cologne, the Dreimonds. This rumour would pursue him to the end of his days: he responded to it with rage and fury – and without the least humour: 'My work is me, and my work is my race, my race is my origin.'[44]

This Bible of hatred is still today, just like *The Protocols of the Elders of Zion* and *Mein Kampf*, a major reference point, throughout the world, for all the proponents of fully fledged anti-Semitism, in all its variant forms.

A mystical, desperate, and profoundly visionary writer, Léon Bloy opposed Drumont in a remarkable work, *Le salut par les Juifs* [*Salvation through the Jews*].[45] He condemned any idea of eradication or persecution. In his view, the Jews, who had inherited the virtues ascribed to the 'first parent', had become debased as a result of the stigmatization they had suffered: 'I have wasted a few hours reading, like so many other people, the anti-Jewish elucubrations of Monsieur

Drumont, and I do not remember him ever quoting these simple words (*salus ex judaeis est*), so powerful, spoken by Our Lord Jesus Christ and related by Saint John in the fourth chapter of his Gospel.'[46]

And to highlight the psychological and physical wretchedness of the Jews and advocate the ideal of conversion to Christianity, which in his view was the only thing that could save Jews and Christians together, by ensuring that the latter were not the orphans of the former, Bloy embarked on an apocalyptic description of the great Jewish market in Hamburg. He simultaneously deployed and rejected the language of anti-Semitism to tell the story of an apparition. In the middle of all the cast-off clothes, the filth, and the second-hand goods, he had seen three horrible old men, 'yids', who, in a sort of transformation of the abject into the sublime, reminded him of the biblical triad of the sacred Patriarchs Abraham, Isaac, and Jacob. 'Imagine them – I scarcely dare to write it – those three great persons, more than human, from whom sprang all the people of God and the word of God himself.'

Against Drumont, Bloy paid homage one last time to a Christian anti-Judaism that was on the point of vanishing, and of which he claimed to be the most desperate follower in a world steeped in anti-Semitism – in other words, riven by a criminal split between the two first monotheistic religions. For, in his view, the abjection in which the Jew lived – 'an old, sordid, hook-nosed Hebrew, scrabbling for gold among piles of garbage' – was also what, in Christianity, made him worthy of compassion. And so, to those three 'incomparable villains' encountered in Hamburg, he addressed the salvation of the crucified Christ, remembering, at the threshold of a godless modernity, that the salvation of the Christians came from the salvation of the Jews: 'I owe them this homage of an almost affectionate memory, since they brought to my mind the most grandiose images that can enter the plain and humble dwelling place of a mortal mind.'[47]

Once his book was published, Bloy was supported by Bernard Lazare, a Jewish writer and journalist,[48] who became one of the main protagonists in the Dreyfus controversy. Between the visionary of the catacombs, haunted by madness, and the radical atheist, who called for a Spinozist revolution, a strange relation developed. Lazare shared Bloy's visceral anti-Drumont feelings.[49] And yet, for several years, he himself had attacked foreign Jews, contrasting their 'barbarous perversion' with the figure of the civilized Jew: the Israelite. Then, abandoning the aestheticism of the literary avant-garde for a greater commitment to the proletarian cause, he had transformed his hatred into a devotion to the poor and wretched. So the encounter with Bloy led him from the self-hatred so pervasive in his *Histoire de l'antisémitisme* [*History of anti-Semitism*][50] to an acceptance of his Jewish identity that would lead him to do a volte-face. Hannah Arendt painted a vibrant portrait of him, depicting him as a 'conscious pariah'.[51]

Such, in any event, was the singular place occupied by Léon Bloy in the French history of the Jewish question.

In the interwar period, the followers of Drumont who admired Nazism unhesitatingly equated some of Hitler's ideas with those of their hero, even though this meant ignoring the differences between the two discourses. So it barely mattered that Drumont was a militant Catholic who had no time for the doctrine of the 'master race', for Nordic mysticism and the visceral anti-Christianity characteristic of Nazism: the main thing was to amalgamate all the European tendencies of anti-Semitism. The two men, Drumont and Hitler, were also akin in their origins and in the way they had converted professional failure into a desire for vengeful insurrection: there was the same exaltation of populism, the same spirit of destruction, the same murderous impulses towards the 'two-faced' Jew, that master of finance, inventor of the Revolution, hatcher of plots, monopolist of intellect and of the secrets of sex. There was one difference, however: in Hitler's case, the passion of anti-Semitism had been transformed, by the end of the First World War, into a cold and rational determination to act out his hatred and exterminate the Jews legally – something that went beyond planning their elimination in fiery rhetoric. 'Anti-Semitism based on purely sentimental reasons', he wrote in 1919, 'will find its final expression in pogroms. The anti-Semitism of reason, however, must lead to a legal and methodical struggle, and to the elimination of the privileges that the Jew possesses, unlike the other foreigners who live among us. But its ultimate and immutable objective must be the elimination of the Jews in general.'[52]

In 1967, after a long eclipse, the admirers of Édouard Drumont gathered at his burial place in the Père-Lachaise cemetery in Paris to celebrate the glorious memory of this 'pure-blooded Frenchman, this true Frenchman of France . . .'. They founded an association which brought together all the variants of neo-fascism, followers of Maurras, and Catholic fundamentalists. What these groups had in common was their hostility to Charles de Gaulle, to the Resistance, to decolonization, and to Algerian independence. It was at this juncture that Emmanuel Beau de Loménie, with the support of the publisher Jean-Jacques Pauvert and the philosopher Jean-François Revel, the future fanatical opponent of Marx, Freud, Sartre, and the spirit of the Enlightenment, had the idea of publishing an anthology of Drumont's texts presented in a positive light and in a somewhat conspiratorial guise. Drumont was depicted not as an anti-Semite, but as an anti-capitalist stifled by the 'grandees of the Sorbonne': his 'rehabilitation would be absolutely necessary, stirring, and likely to shed light for rising generations on the causes of our failures and the means of our potential recovery.'[53]

But the most incongruous post-war commentary is still that of Georges Bernanos, the eternal defender of Drumont. A writer of exceptional talent, but in revolt against everything – communism, democracy, liberalism, and capitalism, the bourgeoisie, the republicans, and the socialists – Bernanos had rejected Maurras, l'Action française, Francoism, the appeasement spirit of the Munich Agreement, and Nazism before going into exile in Paraguay and then, in June 1940, supporting de Gaulle's Resistance.

In the period after the extermination of the Jews,[54] Bernanos – still haunted by his fears of a Europe in decline and the advent of American 'bestiality' – lambasted the new parliamentary administration that had emerged from the Liberation, emphasizing that at least the Vichy regime could state in its own defence that it had placed itself at the service of the occupying forces. And, surveying the Zionist movement and the return of the Jews to Palestine, he reiterated, in exaggerated and simplistic terms, remarks he had made during the interwar period:

> There is a Jewish question. This is not just my own personal view: the facts are there to prove it. After two millennia, the Jewish racist and nationalist feeling is so obvious to everybody that no one found it extraordinary that, in 1918, the victorious Allies imagined they might restore them to a land of their own: does not this demonstrate that the capture of Jerusalem by Titus did not solve the problem? Anyone who talks this way is treated as an anti-Semite. This word increasingly fills me with horror; Hitler has forever dishonoured it [. . .]. I am not anti-Semitic – and in any case, this does not mean a thing, since the Arabs are Semites too. I am not at all anti-Jewish [. . .]. I am not anti-Jewish but I would blush to write, when I do not think this is true, that there is no Jewish problem, or that the Jewish problem is merely a religious problem. There is a Jewish race: they can be recognized from certain obvious physical signs. If there is a Jewish race, there is a Jewish sensibility, a Jewish mentality, a Jewish sense of life, of death, of wisdom and happiness [. . .]. There is no French race. France is a nation, in other words a human product, a creation of mankind [. . .]. But there is a Jewish race. A French Jew who has been incorporated into our people for several centuries will probably remain racist, since his entire moral and religious tradition is based on racism, but this racism has gradually become humanized, and the French Jew has become a Jewish Frenchman.[55]

These notorious words have often been debated. Ever since 1947, Bernanos's admirers have continually striven to deny that the writer was not in any way a proponent of anti-Semitism, since he had so stridently poured public contempt on Hitler's Germany. But they thereby forgot that, in thus expressing his horror of a word that he deemed to be 'dishonoured', Bernanos was condemning Hitler only so that he could rehabilitate Drumont all the more effectively and hate Germany – Germany as a whole, not just Nazi Germany. The implication is that this denial suggested there might be an honourable form of anti-Semitism. But *what* form?

His words are, to put it mildly, ambiguous, expressing as they do a hatred for the other[56] which merely reflects, without ever sublimating it, the sordid self-hatred that marks the characters in his novels. Bernanos was announcing the birth of a new mode of expression for anti-Semitic discourse. This had become, after Auschwitz, unspeakable: it could now be stated, at least in Western societies, only in an 'honourable' – that is, a masked, denying, unconscious – way.

It was in France that political anti-Semitism was invented, culminating in the rabble-rousing venture of General Boulanger in the 1880s, then continuing throughout the Dreyfus Affair and gaining a new impetus after 1930. But it was in Germany[57] that interest was focused on biological anti-Semitism – a racially based, and thus racist anti-Semitism – which, forty years later, fed into Nazism. With it, the former concept of race, in the genealogical sense, assumed a new, purportedly 'scientific' meaning.

At the end of the nineteenth century, the most eminent authorities in German medical science, fascinated by the rise of Darwinism and terrified by the possible decadence of societies and individuals, promoted the establishment of a biocracy. They sought to move beyond political conflict by governing their nations with the help of the life sciences in the same way that their historicist teachers had believed they could explain the origin and hierarchy of races by philology. The medical specialists were more egalitarian and less attached to genealogical myths than the historicists, but they regarded themselves as heirs of the Enlightenment rather than as proponents of a return to the past. And, as they had taken stock of the burden imposed by industrialization on the souls and bodies of a proletariat that was increasingly exploited in grim, unsanitary factories, they wished to purify German cultural structures and combat every form of 'degeneracy'[58] linked to mankind's entry into industrial modernity.

As materialists who were hostile to religious obscurantism, they invented a strange scientific figure: the new man, regenerated by reason and self-overcoming. They were imitated by the communists[59] and by the founders of Zionism, including Max Nordau,[60] who saw in the return to the promised land the only way of liberating Jews from the stultification in which anti-Semitism had immersed them.

Favourable to women's emancipation and a concerted mastery of procreation, these Enlightenment savants – doctors, biologists, sociologists, etc. – set up a state programme for the regeneration of bodies and souls, a eugenicist programme in which they encouraged the populace to purify themselves by making medically controlled marriages. They urged the masses to wean themselves off their vices: tobacco, alcohol, and any form of unbridled sexuality. They also set up large-scale testing for the diseases that were eroding the social body: syphilis, tuberculosis, etc.

Some of them, such as Magnus Hirschfeld, a pioneer in homosexual emancipation, supported this programme, convinced that a new type of homosexual, finally rid of the perverse inheritance of an accursed race, could be created by science. He too, like the founder of Zionism, wished to create a new man: 'the new homosexual'. So, in 1911, he launched an appeal on behalf of the protection of women, the right to abortion, and the physical and psychological improvement of the human race.[61]

When the movement for racial hygiene was set up, it became split between two main trends. The first, represented by the illustrious doctor Rudolf Virchow, drew on a form of medicine oriented towards the natural sciences and designed to promote a progressive programme for the prevention of diseases and epidemics. Liberal in his views on lifestyle, hostile to anti-Semitism, to Gobineau, and to colonialism, in 1869 Virchow founded the Berlin Society of Anthropology, thus bringing this discipline closer to biology. He insisted on the need to work on the diversity of cultures while developing the idea that diseases evolved – in the same way as races.

The second trend, taking its lead from the ideas of Ernst Haeckel, the popularizer of Darwinism in the German-speaking world, was based on the narratives of Gobineau, which thus met with posthumous success. Eager to apply the theory of species selection to human society, Haeckel sought to incorporate the human sciences into zoology. Unlike the Anglo-Saxon Darwinist school, which was preoccupied by competition and based on a liberal – but still just as racialist[62] – conception of natural selection, Haeckel conceived a classification of human races that mixed monogenism with polygenism.[63] Convinced that the human world resembled the animal world, he thought that mankind, in spite of its original unity, was divided into several species. So he stated that the differences between superior and inferior human beings were greater than those that distinguished

inferior human beings from superior animals.[64] And, among the infe-
riors, he included the mentally handicapped, the insane, and peoples
of colour: blacks, Aborigines, Hottentots. Furthermore, he thought
that mankind was divided into twelve human species and thirty-six
races, themselves grouped into four classes: savages, barbarians, the
civilized, and the cultivated. Only European nations comprised, in
his view, the cultivated classes. As a result, it was their task to bring
their civilizing mission to the rest of the world.

All these post-Darwinian ideas spread through the many different
European varieties of the new colonial imperialism of the end of the
nineteenth century. This assumed a commercial and differential guise
among the English, a cultural and assimilationist form among the
French, and an exterminating (but belated and short-lived) guise
among the Germans, who later turned their expansionist drives
against a Europe that had been, they claimed, 'Jewified'.[65]

After 1920, in a broken Germany that the economic slump had
reduced to poverty, the heirs of this biocracy pursued this programme,
adding euthanasia and systematic sterilization to it. They thus moved
from an Enlightenment to an anti-Enlightenment position, and from
a biological scientism to a criminal science whose sole purpose was
the implementation of a will to genocide.[66]

Terrified at the potential prospect of the decline of their 'race', they
invented the notion of 'negative value of life', convinced as they were
that certain lives were not worth living. These included the lives of
people afflicted by an incurable illness, a deformity, a handicap, or
an anomaly, the lives of the mentally ill, and finally the lives of so-
called inferior races. The figure of the new man fabricated by the
most highly developed science in the European world thereby turned
into the abject figure of the master race in SS uniform. In this way,
Nazism, taking over for its own purposes the anti-Christian biological theories propounded by the post-Darwinians and a French political anti-Semitism stripped of its Catholicism, set itself the task of
'depopulating' the world of all non-'Aryan' races, including the worst
of them all, the Jews, defined as belonging to a sub-animal realm:
vermin, lice, microbes, viruses, etc. Anti-Judaism thus fused with
anti-Semitism, since, in the Nazi view, Judaism and Christianity were
merely two faces of the same Semitism of which only the Jews should
bear the emblem, while Christians could free themselves from it only
by converting to 'Aryanism'.

Christian anti-Judaism did not survive the extermination of the
Jews by the Nazis; nor did the anti-Judaism of the Enlightenment.
And this is why, after 1945, any anti-Semitism could be nothing other
than the perpetuation of the passion of anti-Semitism – a passion that

was disguised in states that observed the rule of law but was openly flaunted in the rest of the world.

The Nazis gave the name 'Final Solution' (*Endlösung*) to the genocide of the Jews, and they called the process of extermination 'special treatment' (*Sonderbehandlung*). They assassinated the German language: as a result, certain words can no longer be uttered. And they believed that they had 'solved' the Jewish question by annihilating the Jews: this was their way of obeying the *fin-de-siècle* injunction claiming that anti-Semitism would end only with the disappearance of the Jews. They then eliminated every trace of the act by which they had perpetrated this annihilation. As defeat loomed, they destroyed the instruments of the crime – the gas chambers – and got rid of the witnesses who might 'carry secrets' with them, in the belief that they were creating the conditions for a future, warped reconstruction of the past. In obedience to Hitler, who himself had drawn inspiration from *The Protocols of the Elders of Zion*, they thought they could spread the idea that the war had been willed and provoked solely by international financiers of Jewish origin or working on behalf of Jewish interests.[67]

Against these labels (*Endlösung*, *Sonderbehandlung*) which, in all their bureaucratic banality, aimed to obscure the horror of administered death, and against this destruction of the traces of destruction, history would hold up the generic name Auschwitz – the same in every language – to designate what the Nazis had sought to disguise. And the eye-witness accounts of those who escaped would continue, in spite of the Holocaust deniers, to reverse the effacement of all traces which these deniers had sought.

And so, beyond the shadow of the camps and the smoke of the ovens, Auschwitz[68] would become, over the years, the main signifier of an extermination which the founders of anti-Semitism had dreamt of without believing it could actually be carried out.

3

Promised Land, Conquered Land

The dream of a reconquest of Zion[1] is as ancient as the history of the scattering of the Jews, a history haunted by a messianism of return and withdrawal – witness the episode of Sabbatai Zevi. We might almost say that it is intrinsic to the existence of the Jewish people: an 'ill-fated people', a *schlemihl*[2] people subjected since the dawn of time to the will of an obscure God who continually promises to his chosen people the coming of a better world: 'I am at home nowhere', says the Schlemihl-Jew, 'I am a stranger everywhere. I would like to embrace everything, but everything eludes me, I am wretched.'[3] Moses Hess, the friend of Marx, and Leon Pinsker, the author of a famous pamphlet published anonymously in 1882, also reflected on this question.[4]

And yet Zionism, as a lay movement to emancipate the Jews of the diaspora, did not spring from Judaism, or from any eschatological impulse, but rather from a progressive de-Judaization of the European Jews, which was the consequence of a de-secularization of this same world.[5]

Inspired by the Enlightenment and by the ideal of tearing themselves away from religion, the emancipated Jews of the nineteenth century believed they could integrate themselves into bourgeois society in several ways: as fully fledged citizens in France, as individuals belonging to a community in England and then the United States, as Jewish-German subjects in the Germanic world, and as minorities in the central empires or the Mediterranean and Arab-Islamic world. Many of them changed their names as they migrated to different places: Polish, Russian, Romanian, etc., names were turned into

German or French names. Finally, many of them renounced their circumcision or converted even though nobody was forcing them to do so.

But, as nationalism took over from the ancient ideals of the 'Springtime of the peoples', they were rejected, no longer because of their religion, but because of their race, and thus because of the way they invisibly belonged to a certain identity which resisted various conversions and thereby obliged them to define themselves too as part of a nation. For centuries, the European nations had faced only individual Jews – a people of pariahs[6] aware of the rejection they aroused and viewing their unity and universality without reference to frontiers. But these nations would soon find themselves confronting a people who now claimed to think of themselves as a nation: the Jewish nation. But what is a nation without frontiers? What is a people without territory? What are a nation and a people composed of subjects or individuals who are citizens of nowhere by dint of being citizens of different nations?

After being the greatest vector of any attempt at extermination made by one group against another, anti-Semitism persisted after 1945 in new forms, while Zionism gave rise, in Palestine, to a state beset by perpetual war, as it was regarded by the Arab world as essentially colonial and by Zionist Jews as the consummation of a process of unconditional legitimation.[7] As for anti-Zionism – as a political and ideological opposition to Zionism – it was originally the creation of several European Jews opposed to the conquest of a new land. Among them were persons as different as Lord Edwin Montagu, Charles Natter, and Sigmund Freud, together with Marxists and socialists influenced by the Haskalah, who came together in the Bund, a movement founded in Vilna in 1897 and focused on a fierce struggle against any form of anti-Semitism.

Just as anti-Semitism had been a seed-bed of racism, it also acted as a biological theory for colonial conquest. Colonialism thus contributed to the global spread of anti-Semitism, as Hannah Arendt magisterially demonstrates.[8] Once the Jews had been held responsible for every kind of plot, they were accused of being the agents of one power against another. For instance, England needed only to seize Egypt back from the French for the Jews to be held responsible. Thus arose the thesis of an international set of plots attributed to 'the imperialism of the Rothschilds'.

Throughout the second half of the twentieth century, while Zionism was identified more and more with a new form of colonization, colonialism declined as the peoples who were its victims managed to turn against their oppressors and often with their support, the weapons of an ideal of liberty which had allowed these oppressors to enslave them.

It is worth noting in this connection that none of the three oldest European colonial powers – England, Spain, and Portugal – had forged the actual word 'colonialism' to refer to the imperialist ideology that rested on a racial theory that was a mixture of the ideas of Gobineau and of Social Darwinism. It was in France, in 1902, that the term was invented[9] to justify in retrospect a phenomenon of expansion that had begun mid-century and consisted in subjecting non-European peoples – blacks, Arabs, Asians – deemed to be inferior: there were expeditions to Tonkin, Madagascar, Congo, Morocco, and Tunisia, and the conquered territories of Algeria were turned into French *départements*. The movement had intensified when the anti-Semitism of Drumont flared up and finally spread in the form of a secular and republican conquest at the start of the twentieth century, once political anti-Semitism had suffered its most harrowing defeat with the recognition of the innocence of Captain Dreyfus. Reconstituted in all its splendour, the French Army then brandished, all the more vehemently, and right up until 1914, the weapons of a whole panoply of racial themes.[10]

The Republicans gave the name of 'civilizing mission' ['*mission civilisatrice*'] to this vast enterprise of territorial conquest, which aimed, they said, at extending the rights of man and the citizen to 'natives', i.e., to men whom they considered neither as equals nor as fully fledged citizens.

It was Ernest Renan, the inventor of the infernal couple of Semites and Aryans, and later a defender of the Republic, who in 1870 gave the best definition of what this doctrine would turn into: 'There is nothing shocking in the conquest of a country of inferior race by a superior race [. . .]. While conquests between equal races are to be deplored, the regeneration of inferior races or races ruined by superior races is part of the providential order of mankind.'[11] This thesis was later taken up by Jules Ferry, a great organizer of the colonial epic: 'Superior races', he said in 1885, 'have rights over the inferior races [. . .]. They have the right to civilize inferior races.'[12]

Ferry's argument rested on the idea that republican universalism was superior to any form of diversity, whether regional, linguistic, racial, familial, or cultural. And it was in the name of the combat against this diversity that, in 1881, he had defended the principle of free and obligatory schooling for all French children. As a proponent of colonialism, he was thus inverting the republican ideal that had sprung from the Revolution of 1789, so as to appropriate for his own purposes the inegalitarian ideas of the opponents of the

Enlightenment, thus warding off the obsessive fear of a political division between the two Frances.

Several trends came to light during the Third Republic. For some people, anxious to put the Enlightenment on trial by replacing the universalism of rights with laws on 'heredity', colonialism had to limit itself to a mere enterprise for exploiting wealth and subjecting other peoples, an enterprise deemed necessary to the survival of Europe. In the eyes of other people, conversely, the Enlightenment needed to remain the vector of an egalitarian project that would make it possible to liberate conquered peoples from ancient despotisms: 'France, that generous nation, whose opinions govern civilized Europe and whose ideas have conquered the world', wrote Francis Garnier as early as 1864, 'has received from providence a higher mission, that of emancipation, summoning to Enlightenment and liberty races and peoples who are still the slaves of ignorance and despotism.'[13]

A third, minority trend was hostile to any form of colonization or colonialism. This was true, for instance, of Georges Clemenceau, who was a Dreyfusard and published Zola's *J'accuse*: 'Conquest', he said in 1885, 'is the pure and simple abuse of the strength that scientific civilization gives one over rudimentary civilizations, to appropriate a man, torture him, wrest all his strength from him [. . .] to the advantage of the so-called civilizer. This is not law [*le droit*], but its negation.'[14]

Conquered by Germany in 1870, and forced to cede Alsace and Lorraine,[15] France embarked on a vigorous colonial policy. Victorious at the same date, Germany also turned imperialist, which did not prevent opposition to this policy being just as strong as in France, an opposition voiced by Virchow but also by the geographer Friedrich Ratzel. His views are reported by Sven Lindqvist: 'It has been [. . .] a deplorable rule that long-standing peoples die out at contact with highly cultivated peoples. This applies to the vast majority of Australians, Polynesians, northern Asians, North Americans, and many peoples in South Africa and South America. [. . .] The natives are killed, impoverished, and driven away, their social organization destroyed. [. . .] Land-hungry whites crowd in between the weak and partly decayed settlements of the Indians.'[16]

When Germany was defeated in 1918, it was forced to return Alsace and Lorraine to France, but also to give up its possessions in Africa. From then on, in the context of a general crisis among nation-states, anti-Semitism flared up again across Europe: this was a political and biological anti-Semitism, as we have seen, springing from the alliance between the French tradition inspired by Drumont and German biocracy.

While established anti-Semitism and colonialism at the end of the nineteenth century shared an inegalitarian theory of race, the two doctrines had divergent goals. The first was intrinsically exterminatory and aimed from the start at the annihilation of the 'bad race' – and it would lead to Auschwitz when circumstances were right – while the second was a programme of enslavement, exploitation, discrimination, and 'regeneration' – in the name of which the state would be fully prepared to commit massacres or even to advocate the extinction of so-called inferior races.

So it would be a mistake to see colonialist ideology as a prefiguring of Nazism and Auschwitz. All the same, after 1945, the simultaneous reaction against colonialism and the extermination of the Jews led the colonized populations and the historians of colonization to draw connections between the policies of destruction of native peoples, perpetrated both by slave-drivers and by their successors, and the gradual decline into savagery of the European states.

From the invention of the word 'genocide' by Raphaël Lemkin in 1944 to its adoption by the United Nations (UN) in 1948, in the context of a universal reformulation of the Declaration of Human Rights, a huge debate was started, leading to a new understanding of the phenomenon of colonialism and all previous forms of mass destruction of human beings and their cultures.[17]

Indeed, the critique of so-called Western values continued to gather momentum at the start of the twenty-first century. Within the UN, for example, a new division of the world was gradually established following the process of decolonization. The fall of communism in 1989, then the destruction of the World Trade Center on 11 September 2001, and finally the rise of Asia merely helped this groundswell to come to light.[18]

While Zionism and anti-Semitism have persisted as responses to the Jewish question, other forms of political commitment marked other destinies, embodying, in contrast to a patriotism of the nation, a patriotism of exile: communism, critical and aesthetic intellectualism, feminism, socialism, the redemptive return to Judaism or to its memorial history,[19] and, finally, psychoanalysis, which shares with Zionism the fact that it was invented, between 1896 and 1904, by Viennese Jews in *Mitteleuropa* faced by a very particular historical situation – the death throes of the Austro-Hungarian Empire – so well described by Robert Musil and Stefan Zweig.

In no other place than Vienna, at that period, at that bridgehead between West and East, had there been such a fervent interest in the possible metamorphoses of human identity: research into the relations between sexuality and the death drive, fascination for the decadence of societies and the degeneracy of a mankind doomed to egotism, the haunting fear of the feminization of men and the virilization of women, the cult of foundational myths, the dream of promised lands and conquered lands . . . 'Zionism was indeed born in Vienna in Austria'. said Joseph Roth. 'It was a Viennese journalist who invented it. Nobody else could have done so.'[20]

Born in 1860 in the Austro-Hungarian Empire, Theodor Herzl, the founding father of Zionism, nicknamed the new Moses of the Jewish people, was a mixture of Savonarola and Sabbatai Zevi. He had been brought up in a liberal, assimilated family that did not respect the dietary rules and for which Judaism was a pious memory that led to little more than lip service to the ritual of the festivals.[21] Ruined in the financial crisis of 1873, the father left Budapest and settled in Vienna, where the son followed law studies while dreaming of becoming a famous dramatist, despite his lack of talent – except a talent for transforming his life, with magisterial aplomb, into an ongoing dramatic performance. For Herzl was a marvellous actor, able to fascinate the crowds as well as the individuals he encountered at any one time.

Attached in an infantile way to his mother and suffering from attacks of exaltation and melancholia, Herzl felt a sort of revulsion at sexuality that expressed itself in his hatred of his own circumcised penis and shame at his Jewishness. Throughout his studies, confronted by anti-Semitism, he continually felt humiliated and adopted the arguments used by his enemies: he admired the Wagnerian ideal and 'Aryan' pan-Germanism, seeking – as Stefan Zweig put it – to escape 'through flight into the spiritual' from 'what had shrunk Judaism: the cold will to make money'.[22]

But he was clearly haunted, from an early age, by Jewish self-hatred (*Selbsthass*), a suicidal passion just as tormented and ambiguous as the passion he felt for his wife Julie, who was unstable, choleric, and crazy, and periodically threatened to slit her wrists, poison herself, or throw herself out of the window. From this tumultuous marriage, three children were born. Pauline, the elder daughter, was interned several times and died on her wanderings. Hans, the son, converted several times – he became a Baptist, a Quaker, and a Unitarian – before returning to the synagogue and then committing suicide with a pistol bullet on the news of his sister's suicide. Trude, the younger sister, was manic-depressive: she was murdered by the Nazis in Theresienstadt in 1942, while her son, Theodor's grandson and sole descendant, drowned himself in Washington after refusing to settle in Palestine.

Theodor Herzl moved to Paris in October 1891 as a correspondent for the great Viennese newspaper the *Neue Freie Presse*. Here he witnessed the crisis of Boulangism, the rise of the anarchist movement – and especially the great explosion of anti-Semitism inspired by Drumont. He frequently saw Drumont in Alphonse Daudet's salon, and liked him, admiring *La France juive* as, after Ernst Dühring's piece, the most brilliant contemporary essay on the 'question'. He had obviously internalized his hatred of Jews and himself so much that he thought the anti-Semites were right to try and rid themselves of these intruders: 'Much of my current conceptual freedom I owe to Drumont, because he is an artist.' And:

> I understand the nature of anti-Semitism. We Jews, through no fault of our own, have maintained ourselves as a foreign body among the various nations. In the ghetto we adopted a number of antisocial traits. Pressure has corrupted our character, and it will take counter-pressure to restore it. Actually, anti-Semitism is the consequence of the emancipation of the Jews [. . .] It was an error on the part of the doctrinaire libertarians to believe that people can be made equal by an edict published in the Official Gazette. [. . .] [W]hen the Jews turn away from money and move into professions previously barred to them, they exert terrible pressure on the livelihood of the middle classes [. . .] Yes anti-Semitism, a strong and unconscious force among the masses, will not harm the Jews. I regard it as helpful in building the Jewish character.[23]

These words, taken from a letter written in May 1895, one month after Alfred Dreyfus had been deported to Devil's Island, show how deeply Herzl loathed what had been the main liberating event in the long history of persecution of the Jews. Hating democracy, despising the Declaration of the Rights of Man and the Citizen, and even more the foundational act of 1791 in which the Jews had finally acquired in France, for the first time anywhere in the world, rights that made of them fully fledged citizens, he thereby rejected the Enlightenment as he had previously hated his own Jewishness.

Thus Herzl mobilized the obscure forces of anti-Semitism to accept its diktat and turn his Jewish self-hatred into pride at being Jewish. And since the anti-Dreyfusards had succeeded in getting the most assimilated French Jew sentenced, the one most representative of the great virtues of republican integration, this comprised definitive proof in his view that the emancipation, in all its forms, was the worst of all solutions to the Jewish question. In such conditions, the Dreyfusards' battle on behalf of truth was of little significance to him. The combat of someone like Bernard Lazare was equally irrelevant: all that counted was the words uttered by Captain Dreyfus when he was arrested: 'I am persecuted because I am a Jew.'

Herzl, now obsessed by this plan to transform anti-Semitism into a driving force, did not commit himself in the Dreyfus Affair, but in 1895 decided – following an 'illumination'[24] – to implement a huge programme for the evacuation of the European Jews to some other territory: Argentina, Uganda, then Palestine. The most surprising thing in the story is the way he managed to convince first the colonial powers – the Ottoman Empire, the European states – and then thousands of diaspora Jews that his project was realizable.

This was, indeed, the period in which the Jews were migrating in the greatest numbers. Fleeing the pogroms of the 1880s, the Eastern Jews (*Ostjuden*) from the Russian Empire, separated from the rest by their rituals, took refuge in Vienna, Berlin, or Paris. Rejected as much by the assimilated, de-Judaized Western Jews as by the anti-Semites organized into political parties, they had little choice other than to dream of the promised land – the biblical land. And when, after the shock of the Dreyfus Affair, the assimilated Jews in their turn started to dream of a new exile outside Europe, the moment to turn into reality what was still a mere utopian longing seemed to have arrived. So it is not surprising that, in these conditions, the first to emigrate were the religious Jews from the East in quest of a holy land: these soon came into conflict with the other migrants, secular Jews both conservative and socialist, aspiring to build a nation-state. Thus, between 1882 and 1940, the five great pre-state *aliyahs*[25] took place: these were at the origin of the creation of the State of Israel, a state that would simultaneously be secular, religious, and democratic.

Herzl was clearly the man of the moment. A strange, half-mad Viennese, he turned a dream into reality, just as Freud, at the turn of the twentieth century, transformed the world of dreams into a place of desire so as to desacralize the obscure universe of predestinations and oracles.

It was perhaps because he had no real understanding of Judaism, or geography, or the difference between Eastern Jews (he accused them of fostering anti-Semitism) and Western Jews (whom he hated) that Herzl could launch such a programme. The promised land of which he dreamt – the Eretz Israel – existed only in biblical tradition, especially in the Mishnah. But Herzl barely knew the Bible or the Talmud. He could speak German, Hungarian, English, and French, but not much Yiddish – and even less Hebrew. And he knew nothing of the Mediterranean Jews, the Arab-speaking Sephardim, who had already settled in Palestine. But he yearned for this land, as the place where the Jews might be regenerated, and himself too: not a holy land inherited in direct line from the legend of the ancient Hebrews, but a conquered land which he wanted to turn into a nation-state on the model of the nation-states of the Europe from which he wished to flee. He cared little that this holy land was populated by its 'real' inhabitants: the Arabs of Palestine. In fact, Herzl dreamt of a mythical land whose memory had been handed down in the Jewish world from generation to generation ever since the Romans had sought to eradicate Judaism from Judaea by renaming it *Syria Palestina*.

His obsession finally won out over reality, and his denial of reality was more inflexible than any form of rationality. In a few years (between 1896 and 1904), driven by the vehemence of his imagination and the tenacity of his desire, Herzl managed to transform a myth into a reality, a dreamt-of land into a *Yishouv* (a community of settlers),[26] and to make credible for the present and the future the creation of a 'state for the Jews' – or state *of* Jews, i.e., Jewish state (*Judenstaat*) – without even needing to invent the word 'Zionism':[27] 'This simple desire to act', wrote Hannah Arendt, 'was such a surprising novel element, such a completely revolutionary element in Jewish life, that it spread as rapidly as a bush fire. Herzl's enduring greatness consists precisely in his desire to do something about the Jewish problem, in his desire to act and to solve the problem in political terms.'[28]

And when, after founding in Basel the World Zionist Organization, he encountered vehement opposition from the Jewish elite of the European cities, the banks, and all who preferred the diaspora to the road into exile, Herzl unhesitatingly turned against them the language of the vilest anti-Semitism, calling them 'Yids':

> Yid is anti-Zionist. We've known him for a long time, and just merely to look at him, let alone approach or, heaven forbid, touch him was enough to make us feel sick. [. . .] But who is this Yid, anyway? A type, my dear friends, a figure that pops up time and again, the dreadful companion of the Jew, and so inseparable from him that they have always been mistaken one for the other. [. . .] The Yid [. . .] is a hideous distortion of the human character, something unspeakably low and repulsive. [. . .] The Yid is the curse of the Jews. . . In our own day, even a flight from religion can no longer rid the Jew of the Yid. Race is now the issue.[29]

The stroke of genius of this man who loved anti-Semites so dearly was to draw inspiration from Moses Hess and Pinsker to purify, as it were, the biblical idea of the uniqueness of the Jewish people and to impose it by the celebrated formula in *The Jewish State*: 'We are one people (*Ein Volk*).'

In words that would become famous, Herzl called on the Jews scattered throughout the world to enter history, to emerge from their stagnation, their brooding over Jewish memory and self-hatred: because he regarded them as a people, as *his* people, he summoned them to self-emancipation, to think of themselves as part of a nation and a state on a par with other peoples: 'What is Zionism and what do I want to do?' he said in 1899. 'It means giving Jews of all nations a corner of the world where they may live in peace, no longer hunted, scorned and despised [. . .]. I finally want to rid them of this moral turpitude; to succeed in putting to work their very real intellectual and moral gifts, so that my people will no longer be the "dirty Jew" but the people of light that it can be.'[30]

Though he was the founder of political Zionism, Herzl travelled to Palestine only once, in 1898; but from Europe, where he continued to mobilize his supporters, he turned the Jewish question into a national question, inventing a new homeland and already defining – even before any process of organized emigration began – the way the Jews were to settle in their new territory. In his book he explained how, through the Jewish Company, transport of populations would be arranged, and how real estate would be built, modes of habitat constructed, land acquired, and finally new forms of living devised, necessary for the manufacture of a purified, superb, magnificent Jew, able to free himself from all the humiliations that his ancestors had endured since the dawn of time. So he was ready to help the imperial powers in their vast enterprise of colonization and to turn the new homeland established at the heart of the Arab world into an ally, helping the West to continue to dominate the East: 'A bit of a rampart against Asia [. . .] the reverse sentinel of civilization against barbarism.'[31]

In 1902, Herzl even went so far as to publish a story[32] in which he imagined a future Palestine as the model of a society based on cooperation, without army or prison. In it, he described the perfect harmony that reigned between Jews and natives, explaining how glad the latter were to integrate into a mainly Jewish society, since it enabled them to preserve their way of life and their religion. This text drew the attacks of Ahad Haam,[33] the proponent of a spiritual Zionism, involving the preservation of a non-diasporic Judaism in the holy land rather than the creation of a Eurocentric state for the Jews. While Herzl was inspired by an idyll that led to his detractors saying that he 'did not know there were Arabs in Palestine', those detractors, even though they were much more realistic, also failed to tackle the crucial question for the future – that of the Arab presence in Palestine. And when Max Nordau, defending Herzl, accused them of behaving towards the Arabs like anti-Semites or followers of the Inquisition, he himself produced no solution to the problem.[34] After all, he himself – unlike Ahad Haam – supported the creation in Palestine of a European-type state and not a homeland that had retreated into a Hebraic particularism.

All these polemics clearly show that Zionism played its part in colonial conquest, and this is how the Arabs saw the project. All the same, it is difficult to maintain that Zionism as such, in its various components (cultural, religious, political, spiritual), was purely and simply an alibi for colonialism. Springing from a response to a situation experienced as intolerable, Zionism in fact sought neither to enslave native peoples deemed to be inferior nor to impose on them a culture or a civilization. The fact remains that its aim was to settle a 'people without land in a land without people'.[35] And whatever its various representatives may have said – some favoured cohabitation, others exclusion – the project was inevitably going to lead to its own negation. The Jews, a people without land, actually settled in a land – thus realizing the Zionist plan – but one that was occupied by another people. This meant the tragedy continued: a Jewish tragedy.

Zionism was a revolution of identity within Jewish awareness, a revolt against Jewish memory made up of 'lamentations', and it was simultaneously a colonial phenomenon, aiming at seizing territory against the will of its inhabitants, and a process of self-decolonization, aimed at bringing the Jews to a new form of emancipation. Thus, as Alain Dieckhoff points out, it fitted into 'the long line of defensive movements against the religious persecutions that had led the Puritans to America and the Dutch Calvinists to South Africa'.[36]

Nonetheless, this experience was unique, anywhere in the world. For, by thinking of itself as a nation, and then agreeing to the creation, in 1917, of a National Foyer, the prelude to the foundation of a state in 1948, the European Jews active in Zionism, of whatever trend, finally obeyed the injunction of the anti-Semites who, ever since the end of the nineteenth century, had continually sought to expel them from every country in Europe. Thereby, moving from the status of pariahs to that of conquerors, they could not help but become, for the peoples they had driven out of their lands, persecutors and thus colonialists. And, when over half of them were decimated by the Nazis, victims of an appalling genocide, they were simply hated all the more by the Arab-Islamic world that made them responsible, after 1948, for the destruction of the Palestinian people.

Just as anti-Semitism lay behind a revolution in Jewish awareness and a disengagement from the ideal of the European Enlightenment, so Zionism triggered an awakening of Arab nationalism, supported first by the Christians of the East, then, in the interwar period, by the Muslims, and finally, decades later, by Islamists. This meant that Zionism introduced into the East not the peace of which Herzl had dreamt, but a perpetual and increasingly murderous war, whose consequences for the world as a whole would be alarming.

In 1898, Rachîd Ridâ[37] interpreted Herzl's utopia as the desire to bring together believers for political aims. And since he himself supported an Arab caliphate,[38] i.e., the project of a worldwide union of Muslims designed to restore spiritual and political power to Islam, he claimed to draw inspiration from Zionism in honing his modern vision of Arab nationalism.[39]

However, the first major analysis of Zionism to come from the Arab world was written in 1905 by a Maronite Christian who admired Barrès and lambasted the 'worldwide Jewish peril'. Nagib Azoury was born in Jaffa, brought up in France, became a functionary in the sandjak[40] of Jerusalem, and together with Eugène Jung, himself a former French administrator in Tonkin, founded the League of the Arabic Homeland. Azoury is celebrated for writing a few words of warning in a superbly Hegelian tone in the preamble to a work that was hardly read at the time: *Réveil de la nation arabe dans l'Asie turque* [*The awakening of the Arab nation in Turkish Asia*]:

> Two significant phenomena, akin and yet opposed, have not yet attracted anyone's attention but are at present making their presence felt in Asian Turkey: the awakening of the Arab nation and the latent effort of the Jews to restore on a very large scale the ancient kingdom of Israel. These two trends are destined to clash permanently, until one of them defeats the other. On the final outcome of this struggle between two people representing two opposing principles, the fate of the whole world will depend.[41]

Two opposing principles destined to fight one another to the death: a veritable tragedy, which would give birth to an endless conflict in which the two opposing parties – Palestinians and Israelis – would both have their own equally legitimate causes, just like the Greeks and the Trojans in Homer's epic. It was impossible to choose one camp against the other since the two camps had no choice but to live together – or to die together.

At the same time as this permanent combat, another conflict was unfolding, apparently more redemptive but also more obscure: that within the Jewish people. The premises can be found in a passage of Genesis relating Jacob's struggle with the Angel at night. Alone in the night, the son of Isaac and grandson of Abraham fought until daybreak with a mysterious opponent, whose sex he did not know, and who was – as Jacob was also unaware – both God and God's envoy (Elohim and the Angel). Seeing that he would not overcome the man, the Angel touched him in the hollow of his thigh, thereby rendering him lame. At dawn, as he sought to escape, Jacob asked him to bless him and agreed to reveal his name to him. And the Angel then told him: 'Thy name shall be called no more Jacob, but Israel: for as a prince has thou power with God and with men, and hast prevailed.'[42]

Victorious but wounded for life, the third patriarch embodies the idea that man's highest victory is the one he obtains over himself, over his arrogance, his will to power – a theme which Freud took up. And it was this man's name – Jacob, victor and vanquished – that was given to the state *of* Jews, the Jewish state dreamt of by Herzl: Israel. A state condemned to perpetual conflict with men and to the never-ending struggle against itself.

If there is a secret link uniting the state *of* Jews and Jacob's struggle with the Angel, another, equally obscure link brought together the destinies of Joris-Karl Huysmans, Marcel Proust, and Oscar Wilde at the end of the nineteenth century. Deeply influenced by the decadent movement, these three writers all invented three characters who, each in their own way, belong to the long history of the people of the perverse, in which we find the combined images of the abject and the sublime: Jews, sodomites, sexual criminals, the abnormal, the marginal, the mystical, the insane, and their rebellious creators.

Identified with his astonishingly beautiful portrait, Dorian Gray secretly indulges in vice and crime while leading a life of luxury and preserving the features of eternal youth. On reading Huysmans' *A Rebours*, Gray sinks into abjection. The hero of this novel, Jean Des Esseintes, has withdrawn from the world after an unwholesome life. Surrounded by precious objects and rare flowers, he has changed into a man who has wilfully chosen to be persecuted and to devote himself entirely to a diabolical beatitude that has brought him to the brink of self-destruction. Robert de Montesquiou, the famous Parisian dandy of whom Des Esseintes was the literary double, later served as a model for Palamède de Guermantes, Baron de Charlus, a key figure in Proust's *In Search of Lost Time* and himself an heir of Balzac's Vautrin and the main incarnation of the 'cursed race' of sodomites.[43] Effeminate, powdered, ashamed of his vice, Charlus despises the weak, takes a malign pleasure in destroying people's friendships, and enjoys taking vengeance on those who have not insulted him. He hates the Jews, whom he accuses of destroying society, which does not stop him seeing Charles Swann, an ardent defender of Captain Dreyfus, certain of whose character traits – especially masochism – are taken from Herzl.

And, to bring out more clearly the extent to which the 'sodomites' form a universal people able both to integrate themselves into every other people and to view themselves as a community founded on a decisive difference, Charlus compares them to another 'cursed race', the Jews, who are in turn viewed as inverts by anti-Semites.[44] Like the Jews, the 'sodomists' as seen by Charlus are split creatures, forever at war with themselves. And, like the Zionists, they dream of rebuilding their original city: Sodom. But once they arrived, Charlus prophesies of the Jews, they would leave the city so as not to appear 'one of them'; they would take wives and maintain mistresses. They would go to Sodom only on the days of uttermost necessity. So everything would happen in the promised land as it does in London, Rome, Petrograd, or Paris.

This decadent mind-set fascinated Max Nordau because it seemed to bear within it the stigmas of an ontological self-hatred. Nordau, a Viennese doctor and journalist, moved in 1880 to Paris, where he was a correspondent, like Herzl, for the *Neue Freie Presse* and produced a vile and grotesque vision of the decadent world in a truly perverse work that he published as *Degeneration*,[45] and that – like *La France juive* – was one of the bestsellers of the 1890s.

Nordau, a pupil of Jean Martin Charcot, under whose direction he had written a thesis in medicine on female castration, was a great admirer not only of the psychiatrist Bénédict-Augustin Morel, the inventor of the term, but even more of Cesare Lombroso, the Italian expert in criminology, a socialist and a Jew, who had drawn on Darwinism to create his concept of the 'born criminal'. In his view, crime was the product of an instinctive propensity found in certain individuals who, instead of evolving normally, regressed to the animal state. On the basis of this quite unscientific 'discovery', Lombroso had extended his thesis to all human and social phenomena, convinced that the 'creative genius' was basically the same as the 'criminal genius'.

Indeed, in this period the so-called doctrine of heredity and degeneration had spread to every area of knowledge. It claimed that it could submit the analysis of pathological phenomena – madness, crime, neurosis, neurasthenia – to the observation of 'stigmas' that revealed social or individual 'defects' which led to the decline of mankind and the decay of the nation. From this pivotal doctrine, two opposing paths emerged: the one led to genocide and eugenics,[46] the other to a focus on hygiene and reparation. Selection and eradication meant, on the one hand, to preserve the 'good race', on the other, redemption based on the regeneration of bodies and souls.

This notion of degeneration spread among European Jews so powerfully that they no longer simply changed their names to escape their origins. Convinced that they bore the stigmas of their 'race', the most assimilated of them started to resort to plastic surgery, which was becoming increasingly widespread after the First World War, so as to modify certain aspects of their faces, in particular their noses and ears.

Nordau was a supporter of this doctrine, and throughout his work he lambasted the two *fin-de-siècle* scourges that in his view were responsible for the lowering of European culture: egotism and idiocy. And he laid into all the writers of his time – Zola, Ibsen, Huysmans, Wilde, Nietzsche, and Mallarmé – whom he accused of produced unwholesome works, corrupting the minds of their readers and leading them down a fateful path that would result in a twilight of the peoples. He even stigmatized their physical characteristics, which he judged to be repellent, using terms identical with those of anti-Semitic discourse. Finally, he savaged homosexuals, imagining the catastrophes that would ensue if, one day, they were given the right to marry legally.[47] His positions were criticized politely but firmly by Lombroso who, he stated, had in no case sought to cast aspersions on modern literary geniuses. Far from it, he pointed out: he had sung their praises . . .

When he met Herzl in 1896, Nordau became enthusiastically embroiled in political Zionism. Moving from the condemnation of degeneracy to the cult of regeneration, he persuaded himself that anti-Semitism was a blessing for European Jews, forgetting that he had claimed that small nations could never survive when faced with competition from the great nations organized into empires.

Thanks to Drumont, it was now becoming possible, in Nordau's view, to manufacture a new type of Jew, stripped of the rags and tatters of diaspora Jewishness, a Jew who would henceforth be 'masculine' rather than 'effeminate', a Jew endowed with the qualities of the Aryan, able to plough the fields, to live in the open air, to practise sport: 'Without Drumont', he told *La libre parole* in 1897,

I would never have felt Jewish. I don't go to the synagogue and I haven't set foot in a synagogue since I was fourteen. [. . .] But Drumont's books operated on me by suggestion. Thanks to him, I rediscovered myself. [. . .] What lies [. . .] at the basis of Drumont's doctrines? A nationalist idea. French anti-Semitism would like to renationalize France, Zionism would like to renationalize Israel. Each of us in our own sphere, we are pursuing the same goal. Let us shake each other by the hand.[48]

In spite of its success, Nordau's book was rapidly forgotten, even though it had been given a very positive reception by Charles Maurras:

> You have captured the present situation in our Europe in a very accurate term. There are no other words: Degeneration is the one. It can apply pretty much everywhere [. . .]. Yes, they are all degenerate: the Parnassians and the Symbolists, the decadents and the egotists, the Pre-Raphaelite mystics and the Tolstoyan mystics, the Ibsenites, the Wagner maniacs [. . .]. A nice world of garrulous and degenerate people, to be sure. They are doomed to die, and they are already dead.[49]

However, it would be wrong to see Nordau's prose as foreshadowing the notion of 'degenerate art' developed by the Nazis in 1937. Nordau's position was close to ideas about heredity and psychopathology as propagated at the end of the nineteenth century; he advocated regeneration and not eradication. And, in this respect, he moved towards the spirit of the Enlightenment that he had so vigorously rejected. The fact remains that this prose has become really unreadable, and we owe it to Freud that he completely undermined this doctrine of degeneration, even though it was shared by all the psychologists of his era.

Nordau was a friend and ally of Herzl and played a central role in constructing the Zionist ideal of the new Jew. And while he opposed the supporters of a more universal Zionism, he nonetheless came up with the idea that the Jewish people owed its 'immortality' to an enduring 'secret' transmitted from generation to generation: Jewish pride. His organicist vision of the evolution of societies did not prevent him from remaining faithful to the imaginary of Zionism in which the mythical history that had emerged from the high authority of the Bible needed to be placed at the service of a nationalist policy. Through the invention of a new notion of the Jewish people, it was – for Herzl as for Nordau – a question of historicizing what was merely a great fantasy of origins so as to bring the Jews into the realm of politics.

This meant that the One People needed, once their land had been localized, simply to reunite and impose a new language on the 'new Jews'. And this task was carried out by Eliezer Ben Yehouda, a Lithuanian Jew (born Perlman), who transformed Hebrew, the dead language of the Torah, into a *lingua franca*, spoken Hebrew, which in 1907 was adopted as the official language of the Zionist movement. Together with Arabic and English, it became, under the British Mandate, one of the country's three official languages.

And so, at every *aliyah*, immigrants tended to transform their names. The Hebraization of names became a way for them to break away from their original Jewishness, a source of humiliation, and to feel at last Jewish, physically and intellectually. This led to a split between two types of being Jewish: the Zionists on the one hand, in revolt against the 'diasporic soul', and the Jews of the diaspora on the other, hostile to nationalism – with each group also dreaming, depending on the period, that it might change places with the other.

The heirs of the two founding fathers continued to tear each other apart, but the idea of regeneration had gained ground, and the Zionism invented by Herzl and Nordau then developed into several opposed trends that were evidence as much of its vivacity as of the contradictions within it: liberals, Marxists, spiritualists, social democrats, religious groups, revisionists (ultra-right), and even non- or anti-Zionists.

As a citizen of the Austro-Hungarian Empire living in Paris, Nordau became a national of an enemy power. So he was forced to leave France, taking refuge first in Spain, then in Great Britain. Like Zweig and Freud, he witnessed the dismantling of the central empires and the last days of the European world whose end he had dreamt of without even realizing that he had moved away from it. He did not understand the political development of the new generation of militants for whom Zionism was also starting to become an intellectual, cultural, and spiritual affair.

Before the end of the First World War, the Arab world, whipped up by the martial enthusiasm of the unforgettable Thomas Edward Lawrence,[50] a European utopian thinker who had signed up as a colonel in the British Army, expected the victorious powers to foster the rise of a nationalism that could have led to their independence. But, as a result of the agreements signed in May 1916 by Mark Sykes and François Georges-Picot, France and Great Britain committed themselves, with the participation of Russia, to a policy of breaking up the Ottoman Empire and turning it into colonies – a policy that was denounced, following the October Revolution, by the new Bolshevik power.

The British had Palestine, the Red Sea, and the Persian Gulf in their sights; the French, Libya and Syria. Anxious to ensure that Britain maintained a monopoly over this region, Lloyd George adopted for his own ends the idea of the right of self-determination of peoples, as promoted by President Wilson. He thereby hoped to hasten the United States' entry into the war. So he gave his support to Arab nationalism while encouraging the expansion of Zionism. France, meanwhile, was committed to the safeguarding of the Holy Places and the protection of Christians in the East, and was thus obliged to accept British hegemony, while giving her support to the Arab nationalists (who were hostile to it) rather than to the Zionists.

And it was within this context that, on 2 November 1917, Sir Arthur Balfour, the British minister for foreign affairs, sent a letter to Baron Rothschild with the agreement of Chaim Weizmann,[51] in which he announced the creation of a national Jewish Homeland in Palestine as the prelude to the future establishment of a state. In this way, the British people gave a people without land the land of a third people, a land which was at the time populated by Arab peasants exploited by Turkish officials.[52]

The British Mandate was made official by the League of Nations in April 1922. Neither the Arabs nor the Jewish colonists in Palestine were satisfied by this new territorial carve-up which actually separated them. In spite of meetings between Faysal, Lawrence, and Weizmann, who all sought to unite Zionism and 'Arabness' and to find a solution to the status of the Holy Places,[53] and in spite of a poignant appeal for unity launched by Elie Eberlin, the disciple of Bernard Lazare, the two peoples found themselves face to face, under the iron rule of the European powers: all they could do now was learn to live together or to destroy each other, from within or without.

Gershom Scholem[54] passed a severe judgment on the way the Zionists accepted this as a fait accompli:

> Zionism has decided on its position, either freely or under coercion. Actually, it has done so freely, siding with the declining powers rather than with the rising forces [. . .]. Can a movement of national rebirth remain content with taking shelter in this way in the shadow of those who won the war? [. . .] Either Zionism will be swept away by imperialism, or it will be consumed by the flame of this revolution from the East.

This was also the position of Martin Buber and Hannah Arendt.[55]

Throughout their mandate, the British continually bent their policies to suit Arab nationalism, while, in successive ways of immigration, the Jews, victims of European anti-Semitism, found refuge in the new native land invented by Herzl.[56] From 1927 onwards, the translation into Arabic of *The Protocols of the Elders of Zion* swept through the ranks of Near Eastern anti-Zionists, who gradually adopted the ideas that had sprung up among European anti-Semites – especially since the Zionists themselves had never stopped discrediting the Jews of the diaspora, calling them vile 'cosmopolitans' in thrall to the 'powers of money'.

In 1939, Jewish immigration into Palestine was officially suspended;[57] but it continued nonetheless, clandestinely, during the Second World War. It was during this period that the Zionists began to take Nazism as a point of reference, a crucial signifier that enabled them not just to oppose one another but to stigmatize their Arab enemies. In this way they used anti-Semitism as a cog in the machinery of their own internal and external conflicts, just as Nordau and Herzl had drawn on Drumont to assert their Jewish pride.

And then the 'catastrophe' happened in Europe, the great and murderous acting-out, described for the first time on 19 January by the Rabbi of Grabow:

> The Jews are killed in two ways, either shot or gassed. For several days thousands of Jews have been brought from Łódź and the same thing happens to them. Do not imagine that all this is being written by a man afflicted by madness. Alas! It is the tragic horrible truth. 'Horror, horror, man, take off your clothes, cover your head with ashes, run into the streets and dance.'[58]

4

Universal Jew, Territorial Jew

In August 1929, riots broke out in Hebron during which Arabs massacred one of the oldest Jewish communities of the Yishuv. Faced with the nationalist demands of this people, dispossessed of their land, the leaders of the Zionist movements were divided as to how to react. Some, such as Vladimir Zeev Jabotinsky[1] – whom Ben Gurion nicknamed 'Vladimir Hitler' – deemed that the Arabs were affected by a biological determinism that would always stop them accepting the presence of the Jews and that a military 'wall of steel' needed to be built between the two communities, while others – activists on the socialist left – advocated the creation of a Palestinian Legislative Council composed of an equal number of Jews and Arabs. This meant 'agreeing that the Arabs had equal rights over Palestine', writes Georges Bensoussan, 'a major concession in the view of the Jewish leaders, who were unanimously convinced that the historic right of the Jews was not compatible with the right of residence of the Arabs.'[2]

Neither the insurrections, nor the killings, nor the violence, which continued to intensify, made it possible for anyone to find a solution to the terrible problem of access to the Holy Places, which were still closed to immigrants. And while the Hebrew press was harshly critical of the Orthodox Jews of Hebron, whom it accused of allowing themselves to be massacred without resisting, certain right-wing Zionists, including the famous Abraham Schwadron, an archivist and autograph collector, appealed for the victims to be respected without, however, offering the least solution to the Palestinian tragedy: 'The saints of Hebron', he wrote, '[. . .] did not try to defend themselves, and did not seek to kill a single one of their assailants: they have died an absolutely immoral death.'[3]

At this juncture, Chaim Koffler, a Viennese member of the Keren Hayesod,[4] turned to Freud to ask him, as he asked other intellectuals of the diaspora, to support the Zionist cause in Palestine and the principle of access to the Wailing Wall for the Jews. Since 1925, thanks to the intervention of Chaim Weizmann, who was seeking to organize the official teaching of psychoanalysis in Israel, Freud had become a member of the council of administration of the University of Jerusalem – as had his British disciple David Eder.[5] This did not prevent him from declining Koffler's proposal:

> I cannot do what you wish. My reluctance to interest the public in my personality is insurmountable and the current critical circumstances do not in the least impel me to do so. Anyone who wants to influence the great number of people must have something resounding and enthusiastic to tell them, and my reservations about Zionism do not permit this. Naturally, I have the greatest sympathy for efforts freely undertaken, I am proud of our University of Jerusalem and I am glad to hear of the prosperity of the establishments set up by our colonizers. But, on the other hand, I do not think that Palestine can ever become a Jewish state or that the Christian world, any more than the Islamic world, will one day be ready to hand over its holy places to the safeguarding of the Jews. It would have been more sensible, in my view, to found a Jewish homeland on soil that was weighed down by fewer historical associations; admittedly, I know that, for such a rational design, it would never have been possible to arouse the exultation of the masses or the cooperation of the rich. I also concede, regretfully, that the unrealistic fanaticism of our compatriots bears its share of responsibility in the awakening of the Arabs' mistrust. I cannot feel the least sympathy for a mistaken piety that turns a bit of Herod's wall into a national relic and, for its sake, defies the feelings of the country's inhabitants.
>
> You yourself must judge whether, since my viewpoint is so critical, I am the right person to play the role of consoler for a people shaken by an unjustified hope.[6]

Clearly, the missive of the founder of psychoanalysis did not meet with the approval of the members of the Keren Hayesod, since, in another letter sent to Abraham Schwadron, Koffler emphasized:

> Freud's letter, in spite of its authenticity and its warmth of tone, is not favourable to us. And since here, in Palestine, there is nothing secret, it is probable that this letter will leave the collection of autographs of the University Library and be made public. If I cannot be useful to the

Keren Hayesod, I would at least not wish to harm its cause. If you wish to read this manuscript for your own personal interest, before returning it to me, I will ask Dr Manka Spiegel to show it you, as he is to embark on a tourist visit to Palestine.

Schwadron replied to Koffler in Hebrew, in the form of a postscript to Koffler's letter:

> True, there is nothing secret in Palestine, but since I have not been naturalized, my collection receives no aid, and it is not much consulted by the public [. . .]. [This letter must be] neither shown nor handed to just anyone – in other words, more precisely, to a non-Zionist, this is my responsibility: I 'order you like the heavenly messengers (Daniel, 2/14) to make haste'. I promise you, in the name of the Library, that 'No human eye will see it (Job, 7/8)'.[7]

The promise that no human eye would see this missive, which was judged not favourable to the Zionist cause, was respected for sixty years. But since the best way to conceal an archive is to destroy it, this letter, because of the very mystery that lay on its locality and its existence, gave rise to several rumours. And yet it contained nothing more than an open secret, since Freud had already had an opportunity to express his thoughts on this matter several times. So, the same day (26 February 1930), he wrote Albert Einstein another letter, which repeated the same argument point by point: hatred of religion, scepticism about the creation of a Jewish state in Palestine, solidarity towards his Zionist 'brothers' – whom he sometimes called his 'brothers in race' – and, finally, an empathy for Zionism, despite the fact that he would never share its ideals because of its 'sacred extravagances': 'Whoever wants to influence a crowd must have something resounding, enthusiastic to say, and my sober appraisal of Zionism does not permit this.'

Freud stated that he was proud of 'our' university and 'our' kibbutzim, but he did not believe in the creation of a Jewish state because, he repeated, Muslims and Christians will never agree to entrust their sanctuaries to Jews. Thus he deplored the 'unrealistic fanaticism' of his Jewish brothers, which contributed to 'awakening the suspicion of the Arabs'.[8]

To show that, in other ways, he still felt a sense of solidarity for Zionist enterprises – especially after the Nazis had come to power – Freud was perfectly happy, on the occasion of the fifteenth anniversary of the creation of the Keren Hayesod, to send Leib Jaffé a missive full of praise: 'I want to assure you that I know full well how powerfully and beneficently effective an instrument this foundation has become for our people in the endeavour to found a new home in the old fatherland.' He saw it as 'a sign of our invincible will to live which has so far successfully braved two thousand years of burdensome oppression.'[9] In 1934, he had been glad that Zionism was not an opportunity for bringing the old religion back to life, and had shown a certain enthusiasm for the creation of a secular state. In a word, Freud preferred his position as a diaspora Jew, universalist, and atheist to that of a spiritual guide with an attachment to a new promised land:

> While thanking you for welcoming me to England, I would like to ask you not to treat me 'as a guide of Israel'. I would like to be considered merely as a modest man of science and in no other way. Despite being a good Jew who has never denied Judaism, I still cannot forget my totally negative attitude towards all religions, including Judaism, which sets me apart from my Jewish colleagues and makes me unsuitable for the role you would like to grant me.[10]

Freud was fully aware of the great movement of Jewish regeneration inaugurated by the founding fathers. He was acquainted with its men and its ideas. But, although he never denied his Jewishness, he could not imagine that a return to the land of the ancestors might be any solution whatsoever to the question of European anti-Semitism. In this respect, he had the magisterial intuition that the question of sovereignty over the holy places would one day lie at the heart of an almost insoluble problem, not just between the three monotheisms, but between the two brother peoples residing in Palestine.[11] He feared, with reason, that an unjustified colonization would end up setting anti-Semitic Arabs against racist Jews, all over an idolized bit of wall.

We do not find in Freud any of those great imprecations that punctuate Nordau's reflections on the future of the 'new Jew'. Freud did not regard the Jews of Europe as pathological beings, ruined by centuries of oppression. Since he had never supported the theory of degeneracy, or that of the psychology of peoples, he did not think that – merely by putting down roots in a land – the Jews would be endowed with a renewed biological body or a psychological make-up purified of all the 'tares' due to their abasement.

In 1909, when the unhappy Hans Herzl visited Freud to ask for advice about his future, he was encouraged to free himself from the paternal model:

> Your father is one of those men who have turned dreams into reality. People of that type [. . .] are very rare, and dangerous. I shall say only

that they are at the other extreme from my own scientific work. My job is to strip dreams of their mystery, make them clear and ordinary. They do the opposite: they command in the world, but remain on the other side of the psychic mirror.[12]

Considering Zionism as a dangerous utopia, but also as a pathology, i.e., as a way of making up for national feelings frustrated by anti-Semitism, Freud also – quite logically – detested all forms of Jewish self-hatred. He even considered Theodor Lessing's work as quite abominable. But he knew that the phenomenon existed, and he regarded it as a typically Jewish phenomenon, especially among the Viennese. He also saw the castration complex as the unconscious root not just of anti-Semitism, but of Jewish self-hatred and the hatred of women: 'for even in the nursery little boys hear that a Jew has something cut off his penis – a piece of his penis, they think – and this gives them a right to despise Jews. And there is no stronger unconscious root for the sense of superiority over women.'[13]

Hence, feeling at ease in his identity and not humiliated as his father had been, and having subsequently promised himself in his childhood that he would avenge the latter by identifying himself with Hannibal the Semite, Freud recommended that all his friends should never convert, and accept that they were both Jews and something else. For, in his view, both denial and the belief in a possible metamorphosis of one's identity were the worst solutions to the Jewish question, which in any case had no need of any 'solution'. In short, instead of drawing from anti-Semitism the energy needed to accept its verdict and renounce the emancipation within the diaspora, in the name of some 'Jewish pride' – as did Herzl and Nordau, taking their lead from Nordau – Freud laid claim to his Jewish identity only when he needed to confront the prejudice of anti-Semitism and never in order to escape to some ancestral home: 'My language is German', he said in 1926. 'My culture and my attachments are German. I considered myself intellectually to be a German before noting the rise of anti-Semitic prejudices in Germany and German Austria. Since then, I have no longer viewed myself as a German. I prefer to call myself Jewish.'[14]

Likewise, viewing Jewishness as a transhistorical state – a sort of 'property of the Jew' – he saw it as a source of resistance to all phenomena of massification:

And before long there followed the realisation that it was only to my Jewish nature that I owed the two qualities that have become indispensable to me throughout my difficult life. Because I was a Jew I found myself free of many prejudices which restrict others in the use of the intellect: as a Jew I was prepared to be in the opposition and to renounce agreement with the 'compact majority'.[15]

Thus Freud shared with Hannah Arendt the idea that the Jews had an ability to turn their situation as victims of persecution into the position of a 'conscious pariah' which helped them in adversity, not to retreat – and thus to ensure that mankind as a whole benefited from the force of character of a rebellious singularity. He reiterated this claim in 1930, in the preface to the Hebrew edition of *Totem and Taboo*: 'None of the readers of this book can easily put himself in the place of the author and experience what he experiences, he who does not know the sacred language, who is totally detached from the religion of his fathers – as from any other religion – who cannot share nationalist ideas and yet has never denied that he belongs to his people – and who would not wish to change this.'[16] And he added that he said he was convinced that this book on the origin of religions would be given a favourable reception in a country that had fostered the spirit of modern Judaism and succeeded in bringing alive the sacred language.

Freud was wrong. In spite of the support given him by Weizmann, it was not possible for him to ensure that psychoanalysis was taught at the University of Jerusalem by having Moshe Wulf elected to the post,[17] – Wulf had settled in Palestine at the same time as Max Eitingon. Even worse, on the initiative of Judah Magnes,[18] a fierce enemy of Freud's doctrine and a supporter of the experimental psychology inherited from the American model, psychoanalysis was granted no official recognition, even though the Jewish psychoanalysts of Europe were being persecuted by the Nazis and forced to emigrate. Subsequently, the most distinguished thinkers in Palestine – especially Gershom Scholem and Martin Buber – neglected Freud's work, and only in 1977 was a chair in psychoanalysis created, at the behest of Anna Freud, who mainly favoured clinical work of English-speaking inspiration rather than erudite research into Freud's corpus.[19]

The promised land invested by Freud knows no border and no home. It is surrounded by no wall and has no need of any barbed wire to affirm its sovereignty. Inside human beings, inside their own minds, this promised land is woven out of words, fantasies, and tragic scenes: Oedipus at Thebes, Hamlet before the battlements of Elsinore.

As the heir to a romanticism that had acquired a scientific bent, Freud took his concepts from Greek and Latin civilization and German *Kultur*. As for the territory he claimed to be exploring, he situated it in an elsewhere that could not be circumscribed: that of a subject dispossessed of its mastery of the world, detached from its divine origins, and submerged in the discontents of its own ego.

So it is easy to see why, throughout his life, Freud was eager for psychoanalysis not to be seen as a 'Jewish science', i.e., in his view, a category within the psychology of particularism. He defined it as a scientific and universal theory of the unconscious and of desire. Freud did not want his doctrine to be shut away in a ghetto, even if it were the regenerated ghetto promised by Zionism. He, the faithless Jew, wanted to unite in one and the same people, within psychoanalysis, Jews and non-Jews, 'oil and water'. And, in order to demonstrate that psychoanalysis was not in the least in thrall to a *genius loci*, he was ready for anything – even to entrust Carl Gustav Jung, a non-Jew whom he knew to be an anti-Semite, with the leadership of the International Psychoanalytical Association (IPA) that he had founded in 1910: 'His association with us is therefore all the more valuable. I was almost going to say that it was only by his emergence on the scene that psychoanalysis was removed from the danger of becoming a Jewish national affair.'[20] And again, in December 1908: 'Our Aryan comrades are really quite indispensable to us, otherwise psychoanalysis would fall victim to anti-Semitism.'[21]

But the biggest surprise of all is that, in 1913, when Jung left the movement to create his own trend, Freud, furious and hurt, did a complete U-turn without even noticing his change of mind. For a while, indeed, overwhelmed by a sort of imaginary re-Judaization of his doctrine, he declared that only good Jews – in other words, the disciples of the first circle from *Mitteleuropa* – would in future be capable of carrying out his movement's policies. But, in the end, it was Ernest Jones, the only non-Jew on the Secret Committee, to whom he entrusted the heavy task of directing the IPA.

In 1917, already furiously anglophile, and no less furiously anti-Jungian, Freud said that he was favourable to the creation, under British Mandate, of a national homeland in Palestine: 'The only thing that gives me any pleasure is the capture of Jerusalem and the British experiment with the chosen people.'[22] We should point out that Lord Balfour regarded Freud as one of the greatest thinkers of modern times. Finally, in a letter of February 1926, he told Enrico Morselli that he would not be ashamed if psychoanalysis were seen as the 'direct product' of the 'Jewish mind':

> I am not sure that your opinion, which looks upon psychoanalysis as a direct product of the Jewish mind, is correct, but if it is I wouldn't be ashamed. Although I have been alienated from the religion of my

forebears for a long time, I have never lost the feeling of solidarity with my people and realise with satisfaction that you call yourself a pupil of a man of my race – the great Lombroso.[23]

Like all his contemporaries, Freud frequently spoke of the 'Jewish race', of 'Semitism', of 'racial belonging', or indeed of the 'differences' between Jews and 'Aryans', which shows us, in passing, how seriously the philological manias of the nineteenth century had been taken. And when he felt exasperated by his first disciples in the Wiener Psychoanalytische Vereinung, he called them 'Jews' who were incapable of winning over friends to the new doctrine.[24]

However, his use of such expressions never led him to promote a psychology of difference. In a letter to Sándor Ferenczi on 8 June 1913, he took a definite position on this question: 'On the matter of Semitism', he wrote,

> there are certainly great differences from the Aryan spirit. We can become convinced of that every day. Hence, there will surely be different world views and art here and there. But there should not be a particular Aryan or Jewish spirit. The results must be identical, and only their presentation may vary [. . .]. If these differences occur in conceptualizing objective relations in science, then something is wrong.[25]

Freud's relation with Max Eitingon revealed the situation in which he found himself in 1933 when psychoanalysis was attacked for being a Jewish science, or three years after he had judged Zionism as a dangerous utopia. Of course, he was right to predict a complicated future for the coming Jewish state. But, when it came to Europe, Germany in particular, he showed no great lucidity by opting for Jones's policy rather than the much more clear-sighted position of his Zionist, socialist disciple.

Born in 1881, in Mohilev, in Belorussia, Max Eitingon was the son of a wealthy fur trader. In February 1921, after the collapse of the Central Powers, he carried out in Berlin the greatest task of his life, for the love of Freud and psychoanalysis: the Berliner Psychoanalytisches Institut (BPI), the first training institution, which would be the model for all those founded subsequently throughout the world, and integrated into the IPA. To show his thanks, Freud made him a gift of the golden ring reserved for initiates.

Over the years, Eitingon placed his fortune at the disposal of his institute, while also setting up, in the framework of a polyclinic, free treatment for those who could not afford it (while the other patients paid for theirs). In 1930, he had become, all by himself, in the words of Ernest Jones, 'the heart of the entire international psychoanalytical movement'.

However, after January 1933, isolated within the BPI, he was forced to resign by the few non-Jewish psychoanalysts – Felix Boehm and Carl Müller-Braunschweig, among others – who took advantage of the situation to join the Nazis and take the places of their colleagues who were excluded by the so-called laws on the Aryanization of medicine and psychotherapy.

Conservative, hostile to the Freudian Left in Germany – Otto Fenichel, Ernst Simmel, etc. – and keen to reinforce Anglo-American power, Jones leaned on Boehm to favour a policy of collaboration with the new regime. It consisted in maintaining, under Nazism, a so-called neutral practice of psychoanalysis, so as to preserve it from any contamination from the other schools of psychotherapy, themselves introduced into the new 'Aryanized' BPI.

In 1935, in the name of the so-called idea of 'saving psychoanalysis', Jones agreed to chair the session of the Deutsche Psychoanalytische Gesellschaft (DPG) in Berlin, at which the Jews were forced to resign. A single non-Jew refused to accept this infamy: his name was Bernhard Kamm, and he left the DPG to show his solidarity with the excluded. He immediately went into exile and moved to Topeka in Kansas, to the famous clinic of Karl Menninger, a veritable meeting point for all the exiled psychotherapists from Europe.

Subsequently, psychoanalysis was decreed to be a 'Jewish science', whereupon the Nazis set up, under the aegis of Matthias Heinrich Göring, a cousin of the marshall, a veritable programme of destruction, not only of those of its practitioners who had not fled, but of its vocabulary, its words, its concepts. The adjective which Freud had so feared was applied to his doctrine alone, and never to the other schools of dynamic psychiatry also founded by Jews. And it was probably because psychoanalysis was the only doctrine of the psyche that laid claim to the inheritance of a godless Jewishness, detached from its roots – and thus the patrimony of a universalist humanism – that it was, *for this very reason*, condemned to be eradicated.

So it was entirely as if, by seeking to exterminate the language and vocabulary of psychoanalysis – and not just its Jewish representatives – the Nazis had aimed at the universal element within it. By exterminating the Jew because he was Jewish, they were exterminating Man himself; likewise, by eradicating the language of psychoanalysis, they aimed to suppress through murder what, in this doctrine, involved the universality of Man. At the root of any display of radical, absolute, passionate hatred of psychoanalysis, we always discover the symptom of a repressed or unconscious anti-Semitism.

Eitingon was hostile to this line; but, before he made any decision, he demanded that Freud write to tell him of his own thoughts on the matter. Freud did so, in a letter dated 1 March 1933, emphasizing that his disciple could choose between three solutions: 1 – cease the activities of the BPI; 2 – collaborate on maintaining it under the aegis of Boehm, 'to survive through challenging times'; 3 – abandon ship, at the risk of allowing Jungians and Adlerians to seize the prize, which would oblige the IPA to disqualify it.[26]

At this date, Freud had opted for the second solution. On 17 April, he congratulated himself that Boehm had rid him both of the psychoanalyst Wilhelm Reich, a dissident and Marxist, whom he hated (and who would soon be expelled from the IPA before emigrating to Norway and then across the Atlantic), and of Harald Schultz-Hencke, a Nazi Adlerian, who was soon taken back into the BPI.

Faced with such blindness, which consisted in believing that psychoanalysis could survive under Nazism, Eitingon decided to remain as faithful to Freudianism as to Zionism. Without expressing the least reproach to Freud, he left Germany and settled in Jerusalem in April 1934. Here he found the writer Arnold Zweig and founded a psychoanalytical society and an institute on the model of the Berlin one, thus laying the foundations of a future Israeli psychoanalytical movement. Despite Freud's efforts, he did not obtain any support from the Hebrew University of Jerusalem.

In just a few years, old Europe was emptied of all the German-speaking pioneers of psychoanalysis. They became English-speaking and pragmatic as they were forced to emigrate to the United States and, to Freud's great fury, to transform a doctrine centred on the exploration of the unconscious, subjectivity, and the death drive into a therapeutic tool in the service of a hygienic desire for happiness – the precise opposite of what had constituted the revolution of intimate meaning invented in Vienna at the beginning of the twentieth century by Jews of the Haskalah, gathered around the founding father, who, after the Anschluss, was obliged to take refuge in London with his entire family.

As he separated from his Viennese disciples who rejected Jones's policy, Freud uttered these words: 'After the destruction by Titus of the First Temple in Jerusalem, Rabbi Yochannan ben Zakkai asked for permission to open in Jahné a school devoted to the study of the Torah. We are going to do the same. We are, after all, used to being persecuted, through our history, our traditions, and – some of us – by experience, with one exception.' Whereupon Freud named Richard Sterba, the only non-Jew in the circle who had, like Kamm, said 'no' to Jones.[27]

And so Freud, who had rejected the label 'Jewish science' as a description of his doctrine, and had ended up agreeing to Jones's policies rather than Eitingon's in Germany, laid claim – in Vienna, the birthplace of Zionism and of the theory of the unconscious – to the tradition of Judaism, despite the fact that he had earlier declared himself to be the worst enemy of religion and then shown himself sceptical as regards the idea of creating a Jewish state in Palestine. What had saved Judaism, he essentially said in 1938, will save psychoanalysis too. The transmission of a heritage, the study of the texts, the acceptance of exile and dispersion: this, then, was the Jewish destiny of Freudian universalism, a Jewishness without territory, with its roots in science alone.

How can we fail to be reminded here of the overwhelming scene narrated by Elie Wiesel in *Night*? One day, in Auschwitz, the SS hanged a boy – the little *pipel* with his angel face – just for the pleasure of it, and they forced the prisoners to watch the spectacle. 'Where is God?' asked one man. And the young deportee[28] who had lost his faith said to himself: 'Here He is – He is hanging here on this gallows.'[29] From this event, and from his confrontation with the death drive that had led him to be unwilling to save his father when he was already dying, and then to view himself as a corpse that had survived, Wiesel compensated for the loss of God with the need to bear witness: to pray is to believe in God, to write is to believe in human beings. In Auschwitz, as we know, some Jews decided to put on trial the God who had permitted such things, and they condemned him to death. After passing the sentence, the rabbi summoned those present to a reading of the Torah.

And so, even when God is dead, even when the Temple is destroyed, even when Vienna, the cradle of psychoanalysis, is wiped off the map, there remains something that is handed on – and thus hope: bearing witness, reading the sacred text, preserving memory. For what is eternal among the Jews is not God, but human beings who remember – in other words, the Jew of knowledge, able to perpetuate the covenant through speech and writing.

On his arrival in London in 1938, when the British representative of the Keren Hayesod asked Freud to write a new letter of support, he again replied in the negative. The anti-Semitic persecutions had in no way changed his opinion. He still felt a sense of solidarity with his people, but he still hated religion as much, including the same Judaism to which he had appealed as he was bringing the great Viennese venture to an end. And now he continued to reject the idea that a Jewish state – or a state for the Jews – might be viable, precisely because such a state, by referring to a 'Jewish being', could in no way become, in his view, truly secular.

To Eitingon, he wrote: 'I can no longer understand this world. Have you read that, in Germany, they are preparing to forbid the Jews to give German forenames to their children? They will only be able to respond by demanding that the Nazis give up those popular names, Johann, Josef and Maria.'[30]

If Freud's attitude to Jones's policy had been, to say the least, ambiguous, that of his daughter Anna would be even more so. At the congress of the IPA held in Paris in July 1938,[31] she repeated her father's words on Ben Zakkai to all the European psychoanalysts – whose fate was sealed. Then, in his closing speech, Jones announced the triumph of the policy of so-called salvaging of psychoanalysis in Germany and expressed his delight at the 'autonomy' of the new DPG. From this date onwards, in spite of the genocide, the different presidents of the IPA would never agree to recognize that this policy was disastrous: instead, they always presented it in the most positive light. And only in 1985 was an official exhibition on this past organized – on the condition, however, that Jones's name was not tarnished.[32] This new censorship would have considerable repercussions.

In January 1940, when Anna Freud asked Eitingon to collect together her father's letters, Arnold Zweig forwarded the ones he had received from Freud to his friend. He delicately drew his attention to a missive dated 10 February 1937, in which the master expressed a cruel opinion of his wife, Mirra. Stung to the quick, Eitingon, the most lucid of the two men when it came to Nazism and the need for psychoanalysis to refuse to collaborate with the worst – whatever forms it might take – did not wish to preserve of Freud anything but the memory of the beloved person.

He died three years later, by which time the Berlin world which he had served so well was nothing but night and fog.

After 1933, while he was criticizing Zionism while taking pleasure in its successes and mistaken about the character of Nazism, Freud nonetheless drew from a secular return to Jewish history the ferments of a rational ethics capable of responding to the collapse of the old Europe of the Enlightenment. And this was the period which he devoted to the writing of his last work, *Moses and Monotheism*,[33] which came out in the year of his death, in London and Amsterdam. In some respects, Freud was in this work replying to Herzl, who had identified himself with a prophet forever forced to fight the golden calf so as to drag his people out of slavery. He had even compared his story to the tragedy of a leader (*Führer*) who refused to behave as a seducer (*Verführer*).

In 1922, the Berlin historian Ernst Sellin had put forward the idea that Moses had been the victim of a collective murder committed by his people, who preferred to worship idols. Moses' doctrine had then become an esoteric tradition handed on by a circle of initiates, and it was on this idol that would be born faith in Jesus, another assassinated prophet, and the founder of Christianity. This was more than enough to seduce Freud, who adored all these stories about fathers being murdered. To this he added the idea that Moses was an Egyptian, an idea supported by historians of the *Aufklärung* eager to find a rational (and not religious) explanation for the prophet's story.

In the perspective adopted by Freud, the biblical text had merely shifted the origins of monotheism to a mythical time, ascribing its foundation to Abraham and his descendants. As a great Egyptian dignitary and a supporter of monotheism, Moses had become leader of a Semitic tribe, thereby giving monotheism a spiritualized form. And, in order to distinguish it from others, he had introduced the Egyptian rite of circumcision, thereby seeking to show that God, through this covenant, had elected the people chosen by Moses. But the people, unable to tolerate the new religion, killed the man who claimed to be a prophet, then repressed the memory of the murder – a memory which returned with Christianity.

So Freud was here picking up the thread of the idea of Christianity's old anti-Judaism and interpreting it against its usual grain, that of the deicidal people. He turned Judaism into the religion of the father, Christianity into the religion of the son, and Christians into the heirs of a murder repressed by the Jews: 'The old God the Father fell back behind Christ; Christ, the Son, took his place, just as every son had hoped to do in primaeval times.'[34]

Freud also claimed that Paul of Tarsus, the continuer of Judaism, had been its destroyer as well: by introducing the idea of redemption, he had managed to ward off the spectre of human guilt while contradicting the idea that the Jewish people was the chosen people. Finally, he had renounced the evident sign of this chosen-ness: circumcision. The new religion had thus succeeded in becoming universal and addressing all human beings.

But Freud went even further. He was stating, in fact, that hatred of the Jews was fuelled by their belief in the superiority of the chosen people and by the castration anxiety roused by circumcision as a sign of election. In his view, this rite was aimed at ennobling the Jews and leading them to despise the others, the uncircumcised. From the same viewpoint, he took literally, albeit to shift its meaning, the principal grievance of anti-Judaism, namely the refusal of the Jews to accept that they had put God to death. The Jewish people, he said, insists on denying the murder of God, and Christians never stop accusing the Jews of being deicides because they have freed themselves from the original fault, since Christ, as a substitute for Moses, sacrificed his life to redeem them. In other words, if Christianity is a religion of the son who confesses his murder and redeems it, Judaism remains a religion of the father which refuses to acknowledge the murder of God. And the Jews are still as persecuted for the murder of the son, of which they are innocent. Freud concluded that this refusal exposed the Jews to the resentment of other peoples.[35]

After admitting that the history of the Jews could not be separated from the history of Christian anti-Judaism, Freud explained that the anti-Semitism of modern nations was a displacement onto the Jews of a hatred of Christianity:

> The peoples who today indulge in anti-Semitism have become Christians only belatedly and were often forced to take this step by bloody violence. We might even say that they are all 'badly baptized'; under a thin layer of Christianity, they have remained the same as their ancestors, in thrall to a barbarous polytheism. They have not overcome their aversion for the new religion, but have displaced it onto the source whence Christianity came to them [. . .]. Their anti-Semitism is at bottom anti-Christianity, and it is no surprise that, in the German National Socialist revolution, this intimate bond between the two monotheistic religions finds such clear expression in the hostile treatment to which both are subjected.[36]

In other words, if Judaism, a 'fossil' religion, was superior to Christianity by its intellectual force, but unsuitable to be universalized, they had to be thought of together if a Judaeo-Christian culture could be drawn on to oppose modern anti-Semitism.

The novelty of Freud's procedure actually lay in bringing to light the unconscious roots of anti-Semitism, starting with Judaism itself and not just as a phenomenon external to it. This was a way of moving back to the questions discussed in *Totem and Taboo*, of which *Moses and Monotheism* was the continuation.

If society had indeed been created by a crime committed against the father, putting an end to the despotic reign of the savage horde, then, by the establishment of a law in which the symbolic figure of the father was re-evaluated, this meant that Judaism followed the same scenario. After the murder of Moses, it had created Christianity, based on the recognition of guilt: so monotheism was merely the interminable history of the establishment of this law of the father on which Freud had built his entire doctrine. Thus he obeyed the injunction to return to the great authority of the Bible and the religion of his fathers. But, far from adopting the solution of conversion as a response to anti-Semitism, or of Zionism, he redefined himself as a godless Jew – a Jew of thought and knowledge – while rejecting Jewish self-hatred. Thus he prised Judaism away from the feeling of Jewishness proper to non-believing Jews, thereby getting round both the covenant and the election.

But at the very same time that he was in this way de-Judaizing Moses so as to turn him into an Egyptian, Freud assigned to Jewishness, understood both as an essence and as a form of belonging, an eternal aspect. This feeling by which a Jew remains a Jew in his subjectivity, even while keeping aloof from Judaism, was something that Freud experienced himself – and he did not hesitate to see it as a phylogenetic inheritance.

Placed under the sign of speculation and the critical study of myths, this Freudian testament in the shape of a novel of origins gave rise to many contradictory interpretations.

In 1991, the American historian Yosef Hayim Yerushalmi set out to 'listen to Freud', publishing the most erudite and most complete commentary ever written on this work. While re-Judaizing Freud's approach to Jewishness, he emphasized that Freud had turned psychoanalysis into the continuation of a godless Judaism: an interminable Jewishness.[37] And he accused the IPA of never having said anything either about the genocide of the Jews or about the destruction of psychoanalysis in Germany:

> To my knowledge, between 1939, when there was no longer anything to lose, and the end of the Second World War, no official body of any psychoanalytical organization raised its voice to denounce the destruction of the Jews, nor even that of psychoanalysis, when the one included the other, in Nazi Germany and the lands under its domination. It is as if suggesting there was a direct link between the Jews and psychoanalysis had been taboo.[38]

Freud's work was not highly rated by Israeli scholars, specialists in Jewish history. Martin Buber criticized Freud for his lack of scientific rigour,[39] and Gershom Scholem preferred Carl Gustav Jung – at least for a while – who in turn became a fervent Zionist in proportion as his anti-Semitism and his support for Nazi Germany grew. He also hoped that the Jews would be expelled from Europe, and remained blind to what was starting to happen.

While the collaborationist Freudians were preoccupied by the so-called purity of psychoanalysis, Jung's German disciples adopted various different positions. Gerhard Adler, James Kirsch, and Max Zeller actually opposed the new German regime and went into exile in London and California. But others became militant supporters of the new Hitlerian psychology. They included Gustav Richard Heyer and Walter Cimbal.

Heyer, a racist and an anti-Semite, founded a Jungian group in Munich in 1928, and enthusiastically hailed the advent of Nazism before joining the Party in 1937. At the Göring Institute, he wore Nazi uniform and proclaimed the cult of 'blood and earth', contrasting the healthy, creative character of German psychotherapy with 'Jewish' psychoanalysis, which he viewed as grossly materialistic. As for Walter Cimbal, he was, like Achelis and Haeberlin, a pure representative of the *völkisch* spirit. In his opinion, individuality could be realized only by a return to the primordial roots of a deep unconscious, 'alone able to assure the unity of the members of the same community'.[40]

Jung's case is much more complex.

In 1933, Ernst Kretschmer, a German psychiatrist who was hostile to the regime, resigned from his post at the head of the Allgemeine Ärtzliche Gesellschaft für Psychotherapie (AÄGP). The aim of this association, founded in 1926, was to bring together the different schools of European psychotherapy under the aegis of medicine. One review, the *Zentralblatt für Psychotherapie*, created in 1930, acted as an organ for the spread of the AÄGP's ideas. When Hitler came to power, the German branch of the association and the *Zentralblatt*, published in Leipzig, were forced to undergo Nazification, under Göring's supervision. At this juncture, German psychotherapists, simultaneously anxious to fall in with the regime and to pursue their national and European activities, asked Jung to take over the AÄGP, of which he was already the vice-president. Wishing to ensure the domination of analytical psychology over the other schools of psychotherapy, he agreed to become president. He hoped that, from his base in Zurich, he would be able to protect both therapists without a medical degree – previously sidelined by Kretschmer – and the Jewish colleagues who were no longer permitted in practise in Germany. In actual fact, he had been chosen by German practitioners because he was trusted by the promoters of Aryan psychotherapy who were fiercely opposed to Freud's thought.

And so, at the behest of Cimbal and Heyer, Jung embarked on an adventure from which he could easily have held himself aloof. As is shown by a letter of 23 November 1933 addressed to his disciple Rudolf Allers, he agreed to all the conditions dictated by Göring if he were to become head of the *Zentralblatt*. Jung wrote:

> It must unquestionably be a 'conformed' [*gleichgestaltet* – i.e., one conforming to Nazi ideas – Trans.] editor, as he would be in a far better position than I to have the right nose for what one can say and what not. In any event it will be an egg-balancing dance [. . .]

Psychotherapy must see to it that it maintains its position inside the German Reich and does not settle outside it, regardless of how difficult its living conditions there may be. Göring is a very amiable and reasonable man, so I have the best hopes for our cooperation.[41]

Whereupon, Jung began to publish texts favourable to Nazi Germany in the 'Aryanized' *Zentralblatt*, of which he was now the director of publication, with Cimbal as general secretary. The first text came out in 1933: under the title 'Geleitwort' ('Editorial'), it advocated a 'classical' approach to the difference between races and mentalities, each being characterized, he claimed, by a specific psychology:

The noblest task of the *Zentralblatt* will thus be, while respecting impartially all contributions that may present themselves, to constitute an overall conception that can do more justice to the fundamental facts of the human soul than was the case hitherto. The differences which actually exist, and indeed have long been recognized by far-sighted people, between Germanic psychology and Jewish psychology, cannot be ignored any more, and science cannot gain anything from so doing. In psychology, more than in any other science, there is a 'personal equation', and a failure to recognize this will skew the results in practice and theory. This does not mean, of course – and I would like this to be clearly understood – any depreciation of Semitic psychology, any more than it means a depreciation of Chinese psychology when we speak of the psychology proper to the inhabitants of the Far East.[42]

Aware of the vulnerability of his position, Jung was really seeking to prove that the differential approach that he defended had nothing to do with the differential racism of National Socialism. But he was wasting his time. In the same issue of the *Zentralblatt*, Göring loudly sang the praises of *Mein Kampf*, while Walter Cimbal suggested, in the name of Jung's ideas, that a veritable anti-Semitic programme of Nazification should be implemented in psychology and psychotherapy in Germany.

Far from resigning after this initial affront, Jung carried on down the same path. In a letter to Cimbal of 2 March 1934, he accused Göring of having made a 'grave tactical error by shoving under foreign subscribers' noses a manifesto concerning German domestic politics.'[43] He did not protest against the contents of this manifesto, but against the 'error' of publishing it.

On 26 June 1933, while in Berlin for a seminar, Jung gave a radio interview to his disciple Adolf von Weizsäcker, a neurologist and psychiatrist who had joined the Nazis. Von Weizsäcker introduced the Master of Zurich as an eminent Protestant from Basel and as 'the most progressive psychologist of modern times'. He cunningly declared that his theory of the psyche was more creative and closer to the 'German mind' than were those of Freud and Adler. Then he encouraged Jung to paint a positive picture of Hitler and the fine youth of Germany, and to condemn European democracies that suffered from the 'aimless conversations of parliamentary deliberations [droning] on'. Jung finished his interview by suggesting that nations enrich themselves by implementing a programme to renew the soul on the basis of a cult of the leader: 'As Hitler said recently', he declared, 'the leader must be able to be alone and must have the courage to go his own way [. . .]. [The leader] is an incarnation of the nation's psyche and its mouthpiece. He is the spear of the phalanx of the whole people in motion. The need of the whole always calls forth a leader, regardless of the form a state may take.'[44]

Jung supported the theory of racial difference, and thus viewed the individual psyche as a reflection of the collective soul of a people. In other words, far from being an ideologue of inequality (like Vacher de Lapouge or Gobineau), he presented himself as a theosophist in search of a differential ontology of the psyche. Thus he sought to work out a 'psychology of nations' capable of explaining the destiny both of the individual and of his collective soul. He divided the archetype into three components: the *animus* (image of the masculine), the *anima* (image of the feminine), and the *Selbst* (the self), the true centre of the personality. In his view, the archetypes formed the basis of the psyche: they were a sort of mythical inheritance proper to a mankind organized around the paradigm of difference.

With this notion of the archetype, Jung was obviously deviating from Freudian universalism, even though he claimed to be finding the universal in the great human mythologies and in alchemical or esoteric symbolism. And, admittedly, the esotericism in question probably had more to do with the 'pattern' of American culturalists than with racial differentialism found in National Socialism. But, in the historical context of the advent of Nazism in Germany, the two ideas echoed one another.

Armed with his archetypal psychology, Jung classified the Jews in the category of uprooted peoples doomed to wander, and all the more dangerous as, in order to escape their psychological denationalization, they did not hesitate to overrun the mental, social, and cultural universe of non-Jews.

The appearance of Jung's first article in the *Zentralblatt* caused a scandal among his Swiss colleagues. In February 1934, Gustav Bally, psychiatrist and psychoanalyst, a friend of Ludwig Binswanger and a former analysand of Hanns Sachs in the BPI, published in the *Neue Zürcher Zeitung* a scathing attack on Jung. His main criticism was that Jung had placed his conception of the psyche at the service of Nazism: 'And how, then, does he seek to distinguish Germanic psychology from Jewish psychology? What value would there be, in the human sciences, if the works of the Jew Husserl were considered to be "different" [. . .], if a racial criterion were applied to the work of Gestalt psychologists?'[45] Bally ended his article with these words: 'Jung appeals to the destiny that has given him this position. It is clearly destiny which has ensured that National Socialist policies on science can, thanks to his popularity, meet with success.'

This time, the message was clear. Jung could have seen how he had become trapped in the cogs of the machine, and resigned. Instead of this, he replied to Bally in two articles published in the same journal, in March 1934: 'Zeitgenössisches' ['On our own time'] and 'Nachtrag' ['Postscript']. In them, he compared himself to Galileo and Einstein, 'martyrs' of science, though he also rejected not the contents of the articles by Cimbal and Göring, but their editorial strategy. In particular, he restated his complete and total support for the idea of national psychology, while rejecting the 'uniformizing' psychology of Freud and Adler: 'Universality engenders hatred and bitterness on the part of the oppressed and the misunderstood [. . .]. Where does this ridiculous sensitivity come from, whenever anyone dares to speak of the psychological difference between Jews and Christians?'[46]

Following the polemics unleashed by Bally, Jung started to feel persecuted. He began to blame Jews for the anti-Semitism that was being directed against them. It was within this context that he moved towards an inegalitarian interpretation of the archetypal psyche. Up until then, he had been happy with a simple differentialist view. But, in April 1934, he published in the *Zentralblatt* a long article with the title 'Zur gegenwärtigen Lage der Psychotherapie' ['On the current situation in psychotherapy'],[47] in which he provided an apologia for National Socialism, stating that the Aryan unconscious was superior to the Jewish unconscious. This pro-Nazi, anti-Freudian, and anti-Semitic text was to gain a melancholy notoriety, and it became something of a millstone for the later destiny of Jung and the Jungian movement. All the ingredients were thrown into the pot, transforming Freudian theory into an obscene pan-sexualism linked to the Jewish 'mentality'. Jung seemed to forget, in the process, that a quarter of a century earlier he had defended psychoanalysis against arguments such as these which reduced it to an 'epidemic' produced from the 'decadence' of imperial Vienna. Here is the central passage in this text:

The Jews share one peculiarity with women: being physically weaker, they have to seek out the chinks in the armour of their adversaries and, thanks to this technique, which has been imposed on them throughout the centuries, they are better protected where others are more vulnerable [. . .]. The Jew, who, like the Chinese man of letters, belongs to a race and a culture that is three millennia old, is psychologically more self-aware of himself than we are. This is why he is generally unafraid to depreciate his unconscious. The Aryan unconscious, on the other hand, is charged with explosive forces and with the seeds of a future that is still to be born. So he cannot devalue it or tax it with infantile romanticism unless he wishes to place his soul in danger. The Germanic peoples, still young, can produce new forms of culture, and this future is still asleep in the obscure unconscious of every being, where repose germs gorged with energy and ready to catch fire. The Jew, who is something of a nomad, has never produced, and probably never will produce, an original culture, since his instincts and his gifts demand for their flourishing a more or less civilized host people.

That is why, in my experience, the Jewish race possesses an unconscious that can be compared to the Aryan unconscious only on certain conditions. Apart from a few creative individuals, the average Jew is already too conscious and too differentiated to bear within him the tensions of a future yet to come. The Aryan unconscious has a potential superior to that of the Jewish unconscious: this is the advantage and the drawback of a youthful state that is still close to barbarity. The great mistake of medical psychology was that it indiscriminately applied Jewish categories – which are not even valid for all Jews – to Christian Slavs and Germans. In consequence, psychology has found, in the most intimate treasures of the Germanic peoples – their creative, intuitive soul – nothing more than infantile, banal swamps, while my warnings were suspected of being tainted with anti-Semitism. This suspicion stemmed from Freud, who did not understand the Germanic psyche, any more than did his German disciples. Has the grandiose phenomenon of National Socialism, which the whole world gazes on in amazement, shed any light on it for them?[48]

The same year, remembering his stay in East Africa, ten years previously, Jung gave a lecture on the question of 'primitive peoples' incapable of thinking rationally for themselves. And he claimed, in line with his theory of archetypal difference, that the natives loved it when they were whipped:

At the beginning of my stay, I was greatly surprised by the brutality with which they were treated – the whip was common currency; initially, I thought it was superfluous, but I was then obliged to persuade myself that it was necessary; thereafter, I permanently kept my rhinoceros-skin whip at my sides. I learned to fake emotions that I did not feel, to bellow at the top of my voice and stamp my feet in rage.

This is how you need to make up for the natives' deficiency of willpower.[49]

This was where, in Jung, the genealogical link between racism and anti-Semitism could be located. If the 'nomadic' Jews have a unconscious inferior to that of 'Aryans', Jung's argument essentially ran, then the negroes, much more likable at first glance, since they are 'primitive', do not in the slightest resemble civilized whites, and even less de-Judaized Jews. As a result, they need to be maintained in the only state suitable to their 'archetype': that of being a colonized people, desirous of the whip.

In his correspondence for 1934, Jung stated on several occasions that it was now impossible to talk about Jews without being taxed with anti-Semitism. When the attacks doubled in intensity, he blamed them on anti-Christian polemics, as in his letter to James Kirsch:

> The mere fact that I speak of a difference between Jewish and Christian psychology suffices to allow anyone to voice the prejudice that I am an anti-Semite. [. . .] This hypersensitivity is simply pathological and makes every discussion practically impossible. As you know, Freud previously accused me of anti-Semitism because I could not abide his soulless materialism. The Jew directly solicits anti-Semitism with his readiness to scent out anti-Semitism everywhere.[50]

While criticizing the Jews for creating the conditions for their own persecution, Jung claimed to be helping them become better Jews. In a letter to his pupil Gerhard Adler, dated 9 June 1934, he supported the latter's idea that Freud was in some way guilty for detaching himself from his Jewish archetype, from his Jewish 'roots'. In other words, as his theory laid down, Jung rejected the Freudian model of the universal Jew, the Jew without religion, the Enlightenment Jew. He condemned the modern figure of the de-Judaized Jew, guilty in his eyes of denying his Jewish 'nature': 'So when I criticize Freud's Jewishness I am not criticizing the *Jews* but rather that damnable capacity of the Jew, as exemplified by Freud, to deny his own nature.'[51]

Anxious to bring the Jews within a psychology of difference, Jung, unlike Freud, became a fervent Zionist, and followed with growing interest the evolution of his Jewish disciples exiled to Palestine. Thanks to the new Promised Land, he thought, they could finally become Jungians. He was soon writing to Erich Neumann, now living in Tel Aviv: in a letter of 22 December 1935, he lambasted European Jewish intellectuals, 'always on the way to becoming a "non-Jew"'. Conversely, he lauded the Palestinian Jews, who had finally found their 'archetypal soil': 'I find your very positive conviction that the soil of Palestine is essential for Jewish individuation most valuable. How does this square with the fact that Jews in general have lived *much longer* in other countries than in Palestine? [. . .] Is it the case that the Jew is so accustomed to being a non-Jew that he needs the Palestinian soil *in concreto* to be reminded of his Jewishness?'[52]

From 1936 onwards, Jung pondered whether to resign from his post as head of the AÄGP and the *Zentralblatt*. He did so in 1940, when the association was, for the duration of the war, brought under the control of Nazi Germany. Its seat was transferred from Zurich to Berlin, while the *Zentralblatt* was now run exclusively by Göring.

After publishing his 1934 article, Jung changed his mind about the German psyche. He started to describe Germany in his writings as the 'bad' Germany, the melting pot for every evil spell that was now laying Europe waste. As for Hitler, idealized in 1933 as a magnificent awakener of the Germanic soul, he was now compared to a sinister charlatan, a 'puppet', or an 'automaton', a veritable archetype of German Aryanness. In Jung's view, Hitler had no 'personal psychology', and, since his relations with women could only be unwholesome, he was literally possessed by a maleficent *anima*, Germanic in its essence. This was the implication both of his 1936 study on Wotan and of the long interview he gave in 1938 to the famous American journalist Henry Knickerbocker.[53]

Jung turned against Germany and its Führer, using the same arguments he had deployed to glorify them two years earlier. His psychology was a real sea serpent, submerged in the whirlpools of the archetype: it led to the impasse that befalls all forms of differentialist thinking. It projected onto the figure of the *other* the terms of a negativity that swung between symbiotic inclusion and radical exclusion. No form of real otherness could emerge from this infernal circle.

Convinced by 1940 that Hitler was 'the archetype of German psychology', Jung then came out with a stream of Germanophobic remarks turning the Führer into a headstrong monster, like a Wotan reborn, guilty mainly of murdering Europe and persecuting the Jews. The evil Germany of Jung's fantasies thus owed reparation to non-Germans – in particular to Jung himself.[54]

In the wake of the Allied victory, Jung could not understand why he was being attacked so virulently. How could *he* be guilty, when he had so stridently condemned the wicked Germany? In reply to his detractors, in 1946 he published a short piece in English, *Essays on contemporary events*,[55] in which he reprinted several of his pre-war texts, together with an introduction and an epilogue.

And if Jung did not feel responsible for his actions, this was because he had removed from his system anything relating to a so-called Western conception of conscience. One event, however, shows that he wanted to make up for his past. When a conference was organized in Zurich, in 1946, by Hermann von Keyserling, who was himself the theorist of a character study of different nationalities, he met the rabbi Leo Baeck, who had survived the extermination after following his religious community to Theresienstadt. Knowing of the psychologist's past, Baeck refused to go to his home in Küsnacht. But Jung went to see him in his hotel and, after a lively argument, uttered these words: 'It's true, I did go astray.' Baeck related the conversation to Gershom Scholem, who thereupon accepted Jung's invitation to take part in the Eranos conference in Ascona.[56]

Thus Jung was redeemed by the pardon granted him by the greatest historian of Jewish mysticism, who was himself rather hostile to Freud. Convinced that psychoanalysis and Marxism had contributed to a desacralization of the world that was harmful to Judaism and this Zionism, Scholem even preferred Jung's religiosity to Freud's materialism, even if he sometimes included Freud positively in the category of 'sons of the Jewish people'.[57]

For years, Jung continued to gather around him, at the Eranos conferences,[58] scholars, psychologists, and historians of religion, including Henry Corbin, Mircea Eliade[59] and Lancelot White. His commitment to wide-ranging meditations on possible exchanges between Eastern and Western philosophies allowed him to forget the past. Never did he seem to realize the full extent of his participation in Nazism, never did he abandon his archetypal psychology, never did he produce the least commentary on the genocide of the Jews, and never did he deign to acknowledge that he had made anti-Semitic remarks. His only repentance was therefore this confession: 'I did go astray'.[60]

For opposite reasons to those which had driven Freud to criticize Zionism, Jung embraced this cause only because he hated diaspora Jews – whom he deemed to be debased vagabonds – and wished, in order to 'save' them from their Jewishness, to anchor them in a territory and a race. Jung's 'Zionism' was thus nothing more than the disguised perpetuation of an anti-Semitism whose existence he forever refused to recognize, either in his writings or in his collaboration with Nazism.

As I have indicated, the leaders of the IPA for their part refused to analyse or criticize Jones's politics. As a result, they produced no serious analysis of the Jewish question.[61] Yosef Yerushalmi, who was the only thinker in Jewish history to take Freud's *Moses* seriously, even went so far as to state that the Jewish psychoanalysts who had emigrated to the United States were incapable of taking into account in their treatments the fundamental question of unconscious anti-Semitism:

> How many men and women still lie on couches wondering whether the analyst is or is not Jewish because the name does not reveal the identity, but who will never ask directly because the topic seems far more sensitive and threatening than sex? How much anti-Semitic feeling may be not only repressed but consciously suppressed in the transference to a Jewish analyst, and how much else may be missed as a result?[62]

But there is an even more tragic side to the problem. In July 1977, when the IPA held its congress in Jerusalem for the first time, with a French chairman,[63] and the long-awaited Sigmund Freud chair was finally created at the Hebrew University, Anna Freud composed a speech that was read out in closed session. Its contents caused consternation among many of her listeners. She paid homage neither to Eitingon nor to Wulf, the two founding fathers from old Europe. She spoke only of techniques of treatment, perversions, limit states, the therapeutic values of the clinic, effectiveness, physiology, psychology, methodology, the treatment of children, and so on. She completely forgot to mention her father's work on the Jewish question. She uttered not a word on his *Moses*, or on *Totem and Taboo*, nothing about Vienna or Berlin, or indeed on the joint history of Zionism and psychoanalysis. And, of course, nothing on Auschwitz or on the transformation of the IPA after that event.

And then, all of a sudden, at the end of her speech, remembering that psychoanalysis had frequently been attacked, she laid claim to the category of 'Jewish science': 'Psychoanalysis has been criticized for having imprecise methods, for leading to conclusions that cannot be experimentally verified, for not being scientific, and even for being a "Jewish science". Whatever value one grants these deprecatory remarks, it is, I believe, this last adjective which, in the present circumstances, can act as a title of glory.'[64]

In this way, Freud's own daughter appropriated, in a way which she thought was positive, the abject expression used by the Nazis to destroy the language and doctrine of psychoanalysis. By dint of censorship, amnesia, and repression concerning the black years, the masters of the IPA – Anna Freud first and foremost – had thereby turned psychoanalysis into a 'Jewish science' without even realizing the symbolic impact such a description might have in such a place: in Jerusalem itself, where the children of Herzl and the children of

Freud might, if only for a moment, have remembered their two Viennese ancestors. Nothing of the kind happened: Israel had long since repressed Freud's name, and the Freudian International had just given his teaching a slap in the face.

A great intellectual of American nationality, Edward Said, born in Jerusalem to a Christian family from Palestine, a professor of comparative literature in the same university as Yerushalmi, and, indeed, a member of the National Council of Palestine between 1977 and 1991, remembered this repression when, in December 2001, he gave a magnificent lecture on *Moses*: 'Freud and the non-European'.[65] Said, an assiduous reader of Freud's work, proposed an interpretation of the *Moses* which focused on its deconstruction of the Western conception of orientalism.

In his major work *Orientalism*, published in 1978, which had launched Anglo-American studies into post-colonialism, Said tried to demonstrate that the scholarly work of European orientalists was imbued with fears and a sense of superiority in the face of an East that was more imaginary than real. This was a very interesting idea and was close to Frantz Fanon's thoughts on the phenomenology of the colonized.[66]

Be this as it may, in his lecture at the Freud Museum, Said emphasized how Freud's conception of the Egyptianness of Moses was far removed from the old orientalism – and the obsession with Semitism – of Renan and Gobineau, and how it could open the way to a critical exploration of the non-European world. In other words, since the State of Israel had repressed Freud, and thereby repressed his conception of a Jewishness springing from a non-Jewish genealogy (Egyptianness), it was now possible for the non-Jews of Israel and Palestine, excluded by the Jewish state from their identity – some as Israeli citizens without nationality, others as dispossessed of their territory and of any state – to think of themselves as Freudians – in other words, heirs to the long tradition of dissident Jews, non-Jewish Jews, prophets, and rebels who were forever being excommunicated: Spinoza, Marx, Heine.

It could not be put any better. And this was why Edward Said, while acknowledging the legality of the State of Israel, always supported a two-nation state on Palestinian land that would make it possible to bring together within a single people the three monotheisms (Judaism, Christianity, and Islam) and the two hereditary enemies (Jews and non-Jews) so that they could live together.

But this lesson has yet to be learnt.

5

Genocide between Memory and Negation

The extermination of the Jews was unique in the entirety of human history. For this reason, a word had to be invented to refer to it: genocide. When Raphael Lemkin, a Polish lawyer and polyglot from a Jewish family, used the term for the first time in 1944, in a work with the title *Axis Rule in Occupied Europe*, he was doing so in direct response to a preoccupation of the Allies, including Winston Churchill – the latter had described these murders as 'nameless crimes'. And it was indeed a matter of finding a name, at last, for what was being discovered – an organized mass crime – something which the victors over the Nazis had refused to take into account even when they had been informed of it in January 1942, when the Nazi leaders had taken the decision at the Wannsee Conference to implement the 'Final Solution'. In June 1942, the best-known American dailies had started to spread the news, and, in August, the heads of the Allied powers had received confirmation that, in Occupied Poland, mass exterminations of the Jewish people were being carried out. In December, several accounts had referred to the use of new techniques of killing people with gas.[1]

However, eager to win the war as fast as possible, and already thinking about the way the world would be divided up afterwards, the Allies preferred not to act directly against the convoys, for example by bombing the railway lines. Furthermore, the scientific and technical organization of an administered mass murder was at that time so unthinkable that, in order to be convinced, they decided to wait for 'material proof'. But the longer they waited, the more the process of extermination intensified as the Nazi leaders, aware that they risked losing the war on the military level, strove not to lose the *other war*: the destruction of the Jews, which in their view was more important than all the others.

The 'proof' was obtained only when the various armies of liberation reached the heart of darkness. Cinematography now became an indispensable weapon in establishing the facts, even before the first written or oral eye-witness accounts of the Nazis themselves,[2] then of the survivors from the death camps and the extermination camps: Primo Levi, Jean Améry (born Hans Mayer), Bruno Bettelheim, Robert Antelme, David Rousset, and so on. For years, hundreds of eye-witness accounts followed one after the other.

However, the word genocide was not taken up by the Nuremberg Tribunal, in spite of pressure from Lemkin on the American delegation. The tribunal, which started meeting on 8 August 1945, defined three types of crime committed by the main Nazi dignitaries: crimes against peace, war crimes, and crimes against humanity. These last included murder, extermination, reduction to slavery, deportation, and all inhumane acts perpetrated against civil populations persecuted because of their religion or their race. Of course, the extermination of the Jews fell within this definition, but it was seen as on the same level as all the other exterminations perpetrated by the Nazis.

Only on 9 December 1948 did the UN adopt the Convention on the Prevention and Punishment of the Crime of Genocide, which was now defined as an act committed with the intention of destroying, wholly or in part, a national, ethnic, racial, or religious group as such:

(a) Killing members of the group;
(b) Causing serious bodily or mental harm to members of the group;
(c) Deliberately inflicting on the group conditions of life calculated to bring about its physical destruction in whole or in part;
(d) Imposing measures intended to prevent births within the group;
(e) Forcibly transferring children of the group to another group.

As we can see, the term applied to a broader crime than that of crime against humanity, since it involved the idea that the perpetrators were attacking not just civilians because of their race or religion, but a group as such, in its very existence. And it then became clear that only a state could be accused of the crime of genocide, since no individual was in any position to commit such a serious crime, even if he was helped by accomplices. The idea of a state acting intentionally was therefore included in the notion of genocide. As for the Universal Declaration of Human Rights, promulgated on 10 December 1948 by the General Assembly of the UN, it took into account both the sentences handed down at the Nuremberg Tribunal and the adoption of the notion of genocide.

In the preamble to the declaration, men are defined as belonging to a single 'human family' and thus to a *genos* (species, type, birth), and any failure to respect their rights is viewed as an 'act of barbarism' that revolts the human conscience (deemed to be universal).

Though the invention of the word was useful to describe a new kind of crime, it was not really adapted for defining the specific nature of the genocide of the Jews committed by the Nazis. And, in any case, this had never been Lemkin's intention – far from it. He wished to link the extermination of the Jews with the long history of massacres perpetrated by men against men: he thus included within his definition not merely the genocide of the Armenians by the Turks – which Hitler regarded as a model – but also all the crimes of Stalinism, for instance the organized famine in Ukraine, as well as all the cultural consequences of such crimes. Thus he envisaged revising the entire history of mankind in the light of this new paradigm and writing a major three-volume history of genocides since antiquity.

The difficulty lies in the fact that it is difficult to rewrite history with the help of a conceptual apparatus that is not suitable for what one is trying to describe. If, as we have seen, it is already dangerous to describe in retrospect all the old forms of anti-Judaism as anti-Semitism, it is almost impossible to transform into a genocide any massacre perpetrated by human beings since the dawn of time – however great the extent of the massacre, and however cruel it was. Apart from the risk of falling prey to anachronism, such an enterprise also runs the risk, firstly, of turning history into a law court, bringing all murders under the rubric of a retrospective accusation of genocide, and, secondly, of losing sight of the way that, for a real genocide to have occurred – distinct from all previous forms of collective massacres – the Constitution of the United Nations would have needed already to be in place, and anti-Semitism, then modern nationalism, colonialism, and racism, and finally science, would have had to come into being – since only then did states have at their disposal the means to pervert this same science to the goal of extermination.

It was Lemkin's error to underestimate these historical givens when he claimed that genocide could assume its place in the family group of tyrannicide, homicide, and parricide, and that the destruction of Carthage, the massacres of the Albigensians and Waldensians, or the Crusades fitted into the legal category of genocide.[3] In this respect, we should note that the UN was more sensible than the inventor of the concept when it gave a less extensive definition of this new type of crime.

Ever since this description was adopted, only four genocides have been recognized by the UN, and only three of them on the juridical level: those of the Armenians, the Jews and the gypsies (by the Nazis), the Tutsis in Rwanda (by the Hutus), and the Bosnians (by the Serbs). But Serbia as a state was not designated as guilty of genocide.

Considered as crimes against humanity, certain great massacres perpetrated by states in the twentieth century were not viewed as genocides by the UN, in spite of the expectations of the victims and the vehemence of the debates surrounding the decision. As can be seen, while it has been necessary over the years to redefine the notion of genocide – now extended to all sorts of planned exterminations – it is difficult, without emptying it of its content, to include for example the massacres ordered by Pol Pot, in the name of Democratic Kampuchea, against his own people: was this a case of trying to destroy the *genos* of the Cambodian people or to exterminate what was allegedly a social class? To give the name 'genocide' to such a massacre, we would need to view belonging to a particular class as an identity bound up with a *genos*, and thus talk of auto-genocide – which is hardly appropriate. And yet, of course, the horror was the same, so these days we tend to use the term 'genocide' to describe such massacres.

In the case of French colonization, the massacre of the American Indians, or slavery, it is preferable not to describe them as genocides however much their victims may demand this. For this term presupposes the pre-established desire on the part of the state to exterminate a people because it does not wish it to exist any more, and the implementation of this desire: it is not just about enslaving it or persecuting it. This is a significant difference.[4]

On closer inspection, the term genocide also describes a crime against humanity aiming at the annihilation by a state of a people not merely for what it thinks but for what it is – in other words, for its *genos*, its identity, its being, its history, its genealogy. In this respect, the planned destruction of the Jews of Europe corresponded perfectly with this definition, and it is no coincidence if the term was invented by a Jewish Pole who, in order to grasp the immensity of the crime, had been forced to conceive of it on the basis of the extermination of his own people.

As we know, the Nazis did not seek simply to destroy the Jews residing within a particular set of borders. They wanted to eliminate *all* the Jews, irrespective of *any* geographical limit and *any* real presence of the victims. What the 'Final Solution' aimed at was not merely the destruction of the very origins of the Jew, genealogically defined – ancestors, grandparents, parents, children, children yet to be born,

Jews already dead and buried[5] – but also the destruction of the generic Jew, outside any territory, with his or her territory, culture, and religion: a vertical extermination starting with the first parent, a horizontal extermination starting with the scattered people (the diaspora). And in the Jewish *genos*, now the paradigm of the evil race, was included everything that was not the Aryan *genos*. In this way, the Nazis aimed to replace the Chosen People by fabricating, in the Aryan myth, a perverted figure of the doctrine of chosenness: 'Nazism', wrote Pierre Vidal-Naquet in 1987, is a *'perversa imitatio,* a perverse imitation of the *image* of the Jewish people. What was needed was to break with Abraham, and thus with Jesus, and seek another lineage for oneself among the "Aryans". Intellectually, this is the line of argument put forward by the New Right these days.'[6] As for the decision to exterminate the Jews in gas chambers, it was evidence of the overlap within Nazism between an anti-Semitic policy and a programme of euthanasia applied to all categories of 'non-Aryan' humans.

In this respect, we might claim that there is a specific character to this destruction of the European Jews by the Nazis: it is the only one in the whole history of mankind that corresponds strictly to the notion of genocide insofar as, over and above the Jews, the crime of which they were the victims included all others. In Auschwitz, man did not kill his fellow merely for human reasons, but in order to eradicate man himself and with him the 'concept of humanity'.[7] Thus, the genocide of the Jews was, as such, the genocide of Man, and that is why there is a *before* Auschwitz and an *after* Auschwitz. And this is why, if Auschwitz *names* the singularity of the Nazi crime, it is because this very singularity thereby *names* the crime against humanity itself. The gas chamber was indeed invented *for* the Jew, because, through the Jew, Nazism aimed at the annihilation of humanity.[8]

This caesura, which makes of Auschwitz a unique event, is linked to the fact that the extermination of the Jews served no other aim than that of satisfying a perverse, pathological, indeed paranoid hatred of the Jew insofar as he was excluded from the human world. No other reason lay behind this project: neither the elimination of an enemy, nor the conquest of a territory, nor the enslavement of a people, nor even the desire to appease an ancestral power.[9] Probably only Freudian categories allow us to think of a genocidal action of this kind in its collective and individual dimension.

In the wake of the Allied victory, several intellectuals, far from the scene of the crime, were in a position to think these events through and, above all, to put them into words: Hannah Arendt, Karl Jaspers,

Theodor Adorno, Max Horkheimer, Jean-Paul Sartre, Günther Anders, Maurice Blanchot, Jacques Lacan, and Dwight Macdonald.[10] Freud had, of course, died before he could move on from the publication of his unfinished *Moses* to grasp the reasons for the tragedy.

In 1947, Adorno and Horkheimer embarked on a long digression on the limits of reason and the ideals of progress.[11] They maintained that mankind's entry into mass culture and the biological planning of life ran a serious risk of creating new forms of totalitarianism unless reason managed to critique itself and surmount its own destructive tendencies: this, indeed, had already been Freud's message in 1930.

For his part, Anders[12] compared Auschwitz to Hiroshima, and emphasized that the two events showed how the most sophisticated science could be used to wipe out mankind. But he also demonstrated that the use of atomic power, in such circumstances, was not part of a programme of genocide; in any case, Claude Eatherly, the pilot of *Straight Flush* who had reconnoitred the site before the bomb was dropped, had 'expiated' America's guilt by refusing to become the 'hero of Hiroshima'. He periodically slipped into depression. No Nazi had ever reacted in such a way.

Sartre, meanwhile, wrote the first major book in France on the Jewish question after Auschwitz, pondering both what it meant to be Jewish, authentically or inauthentically, and on the passion of anti-Semitism.[13] He referred much more to the heritage of Drumont than to the extermination as such: as a philosopher, rather than a historian, he reckoned that genocide did not alter the *nature* of the problem. Any real anti-Semitism could not fail, in his view, to lead to the most abject positions. This is surely undeniable. And, at the heart of his work, he pointed to Louis-Ferdinand Céline as the prototype of the consummate French anti-Semite, even though he had been one of the most strident defenders of the latter's novel *Journey to the end of the night*.[14] Céline responded in the purest tradition of the virulent anti-Semitic insult: 'Murderer, cursed, hideous, shitty pimp, bespectacled ass [. . .] little turd from my brilliant anus [. . .], fucking little Piece of shit, drooling sucker, Anus Cain pah [. . .], tapeworm, dam rotten backside [. . .] cobra, ungrateful, damned ass.'[15] And so on.

Dwight Macdonald, a figurehead of the left-wing New York intelligentsia, renounced Marxism so as to embrace the libertarian cause just as Sartre was discovering Marxism.[16] And he then started to claim that the extermination of the Jews was the great moral issue of the time, that it drove a wedge into the history of anti-Semitism and that Stalinism was not of the same nature as Nazism – an idea that Arendt would take up.[17]

Maurice Blanchot's attitude was different but, in its extremely radical stance, just as interesting. Born in 1907 to a Catholic family in the rural heartland of France, Blanchot discovered German philosophy in 1925 as a student at Strasbourg attending the lectures of Emmanuel Lévinas. Between the future great philosopher of Judaism and Jewishness and the young student who was to become one of the main writers of the second half of the twentieth century, a friendship sprang up that would only intensify in the course of the next fifty years – a state of grace to which Jacques Derrida, the friend of the two men and the youngest of the trio, later paid homage. As a nationalist, a Robespierrist, an anti-capitalist, and, above all, a fervent monarchist, Blanchot entered politics as a leader-writer in different newspapers of the Maurassian far right. And it was during this period that he composed articles in which he attacked Jews, Freudians, communists, Stalinists, Hitlerians – and, later on, Léon Blum and the Popular Front. Rather like Bernanos, he called, against all the moderates, for a purification of the French nation, which in his view had become a 'caravanserai', an 'abjection'.[18]

During the Occupation, Blanchot became a different man as he turned towards fiction. When Lévinas was taken prisoner by the Germans and incarcerated in a stalag, Blanchot took Lévinas's wife and family into his home and then ensured they were brought to safety. While continuing to collaborate with Pétainist reviews (where he wrote nothing but literary criticism), he became aware of the need to make a clean break with the person he had been before. His meeting and subsequent friendship with Georges Bataille, and then with Dionys Mascolo, Marguerite Duras, and Robert Antelme,[19] played a significant role in this transformation. And we find an echo of it in *Thomas the obscure*, many of whose pages, written from 1932 onwards, were revised twice over: in 1940, when France was defeated, then in 1950, after Auschwitz. The novel, a veritable manifesto for an anti-psychologizing literature, was inspired by a whole modernist tradition, from Proust to Kafka via Thomas Mann, and it began with a sentence that was to become famous: 'Thomas sat down and gazed at the sea.'

A human, monstrous hero, immersed in nocturnal forces, Thomas – whose name is reminiscent of Jesus's unbelieving disciple – confronts death: his own death and that of two women, one of whom decides to slit her throat with a stiletto, while the other dies of anorexia. He then allows himself to be swallowed up by the void: 'I think', said Thomas, 'and this invisible, inexpressible, inexistent Thomas that I became, meant that henceforth I was never there where I was, and there was not even anything mysterious about this. My existence became entirely that of an absent person [. . .] my life was then that of a man wholly walled up in concrete [. . .].'[20]

Subsequently, Blanchot never stopped writing about death, about the instant it occurs and the way it burrows through a life: he refused for forty years to intervene in the public arena, he allowed no photos of himself, and he took part in no debates. He lived withdrawn from the world but, as an 'invisible partner',[21] was ubiquitous through his writing: in the letters he sent his friends, his enemies, the press, or various interlocutors; in his texts; and in his commitments. Through this absence from the world, he seemed to be expiating his past misdeeds while expiating the collective misdeeds of Europe towards the Jews. And yet he had never committed the least crime or denounced anyone. In his private life, surrounded by his family and friends, and without ever forming a school, he was the most living writer imaginable, and the most influential.

In the post-war period Blanchot was active in the struggle against colonialism and in 1960 composed the celebrated *Manifesto of the 121* 'on the right to absence without leave in the Algerian War', which ended with these words: 'The cause of the Algerian people, which is making a decisive contribution to ruining the colonial system, is the cause of all free men.'[22] The signatories were called 'bourgeois' by the far left and 'anarchists' by the right, while the heirs of Maurras's France, who supported French Algeria – including Thierry Maulnier, Blanchot's former companion – responded with a counter-petition insulting Sartre.[23] As for the text on disobedience, it was directly inspired by the Declaration of the Rights of Man and Marx's *Manifesto*: a literary masterpiece. And Blanchot stated that he had signed it as a writer and not 'as a political writer'.[24]

It was through this struggle against colonialism, and then by his political stance in May 1968, that Blanchot began to theorize the question of the extermination of the Jews as a historical absolute, as a break which left a deep imprint on the very conditions for producing philosophy and literature. While agreeing with Adorno, he emphasized that at Auschwitz humankind had died, for the first time, as a whole, so that from now on any narrative would be 'pre-Auschwitz', whatever the date at which it was composed. For, if life continued after this event, it could be nothing other than a survival to which each text would bear witness.[25]

Hence the idea that Jewish existence should be thought of as a wandering or as a culture of refusal: a difference. Opposed to all anti-Zionism, which in his view always threatened to turn into anti-Semitism, and staying close to Derrida, who warded off the risk of any over-hasty moves by shifting towards a way of thinking that was able to include within Judaeo-Christianity the third monotheism (and thus the Arab-Islamic world as being partly inside and partly outside the Western world),[26] Blanchot gave his support to Israel: not to the policies of its government but to the signifier 'Israel'. He viewed this term as covering something more vulnerable than the signifier 'freedom' brandished by the Palestinians: 'Whatever happens, I am with Israel. I am with Israel when Israel suffers. I am with Israel when Israel suffers by making others suffer.'[27]

Adopting the word 'genocide' opened the way, for colonized or oppressed peoples, to a new appropriation of their history and the establishment of a memorial of their past sufferings that would soon be competing with that of the Jews, especially after the creation of the State of Israel, experienced by them as the victor of oppressors over the wretched of the earth: the Arabs of Palestine. Now, the 'peoples without history' exploited by a West that had vanquished barbarity, and declared to be equal to their exploiters by the Universal Declaration, would soon be awakening and laying claim to their own rights.

Within this context, the word 'genocide', whose meaning was clear enough, had to compete with other terms of a religious connotation. In the English-speaking world, dominated by a Protestant reading of the Bible, the habit developed of calling the extermination of the Jews the 'Holocaust'. This word refers to 'the sacrifice by fire of a male animal with an unblemished skin', and it also alludes to the mediaeval accusations of ritual crimes practised by the Jews, as well as to the stakes at which they were burned for imaginary crimes. So the word was not suitable, but it caught on. Likewise with the term 'Shoah', which alluded to the history of Judaism and the different catastrophes which God had inflicted upon his people to punish them. Thus the word was officially adopted by the State of Israel on 12 April 1951, when the national day of memory was fixed.

It subsequently became current, though it never supplanted the world 'genocide'.[28] And yet, the extermination of the Jews of Europe was neither a sacrifice nor a catastrophe sent by God, but a concerted act of destruction conceived by men hostile to Judaeo-Christianity and now radically estranged from any idea of God. And the adoption of the terms 'Holocaust' or 'Shoah' tends to favour the cult of memory, the remembrance of suffering, rather than the rational study of this unprecedented historical event – memory rather than history.

Just as Zionism had contributed to the awakening of Arab nation-alism, the civil war of 1948, in which the Palestinians were forced into exile, was experienced by its victims as the equivalent of the

Shoah. They gave the name '*Naqba*' ('catastrophe') to the destruction of their society, and also cultivated a memorial history through which they viewed the Jews as genocidal racists. This painful experience of memorial history was denied by the Israeli authorities: the *Naqba* does not exist, they said, it is a fiction created in every detail by Arab propaganda, by anti-Semites and anti-Zionists. And the truth of the *Naqba* was not established until the new Israel historians started to work on it, drawing on the archives of their own country.[29]

Be this as it may, during a war that was of course in no way comparable to the Shoah but had still been murderous, around 800,000 Palestinians had been brutally driven from their homes, their goods confiscated and their houses wrecked. What form can a state founded in such conditions take?

The Declaration of Independence on 14 May 1948 proclaimed that the State of Israel, which did not have a constitution, was simultaneously Jewish and democratic. As Jewish, it drew partly on the Bible, and thus on a mythical and religious origin (the first monotheism), and partly on Zionism, a spiritual, secular, and nationalist movement. But, as a democratic state, it also sought to be a state ruled by law founded on an inclusive right of citizenship. Open to Jewish immigration from all the lands of the diaspora, as a Jewish state – and a state *of Jews*, as Herzl had put it – this state also claimed that it could ensure the most complete social and political equality to all its inhabitants without distinguishing between race, religion, or sex – in other words, to non-Jews as well. But, while it also drew, of course, on universal principles guaranteeing each citizen full freedom of conscience, worship, education, and culture, it defined this freedom not on the basis of the definition in the Declaration of the Rights of Man, but in reference to the teaching of the prophets of Israel.

From its foundation, then, this state was riven by a contradiction proper to the very history of the Jewish people: it drew on a particularism (Judaism) and a universalism (democracy). But it was also shaped by the Jewish question – in other words, by anti-Semitism, especially in its most criminal version: that which had produced the Shoah. Originally conceived to give a nation to the Jews who were victimized by anti-Semitism at the end of the nineteenth century, this state, as its Declaration of Independence laid down, was also to be a state for all those who had survived the genocide.

But how could a Jewish state – established in favour of the Jews – ensure equality between all its citizens? This question was never resolved, in spite of the many attempts of various Israeli lawyers who for several centuries hunkered down to the task of enabling the state to escape from its hybrid character. As a consequence, non-Jewish minorities – Druze, Circassians, Armenians, and, in particular, Israeli Arabs, the most numerous, who were also called 'homeland Palestinians' (whether Muslim, secular, or Christian) – did not enjoy the same status as Jews. Recognized as citizens, they did not gain full nationality, which was reserved for Jews. So the Israeli state can be described, as the lawyer Claude Klein says, in the great tradition of Jewish humour, as a democratic state for Jews and a Jewish state for Arabs.[30]

On the eve of the foundation of this state, which would sometimes be labelled 'Jewish', because it had been conceived for the Jews, and sometimes 'Hebrew' in reference to the national language, several debates sprang up around the question of what exactly to call it. The word 'Judah' seemed to make the running for a while, but eventually 'Israel' was preferred, from the name given by the Angel to Jacob, the third patriarch. The choice was far from innocent, since the name bore within it an ancestral memory of the struggle between the Angel and the son of Isaac, between God and God's chosen: an interminable struggle fought within the Jewish people itself. As for the national emblems, they drew inspiration from the biblical tradition: the flag, emblazoned with a Star of David, has the blue colour of the prayer shawl (the tallith); the official seal reproduces the seven-branched candelabrum, a symbol of the Jewish people's aspirations for peace. As for the national anthem (Hatikva), it expresses the 2,000-year-old desire of the Jewish people to recover Jerusalem and the promised land of Zion.

Forced to make concessions to the ultra-Orthodox, who wished to ensure that Judaism had a major presence in the state, Ben Gurion entrusted the rabbinical authorities with the management of civil rights, creating a specific judicial apparatus – twelve tribunals and a court of appeal – to settle the matrimonial affairs of Jewish citizens on the basis of religious law (Halakha). In this way, Jewish law was applied to designate who is a Jew: according to this law, a Jew is Jewish only if he is born to a Jewish mother or has converted to Judaism. Likewise, a Jew who is born in the same conditions but no longer practises the Jewish religion (even if, for his personal status, he is obliged to obey the religious rites) is still a Jew.

Furthermore, to reinforce the 'Jewish character' of the state – in the sense of national identity – and thereby to ward off the inevitable conflict between religious and secular Jews, Ben Gurion promulgated laws which guaranteed the observance of the dietary rituals, the Sabbath, and the festivals in every sector of public life. And when, in 1953, the Yad Vashem memorial was set up to list and honour the victims of the Shoah, the habit grew of commemorating at the same time the Jewish Passover (Pesach), the creation of the State of Israel

(Independence Day), and the memory of those who had died in the genocide, as well as in the heroic uprising of the Warsaw ghetto. In this way, very different events were woven together in one and the same complex of memories: the cult of the dead and the celebration of a rebirth, the memory of a heroic action, and the invocation of religious tradition: 'If this is really the case', Pierre Vidal-Naquet later wrote, 'and I have every reason to fear that it is, I do not just think that it is politically dangerous but that it is historically dangerous.'[31]

Over the years, with the issue being 'revisited' often, the question of who is Jewish continued to raise its head: for instance, can you continue to say that you are Jewish when you willingly practise another religion? In 1970, an amendment to the law on return was passed, defining a Jew as 'born to a Jewish mother or having converted to Judaism and not practising another religion'. This choice of words respected the division that had, ever since the Haskalah, lain at the heart of Jewish awareness: what it really meant was that you could be Jewish without being a believer (in other words, without practising Judaism) but that it was impossible to remain Jewish once you adopted another religion without being forced to do so. However, this amendment did not resolve the still intractable problem of children born in Israel to a Jewish father and a non-Jewish and non-converted mother. In such cases, mixed marriages were proscribed by Jewish law. But, as the state was democratic and civil law courts existed, living together openly was not prohibited. As for the rights of homosexuals to live together and adopt children, they were eventually granted – to the wrath of the Orthodox Jews.

Now, and for the first time in history, there was a split in reality between the universal (diasporic) Jew and the territorial Jew who had become the citizen of a nation through the creation of a Jewish state. And in fact the conflict within this state turned out to be almost as serious as that which set it against its enemies, since it was perceived as a threat not just to the future of Israel society, but to the destiny of a Jewish diaspora that had survived the camps.[32]

For some (secular) people, the State of Israel was, from its origin, doomed to fall prey to fundamentalism and thus to perish, while for other (religious) people it was threatened by a new destruction if it lost its 'Jewish soul' and its covenant with God.[33] In both cases, the terror of disappearance was still there: either through some catastrophe, or through a new scattering. As for the memory of the Shoah, it was omnipresent: as Idith Zertal wrote in 2002:

> According to circumstances of time and place, the Holocaust victims were brought back to life again and again and became a central

function in Israeli political deliberation, particularly in the context of the Israeli–Arab conflict, and especially at moments of crisis and conflagration, namely, in wartime. There has not been a war in Israel, from 1948 till the present ongoing outburst of violence which began in October 2000, that has not been perceived, defined, and conceptualized in terms of the Holocaust.[34]

Ultimately, it was all as if modern Jews – the Jews 'after the catastrophe', or Jews of the Shoah – were haunted by the terror of their own disappearance. At the beginning of the nineteenth century, the philosopher Nachman Krochmal had already focused on the question before Freud turned to it, and had attempted to give a full and detailed answer. His conclusion had been that the Jews ran no risk of disappearing since, having no territory or national identity, they had continued ever since their origins to go through a cycle of growth and decline, being reborn each time through the force of their spirituality.[35]

But this prophecy became null and void once half of the Jews had become part of a nation like any other, with their own territory and state. Before that, when there had been no state, they were the victims of persecution, pariahs, wanderers, parvenus, assimilated within other nations. But later, as a people with their own state, the Jews of Israel were hostile to one another and had enemies or adversaries just like all citizens integrated within a state. And, on closer examination, if no catastrophe of any significance menaced the Jews of the diaspora after 1945, now protected by laws against racial hatred, the only threat which hung over the Israeli Jews was created by the policies of their governors, which would, after a golden age, become increasingly disastrous and increasingly criticized by the Israelis themselves, especially the brilliant intellectuals, historians, and writers among them: 'If war threatens the *physical* survival of Israel', writes Ilan Greilsammer, 'its territorial existence, then peace poses a deadly threat to the Israeli social fabric and risks causing its dissolution or implosion. Some people even advise Arabs hostile to the existence of Israel to make peace [. . .] so that the Jewish state will cease to exist by self-destruction at the end of an internal process.'[36] This is an alarming idea.

All the debates on genocide and the fear of disappearing clearly show that it was at the very moment of composition of the Universal Declaration of Human Rights, aimed to bring to an end any form of racism and to extend to all peoples the benefits of the French Declaration of 1789, that a huge movement started to spread that was critical of its universality. This criticism continued to intensify over the years. The more stridently this universality was asserted by democratic countries which continued to flout it by policies that exploited poor countries, for example in Africa, the more the peoples of those countries started to relativize, to an extreme degree, these principles of justice, law, and equality which stemmed from the declaration, instead of appropriating them.

We should point out at this point that, after successfully imposing the Zionist idea on the Western world, and unhesitatingly cooperating with colonial imperialism, Herzl, as visionary and paradoxical as ever, had dreamt of solving the racial question at the same time as the Jewish question and had laid out his project in 1902, in his incredible novel *Altneuland*:

> There is a problem, a national distress, of which only a Jew can gauge the profound horror and which has found no solution hitherto. This is the problem of the Negroes [. . .]. Certain men, just because they were black, have been captured like animals, deported, sold. Their descendants have lived far from their countries, hated and despised because they were another colour. I have no compunction in saying it, even if I am mocked: after seeing the return of the Jews, I would like to help to prepare for a return of the Negroes.[37]

On this issue, Herzl was not followed by his successors.

In 1952, Claude Lévi-Strauss wrote a famous text, *Race and history*, in which he warned the proponents of universal rights of the risk they were running of claiming that any race could be superior to any other. And he went so far as to reject the very notion of race – the source of all racism, and a notion that was subsequently abandoned[38] – to emphasize that no cultural or psychological property could be deduced from any biological substrate. He did not reject Darwinism, but he did denounce the aberrant tendencies of an evolutionism that was always threatening to turn an absolutized idea of progress into its opposite, too prone as it was to deny the positive values of cultural diversity. For, without respect for these diversities, no universal theory of man could provide an adequate account of the unity of the human race. And Nazi barbarity proved as much, since it had been based on an inegalitarian worldview taken to such an extreme that it aimed at the extermination not just of the Jews, but of the human race as a whole.[39]

Within this context, the creation of a Jewish state for the Jews was increasingly sensed by the colonized peoples as an act of oppression. After having been almost totally wiped out, the Jews were now driving from their land Palestinians who had not been in any way responsible for the great massacre: the Western democracies were making these Palestinians pay for their own guilt at not having been able to halt the process of the 'Final Solution'. And the founding father of this new state, David Ben Gurion, was fully aware of this: in the wake of his victory, he made this stupefying declaration: 'If I was an Arab leader I would never make terms with Israel. That is natural: we have taken their country. Sure, God promised it to us, but what does that matter to them? Our God is not theirs. [. . .] There has been antisemitism, the Nazis, Hitler, Auschwitz, but was that their fault? They only see one thing: we have come here and stolen their country. Why should they accept that?'[40]

This is how Edward Said described, just before his death, a world that had, for Siri Husseini Shahid, the mother of Leila Shahid, been Palestine before the *Naqba* – a near equivalent of the world of European Jews of the years 1905 to 1914, that 'world of yesterday' reconstructed by Stefan Zweig in his memoirs:

> We can see shepherds, cooks, aunts, cousins, peasants, [. . .] relatives, lovers, favourite objects: houses, schools, farms, places for picnics and social gatherings that were conquered by Israel and transformed into 'foreign goods' or purely and simply destroyed. [. . .] This book deserves to find a place in the museum of memory, next to other memories, so that neither amnesia nor so-called historical progress can ever obliterate their testimonies.[41]

The work of the Nuremberg Tribunal also paved the way to studies on the question of the extermination. And even if, during the years following the Allied victory, the survivors kept their silence, preferring to repress the horror rather than to transmit it to their family and friends, at a time when no distinctions were drawn between the different victims of Nazism, historians again focused on the Jewish question. In the second half of the twentieth century, anti-Semitic discourse was officially banned from all democratic countries and made impossible by a series of laws forbidding incitement to racial hatred and punishing insults against Jews, blacks, Arabs, etc. While diaspora Jews, protected by these laws, rediscovered their pride in being Jewish, their attitude towards the principles of assimilation changed, particularly in France, where assimilation had been derided by the Vichy regime. Instead of giving a French twist to their names or disguising their origins, they flaunted them, just as – even when they were neither believing nor practising Jews – they attempted to bring back to life, through secularized rituals, a memory of the old Yiddishland that had been swept away in the cataclysm.

Like the first Zionists, some of them, including (but not only) the children of deportees, engaged in progressive struggles by becoming anti-colonialists and communists, Trotskyists, or Maoists. In this way they refurbished the revolutionary idea that had led to the emancipation of the Jews in France. But it was through psychoanalysis that many Jews, born after the war, joined the venture of so many diaspora Jews, either as practitioners or as patients: treatment was their way of confronting *their* Jewish question. And Lacan's role here was decisive in France, at a time when psychoanalysts of the International Psychoanalytical Association (IPA) had come to a dead end over Jones's collaborationist past. Heavily influenced by the great text by Adorno and Horkheimer, Lacan continually placed his return to Freud under the sign of the post-Auschwitz period.

Lacan had been opposed to the Nazis from the outset, and had remained completely lucid in the period between the two world wars: admittedly, he had not joined the Resistance, but he was repelled by anything that resembled racism and anti-Semitism – so much so that he was not in the least embarrassed about having tried to meet Maurras in his youth, or of having frequented Pierre Drieu la Rochelle in 1932, or, indeed, of having all his life long shown great admiration for Heidegger as a man, even though he twisted the meaning of the latter's writings when he drew inspiration from them, especially when he produced a highly idiosyncratic translation of *Logos*, making this text say the complete opposite of what was written in it.[42] In 1932, he had attended – and been shocked by – the Berlin Olympics, and in the wake of the Second World War he planned to write a clinical study of the Rudolf Hess 'case'.

Nonetheless, he considered that Freud's message of origins needed to be heard afresh in the light of the event of Auschwitz, which – he said – confirmed how right Freud had been about the death drive.[43] But Lacan also thought – as indeed Freud had – that the emigration of almost all European psychoanalysts to the United States had been a catastrophe for Freudianism, which had completely changed character. Forced to adapt, the immigrants had ended up espousing the pragmatic ideals of a hygienist psychiatry centred on the subject's adaptation to society, forgetting that the quest for desire and the unconscious was entirely foreign to any doctrine of social happiness.[44]

And this is why, when he founded the École freudienne de Paris in 1964, Lacan stated that Marxism and Hegelianism were not enough to understand the Holocaust. In this modern tragedy, he said, appeared the supreme form of the sacrifice to the *Obscure God* (identified with the big Other). And he cited Spinoza as the only philosopher capable of thinking the eternal meaning of sacrifice in the *amor intellectualis*. But, after assigning an exceptional position to this philosopher, he also called for an overcoming of philosophy by psychoanalysis while emphasizing the importance of the ideas in his famous article 'Kant with Sade',[45] inspired by a reading of Adorno's text in which the latter showed how the perverse reversal of the Law leads to turning the law into the law of crime. But he also rejected, in spite of the use of the word 'holocaust', any theologization of the question of the genocide, whether religious or atheistic: it was neither a sacrificial abasement of man nor a meaningless event which abolished the divine order. Lacan universalized Auschwitz by turning it into the tragedy of the century, something which belonged to mankind as whole.[46]

Lacan, the non-Jew who identified with Spinoza, had come to tell the notables of the IPA, trapped in their adaptive ideal, that they were no longer the bearers of the message of Jewish universality bequeathed to them by Freud – a message which, after Auschwitz, needed to be radically rethought.

The attempt to locate the causes behind the genocide and the interest in the evidence of the victims came with the need to punish the perpetrators of the genocide, and thus to hunt them down in the countries where they had taken refuge. But, in Israel, the question of punishment took a paradoxical form. The law of 1950, for instance, which made it possible to prosecute war criminals and those who had committed crimes against humanity, could be applied only to Jews who had survived the camps and been forced to cooperate with the Nazis. These included the members of the Jewish councils (*Judenräte*), the Kapos, and other auxiliaries in the concentration camp system – and, of course, the Sonderkommandos.[47] Initially, then, the quest for 'accomplices' was yet another attempt to purify Israeli society of any stain from the European world. But there was a risk that hunting down these survivors would lead to the worst injustice of all: that of passing judgement on victims rather than on murderers. For the Jews who had cooperated with the Nazis were completely different from the standard collaborationists – those of the Vichy regime, for example. After all, they had had no choice other than death: even if they collaborated, they were merely delaying the time when they would be themselves exterminated, and they knew it.

In 1950, a young woman of twenty-six, Elsa Trank, was put on trial for 'crimes' which she had committed at Birkenau, eight years earlier. On Nazi orders, she had maintained order and discipline in the ranks of the deportees, which sometimes involved hitting them.

But, as she gave her evidence, the judges started to view her as a victim forced to become an oppressor.[48] Thus, the only verdict that could be reached on those who, in any event, were doomed to die in the camps was acquittal.

More serious was the case brought against Israel Kastner, a former socialist leader from Hungary, by Malchiel Grünwald, a Hungarian by birth who had emigrated to Palestine before the genocide. The accuser, a right-wing Zionist from a modest background, had lost part of his family in the extermination camps. The accused, a culti-vated intellectual and indisputably a charming man of the world, had become an important political figure in the Israeli establishment. In the dark hours of the extermination, he had cooperated with the Nazis to organize the rescue of 1,685 privileged Jews, including his own family, abandoning a great number of Jews from less well-off backgrounds. His quest for recognition was to some extent the symptom of the terrible guilt from which he had been suffering ever since that episode. His rival, who called him a 'stinking corpse', simply wished him to be 'exterminated'. The state decided in favour of the accused rather than the accuser, who was sentenced for defa-mation. But the question of the Jewish councils was still unresolved. In March 1957, in a street in Tel Aviv, Kastner was shot down with a pistol.

It was high time to put an end to this type of procedure and to put on trial a real killer. As Idith Zertal writes,

> Out of the same trial was born the Eichmann trial, which was intended as, and indeed became, the great redress for the Kastner affair, the show of power of the new and 'another' Israel prosecuting now, not Jewish victims, but a Nazi criminal for war crimes and crimes against humanity – Ben Gurion's last great national undertaking.[49]

When Ben Gurion ordered the capture in Argentina of Adolf Eich-mann, who was responsible for the 'Final Solution' in Germany and all the occupied countries, his first objective was to exalt the warlike heroism of the Israelis, contrasting their feats of arms with the sup-posed passivity of the European Jews who, it was said, had allowed themselves to be led to the slaughter. But he also wanted to give added legitimacy to the State of Israel, to remind the Allies that it was their duty to support it, and finally to show the world that never again would the least justification be given to those who sought the destruc-tion of the Jews.

In this respect, the trial was an undoubted success in spite of all the criticisms that were made of its alleged illegality, starting with that of Erich Fromm. In a letter published by the *New York Times*, Fromm claimed that the kidnapping of Eichmann was an illegal act, 'of the same kind as those which the Nazis themselves (and the regimes of Stalin and Trujillo) committed. It is true that there are no worse provocations than the crimes committed by Eichmann. But it is precisely in the case of extreme provocations that the respect for law and the integrity of other countries must be tested.'[50] Fromm, a dissident from classical Freudianism and a militant anti-universalist, had been driven out of Germany by Nazism: he had moved from Zionism to anti-Zionism.

In 1948, like Hannah Arendt, Fromm had called for Palestinians to be given the possibility to return to their own countries. But, in 1963, he unhesitatingly compared the situation in the United States to that in Germany in the 1930s, emphasizing, after a trial that he had not wished for, that Eichmann had been unaware of the true nature of the orders he had obeyed and was basically just an ordinary man. Every man bears a repressed Eichmann within himself: this was the tenor of Fromm's argument. Nothing could have been more mistaken than this conclusion: drawing on a behavioural psychology, it suggested that anybody can become a genocidal killer if the circumstances lend themselves to it.[51] This idea was later – and wrongly – confused with Hannah Arendt's thoughts on the banality of evil.

But the real scandal surrounding this trial lay in the grossly exaggerated reaction on the part of certain Israeli, American, German, and French Jews to the comments on it made by Arendt herself, who had been sent to Jerusalem by the *New Yorker* to cover the event.

A Zionist right from the start, although always ready to criticize the errors of Israeli politics, Arendt was, like Judah Magnes, in favour of coming to an understanding with the Arabs, though she continued to think that there was indeed a 'Jewish people'. While she rejected the chauvinistic twist that could be put on the doctrine of a chosen people, she drew on the work of Gershom Scholem and was quite ready to consider that spirituality was indispensable for the transmission of the Jewish culture and spirit. However, she could not imagine that the Jews would content themselves just with writing commentaries on the sacred texts. Far from it: it was their duty to enter real history.

In 1944, Arendt had written a text which aroused an intense polemic.[52] She noted that Zionism was the bearer of two contradictory notions of Jewish politics – one progressive, the other nationalist – and that the latter had, unfortunately, won. As a result, indifference to the diaspora among the Jews of Palestine, in her view, came with a failure to understand imperial policies in the Near East. The text was turned down by Clement Greenberg, the editor of the highly conservative review *Commentary*: 'It includes too many anti-Semitic implications, not that you deliberately put them there, but a malevolent reader will easily be able to deduce them.'[53]

And so, for the first time since the creation of a Jewish state, an accusation of anti-Semitism was brought by one ultra-conservative Jewish man against a Jewish woman who knew much more about the subject than he did – one who had dared to criticize Zionist nationalism. And this accusation was especially malicious in that it posed as sympathetic and protective: Hannah Arendt, said Greenberg, did not even realize that she was anti-Semitic. This was, so to speak, the starting point of what would become (as we shall see) the common tactic of revisionist and conservative prosecutors in the second half of the twentieth century, which consisted in denouncing anti-Semitism where it did not exist – more particularly among the proponents of the Enlightenment.

This accusation seemed all the more plausible in that Arendt, as a young woman in Germany, had been involved in an affair with Martin Heidegger. And not only was the philosopher anti-Semitic: in 1933, he had given his support to the Nazi regime in his 'rectoral speech'.[54] This all made Arendt an easy target for her enemies: she was guilty of having loved a Nazi and showing no remorse; she was guilty of anti-Zionism for merely criticizing one form of Jewish nationalism (one which had already been criticized by other Jews before her). Heidegger was hateful, and his wife Elfriede was even worse. And, however much he despised her, Arendt never attacked him. She refused to accept the arguments of her close friend Karl Jaspers, who urged her to show greater lucidity.[55]

At the end of a profound study of different revolutions, Arendt had clearly stated her preference for the American concept of freedom, based on the firm ground of communities, rather than the French concept, which – through the idea of the nation-state – linked freedom to equality. But, ever since she had emigrated to the United States, she had identified with the position of Bernard Lazare, a deliberate and rebellious pariah, and she had not stopped criticizing the policies of the country of which she had become a full citizen. Thus she denounced McCarthyism with the greatest firmness. Feeling neither truly Jewish nor truly German, but often more Jewish than German, she still preferred to define herself as 'the woman from somewhere else', always foreign to any integration – something she felt to be too normative. On this basis, she had simply taken the risk of being considered as an anti-Semite by Jewish nationalists, as a Jewess by anti-Semites, as a conservative by Marxists, and as a communist by conservatives. Be this as it may, for some people she was a dangerous Zionist, for others an implacable anti-Zionist.

Over and above any expression of compassion for the ancestral sufferings of her people, Arendt had been the first theorist of Jewish history to think through the question of modern anti-Semitism (which she distinguished from Christian anti-Judaism) in a rigorous way. In her view – and quite justifiably – anti-Semitism, born in the middle of the nineteenth century, had been not merely a weapon against the Jews but the greatest and most tumultuous process of decomposition ever experienced in Europe: it had led to the destruction not only of the Jews but of Germany and of European humanism.[56] Even before the publication of modern studies on the history of colonialism and the slave trade, Arendt had been the first to condemn these latter phenomena, but also to distinguish them from genocide, as Pierre Vidal-Naquet later did in his response to those who proposed to see all forms of massacre and oppression committed by men against other men as the same. She could even entertain the idea that the genocide of the Jews did not have the same meaning for the peoples of Asia or Africa as for those of populations in the Western world.[57]

Like Freud, whose work she knew but little (she even confused it with the work of his paltry exegetes), Arendt rejected the Zionist idea of the supremacy of the territorial Jews over the Jews of the diaspora. So she did not draw a contrast between 'being Israeli' and 'being Jewish', any more than she could accept that the creation of a state could be the equivalent of a Copernican revolution in the history of Jewish consciousness. Having already laid down the bases for a reflection on the genocide, she considered it her duty as a Jew to attend the trial of a man who had been one of the major figures responsible for the extermination of the Jews and the destruction of the European world. She was also in agreement with the way this trial was conducted, and did not even wonder whether the death penalty were a problem here. At no time did she confuse the victims with the executioners, even when she showed some severity towards the Jewish councils – here, she drew on the work of Raul Hilberg,[58] the first version of whose book had just been published in the United States. Furthermore, she drew a distinction between the leaders of the Jewish councils – whom she criticized, without claiming to stand in judgement over them, for cooperating in various degrees with the Nazis – and the detainees, who, once they had been integrated within the machinery of genocide, had no choice other than death, a death which could never resemble the 'beautiful death' of the Greek tradition.

From this point of view – and just like Hilberg – Arendt mainly attacked Leo Baeck, whom she had already met and who saw Nazism as the continuation of the eternal persecution of the Jews, a people chosen by God and distinct from the rest by its talent. This led Baeck to deny that there was any distinction between anti-Judaism and anti-Semitism: indeed, he ignored the specific historical break represented by the genocide of the Jews.

When he had realized that the extermination of his family was inevitable, he had decided to lie to them so as to make their final trials more bearable: 'But later, when the question arose whether Jewish orderlies should help pick up Jews for deportation, I took the position that it would be better for them to do it, because they could at least be more gentle and helpful than the Gestapo and make the ordeal easier. It was scarcely in our power to oppose this order effectively.'[59] Not only had Baeck thereby deprived his family of the right to confront their deaths: his attitude had contributed to shaping the legend that the Jews had allowed themselves to be led like sheep to the slaughter, an idea that was later taken up by the perpetrators of the genocide at their trials. Eichmann, Höss, and many others thus claimed that the Jews themselves desired their own extermination – or, at the very least, were the ones mainly responsible for it.[60]

Arendt very quickly realized that neither the prosecutor Gideon Hausner nor his team were up to the task entrusted to them. They had expected to see a monster straight from the long tradition of vampires and other sadistic murderers gorged with blood; they were disappointed when the man appearing before them turned out to be an idiot, a failure who claimed that he had never persecuted the Jews 'for pleasure or passion', and who presented himself not only as a good Zionist seeking a 'humane solution' to the Jewish problem but also as the 'victim' of his superiors, men who had 'exploited his obedience' by turning him into an unwilling executioner. And he complained as sincerely as anyone could have done at the atrocities inflicted on him when he was kidnapped in Argentina: 'They flung themselves on me and, rendered unconscious by the injections they gave me, I was then taken to the aerodrome in Buenos Aires; from there, I was taken out of Argentina by plane. Obviously, this can be explained only by the fact that they held me responsible for everything.'[61]

At that time, there was a considerable literature drawing inspiration from psychiatry and psychoanalysis to study Nazi criminals, inventing for them a childhood that fitted an erroneous conception of perversion, which they understood as a monstrous deviation of the sexual instinct. Thus it was that several authors compiled amazing clinical catalogues of the different sexual practices of the perpetrators of the Holocaust. So Hitler was viewed by his biographers as a mentally deficient çoprophagist.[62] As for Eichmann, he was depicted as having, at the age of ten, created a machine for torturing children. He was also accused of cases of sexual abuse and rape.[63] It is impossible to exaggerate the extent to which the so-called clinical approach to the murderers, fabricated by unscrupulous authors with the frequent support of psychoanalysts, helped for years to ensure that a mistaken view of the Freudian categories prevailed: this also affected the structural definition of perversion and its different metamorphoses.

Thus, in Jerusalem, the judges, influenced by a whole ideology of the alleged 'monstrous inhumanity' of Nazism and its mass murderers, were amazed to see appear before them a banal civil servant, an assortment of tics and obsessions, fundamentally grotesque and stupid, and in any case incapable of any form of emotion or any real sense of responsibility. The murderer was aware of his acts and admitted that they were dreadful, but he accused other people of being really responsible. Thus he pleaded not guilty because he did not *feel* guilty of the crimes of which he stood accused.[64]

At Nuremberg, several psychiatrists had described the perpetrators of the genocide as 'murderous schizoid robots', men of terrifying ordinariness: they also showed that it was the Nazi system that, by inverting the values of good and evil, had given birth to this type of criminal. Arendt did not endorse these assessments, which she deemed to be inadequate; she did note, however, that Eichmann was terribly normal:

> it would have been very comforting indeed to believe that Eichmann was a monster. [. . .] Surely, one can hardly call upon the whole world and gather correspondents from the four corners of the earth in order to display Bluebeard in the dock. The trouble with Eichmann was precisely that so many were like him, and that the many were neither perverted nor sadistic, that they were, and still are, terribly and terrifyingly normal. From the viewpoint of our legal institutions and of our moral standards of judgement, this normality was much more terrifying than all the atrocities put together, for it implied [. . .] that this new type of criminal [. . .] commits his crimes under circumstances that make it well-nigh impossible for him to know or to feel that he is doing wrong.[65]

For this reason, Arendt judged that Eichmann was 'unaware' of the meaning of his actions while still being aware that he had committed them. As a result, she said, he did not deserve to live, since he denied human diversity: if Nazism is radical evil, she added, evil in Eichmann's case was 'banal' and never demonic. That evil came not from God but from men, and the Nazis were human beings who, through the genocide of the Jews, had declared that human beings were superfluous as human beings – so that the human being as such could become superfluous.

But Arendt also remarked that the actions of such a criminal defied punishment, and it was absurd to punish with death a man responsible for such appalling crimes. In any case, this was precisely what Eichmann dreamt of: he wanted to be hanged in public and enjoy his own execution so that he could believe himself to be immortal, the equal of a god. Indeed, at the gallows, he taunted his judges, claiming that he would see them again one day, forgetting that he was there for his own death: 'It was as though in those last minutes he was summing up the lessons that this long course in human wickedness had taught us – the lesson of the fearsome, word-and-thought-defying *banality* of evil.'[66]

⌐ So it was by demonstrating an extreme normality that Eichmann embodied the very essence of perversion: an enjoyment of evil, the absence of emotion, the gestures of an automaton, implacable logic, the cult of detail and the most insignificant anecdote, an unparalleled ability to endorse hateful crimes by making them into something theatrical, so as the better to flaunt the way Nazism had turned him into an abject creature. In claiming to be Kantian, he was telling the truth, since in his view the vile character of the orders he was given counted for nothing in comparison with the imperative character of the orders themselves. Thus, he had become a mass murderer without sensing the least guilt.

Arendt's stroke of genius – despite the fact that, as I have said, she had never read a line of Freud's work – lay in understanding the extent to which anti-Semitism was also a matter for the unconscious. Eichmann's anti-Semitism was not in doubt, and yet he denied it and claimed to be the friend of Jews. Quite obviously, he was one of the men in charge of the genocide, but he denied this responsibility while at the same time acknowledging that he had carried out an appalling extermination. He did not lie, he did not pretend, he was not evasive: he offered the spectacle of an atrocious sincerity combined with complete stupidity.

This was all of great interest to Arendt, this Jewish and German philosopher who had avoided hell and, far from Israel, did not hesitate to criticize the nationalist excesses of Zionism as well as the exaggerated cult of the memory of the victims. Arendt was doubtless wrong about one point: she forgot that those involved in the

Judenräte had not been aware of their 'cooperation' with the Nazis; even if they had been, this would have changed nothing – so she believed – in the process of extermination. Probably, too, her understanding of the banality of evil could lead to confusion and imply, for example, that *any* civil servant could become a mass murderer. In actual fact, the notion of the banality of evil can be a perfectly good example of Bebel's notion that anti-Semitism is the socialism of imbeciles. An anti-Semite is always and primarily full of stupidity,[67] whatever may be his degree of pathology or criminality. And Arendt clearly shows that Eichmann was, before all else, a perfectly stupid person.

That fact remains that her book, far ahead of its time, presented a magisterial analysis of the phenomenon of genocide and of its main organizer – an analysis that did not in the least suit the Jews of the 1960s – neither those in the diaspora, in search of a new identity between community and universalism, nor those in the State of Israel eager to promote a heroic image of themselves. And then, at this date, it was unthinkable that anyone could devote their energy to portraying a murderer at a time when the victims were starting to present their eye-witness accounts.

Thus, Arendt's account of the Jerusalem trial was met with a hail of brickbats throughout the world – which does no honour to her detractors. Stupefied by the calumnies raining down on her, which made out that she was saying the complete opposite of what she had actually written, Arendt decided to respond. But she was forced to realize that every press article produced by her enemies imitated another one, thereby compounding its errors – an unavoidable process at a time when the power of the media was growing, as was their intrusion into intellectual debates hitherto reserved to a small and cultivated public.

In the United States, conservative Jews accused Arendt of being fascinated by the mass murderer, of neglecting the victims, and of vilifying the members of the Jewish councils.[68] They claimed that her book would become a bible for anti-Semites eager to make the Jews responsible for the crimes of the Nazis. In Israel, Hausner's family criticized her for turning the meaning of the Shoah upside down, turning the criminal into a virtuous man and the victims into murderers. In France, the translator of the work, Pierre Nora, saw fit to add an ambiguous preface, in which he noted the polemics while abstaining from taking any position himself.[69]

And when *Le nouvel observateur* produced an excellent number to the trial, several intellectuals of note published a collective letter in six points to express their indignation: 'Is Hannah Arendt a Nazi?'

Such was the question asked by Robert Misrahi, Vladimir Jankélévitch, Madeleine Barthélemy-Madaule, Olivier Revault d'Allones, and several others.[70] They criticized the philosopher for being a masochist, a malevolent person; they accused her of lying, of putting forward untruths, of being indifferent to the fate of the Jews, and so on. Éliane Amado Lévy-Valensi invited people to 'raise the level of the debate' and to restore to the book its unconscious meaning. The implication was that Arendt was judged to be both schizophrenic and paranoid, haunted by Jewish self-hatred and anti-Semitism, incapable of understanding the self-sacrifice of the members of the Jewish councils.

In the midst of this wave of negative interpretations, which clearly showed that the accusers had understood nothing of Arendt's pathbreaking analysis, Pierre Vidal-Naquet alone had the courage to side with her. He declared that the book had not been properly read, that most of the facts about the Jewish councils were accurate and already known, and that the author's stroke of genius lay in drawing a portrait of a mass murderer that completely fitted in with her previous analyses of totalitarianism. And he emphasized the brilliance of this report on the banality of evil: indeed, it made it possible to understand that totalitarian language – that perversion of the German language, as Saül Friedlander later put it – was also a mystification that had authorized the murderer to believe that he was a Kantian and to judge himself to be innocent of the crimes he had committed.[71]

The real critique, the most painful for Arendt, came from Gershom Scholem. True, Scholem did not share Arendt's conception of Zionism, but they were after all bound by mutual admiration, by family exchanges, and by their friendship with Walter Benjamin. Scholem had demonstrated his brilliance by debating the question of the madness of Sabbatai Zevi, who converted to Islam. He had proposed a subtle interpretation of the way the mystical discourse swung between darkness and light, and he had powerfully raised the question of redemption through sin while advocating the need for Judaism to find room once more for a messianic trend that had been repressed by rationalism. Furthermore, he had been one of the few people to analyse – especially with regard to the destiny of Walter Benjamin, of whose Marxism he did not approve – the paradoxes linked to the dual quest for universality and for territory, for materialism and for spiritualism.

Scholem knew that exile was one of the great issues at stake in Jacob's struggle with the Angel, the combat between the spiritual man and the natural man, the one who does not say his name (God) and

the one who, at the same moment he is both wounded and trium-
phant, receives the name of Israel, the name of the man who is able
to fight with God. He also knew – better than anyone – the *Angelus
Novus* painting by Paul Klee, the angel with whom Benjamin had
identified, the angel whose eyes are turned simultaneously to the
future and to the past.[72] In short, he was the person best placed to
understand what was at stake in this trial: the need for those who
had survived the Shoah – Jews from the diaspora and from Israel – to
establish, by passing judgement on the murderer, a link between
history and memory and, for researchers across the world, to encourage new thinking about the Jewish question, anti-Semitism, Nazism,
and totalitarianism.

However, having moved towards a certain nationalism, Scholem
was convinced that the only answer to the Jewish question lay in a
return not to Orthodox Judaism, but to a Jewishness centred on a
voluntary acceptance of faith, religion, and the doctrine of the chosen
people:

> I have always considered secular Zionism as a legitimate path, but I
> reject the stupid idea that the Jews should become a 'people like
> others'. If this were to happen, it would be the end of the Jewish
> people. I share the traditional opinion that, even if we did desire to
> become a people like the others, we would not succeed. And if we did,
> it would be the end of us [. . .]. I cannot understand the atheists, I have
> never been able to understand them, either in my youth, or in my old
> age. I think that atheism is understandable only if you accept the
> domination of unbridled passions, a life lacking values.[73]

In other words, Scholem was very far from the position of the de-
Judaized Jews of the diaspora who led the 'Galutic existence' of
'non-Jewish Jews' or of godless Jews:[74] he could support neither
Marxism, nor Freudianism, nor secular Zionism.

As a result, Nazism was for Scholem nothing more than the experience of a systematic destruction of the image of God in man. Admittedly, he did think that Eichmann could be judged, but it would have
been preferable in his view not to execute him. Though he did not
seek the abolition of the death penalty, the great theorist of mysticism
thought that an execution in this case would be of no use to the State
of Israel and would not solve the question of knowing why so many
Jews had allowed themselves to be slaughtered.[75] Was there not a
risk, he said, that people would later accuse the Jews of having sought
to take vengeance for their own weakness?

This was the angle from which Scholem sent to Arendt a critique
that, unfortunately, did not contain anything by way of serious

argument. He reproached her for lacking love for the Jewish people, for being a Marxist, and for having no empathy for Leo Baeck. He rejected – without any real analysis of it – the concept of the banality of evil, and he also acknowledged that he quite failed to grasp the perverse idea that Eichmann had dared to claim he was a Zionist by seeking a solution to the Jewish question.[76]

Wounded by this letter from an old master, Arendt replied tartly. She pointed out that she was not a Marxist, that her fidelity to Zionism and to her own Jewishness was entire, that her position was that of a foreigner in permanent exile, and that, finally, her conception of love drew her to individuals, which meant that she could not love one people to the detriment of another. She said she was distressed to see that her detractor, for whom she had so much respect, could misunderstand her ideas so badly that he was quite unable to criticize the disastrous absence of any separation, in Israel, between the state and religion. And she added: 'The evil committed by my people naturally causes me more sorrow than the evil committed by other peoples.'[77]

In this exchange of letters, the examination of the Jewish question took a new turn: here was a Jewish philosopher desacralizing the Zionist cause, not only by analysing the personality of the murderer but by bringing out, with regard to a trial that was intended to be a new 'foundation', a profound division between the Jews of the diaspora and the Jews of Israel, and between those Jews who wished to accept the ideal of a redemptive state and other Jews who sought, on the contrary, to remain detached from this reference to territoriality.

Arendt's work was not recognized by the greatest French philosophers – from Sartre to Derrida, via Foucault, Canguilhem, Deleuze and Althusser – and it was not until the 1980s that it started to be read.[78] For Freudians she was an anti-Freudian, for Marxists and feminists she was conservative, for conservative Jews she was anti-Zionist, and for all those who reduced Heidegger's philosophy to a Hitlerian epic she was, because of his own silence on the topic, an accomplice of Nazism. For historians she was a philosopher, for philosophers she was a political scientist, for specialists in Judaism she was not Jewish enough, and for materialists of every stripe, atheistic and anti-religious, she was too heavily influenced by Judaism. In short, there was really no room in the French intellectual field between 1960 and 1980 for such a paradoxical body of work and for a woman who was free in her judgements. In this respect, Vidal-Naquet, yet again, had proved a pioneer.

We should also note that the French and German debates on totalitarianism later espoused different positions from Arendt, especially when Ernst Nolte and François Furet equated the two forms of totalitarianism: they both saw communism and Stalinism as the same, as if Stalinism were already present in Marx's work and in the communist ideal. Indeed, they both thought that communism was far more criminal than Nazism, since it was possible to ascribe to that 'nefarious ideology' a much higher number of deaths than Nazism had caused. Reading them, it would have been easy to deduce that communism was responsible for all the massacres that had occurred in Europe since 1917, then in China, Cambodia, Vietnam, and so on – the deaths caused by the civil war, by the several famines, by the two world wars, by the colonial wars, etc.

Nolte, a pupil of Martin Heidegger and Eugen Fink, maintained not only that communism and Nazism were two identical systems, but that Nazism had been the consequence in Germany of the victory in Russia of the Bolshevik Revolution. He relativized Nazism, making of it a mere anti-communism; in the same way, he underlined the way that the Gulag – which had come before the Shoah – had provided a first model for the extermination of the Jews. This revisionist idea was attacked by Jürgen Habermas: it tended to exonerate Germany from all responsibility in the genesis of Nazism and to reduce communism to Stalinism.

Furet endorsed this approach, revising the history of the French Revolution and claiming that, if the Terror of 1793 was already at work in the uprisings of 1789, this meant that Bolshevism was present in the Declaration of the Rights of Man and then in Robespierrism – and that the Revolution of 1789 therefore led straight to the Gulag. This idea would be taken up by several French philosophers eager to transform the Enlightenment into an obscurantist ideology that led to anti-Semitism.[79]

Alain Besançon had, like Furet, been a member of the French Communist Party before 1956, and was thus imbued with a thoroughgoing Stalinism: he put forward a more or less identical thesis, based on an equally aberrant comparativist view. But he added to his approach a purportedly 'psychoanalytic' angle. Describing Nazism and communism as 'heterozygotic twins', he regarded the first as the product of an instinctual romanticism, explaining that genocide was nothing but the carrying out of this instinct; and he turned communism into the greatest perversion of the century. Unlike Nazism, he claimed, communism did not ask men consciously to take the moral step towards becoming criminals. So it was intrinsically more perverse than Nazism, since it passed off the extermination of its victims as a moral necessity. In one case (Nazism), the victims were honoured; in the other, they were forgotten.[80]

Once the polemics had subsided, Arendt was given, in the United States, the support of a new generation of left-wing intellectuals, both Jewish and non-Jewish, who opposed both the deployment of American imperialism in the Third World and the increasingly imperialist policies of the State of Israel towards the Palestinians. In the proclamation of the Charter of the PLO in 1964, the Palestinians described the creation of the State of Israel as 'illegal'.[81] After the Six-Day War, which marked the triumph of Israeli military power in the Middle East,[82] the Jews of the diaspora felt obliged to choose sides: either to become unconditional allies of Israel, at the risk of moving towards a nationalism of identity, or to commit themselves to protest, at the risk of cutting themselves away entirely from Zionism or of protesting against it in such a way as to deny the perfectly real rise of Arab anti-Semitism.

On both sides, yet again, the great Jewish obsession with disappearance, dispersion, and catastrophe loomed. Some wished to 'forget the Shoah', while others sought to establish it in memory so that the 'foul beast' would never again arise from the recesses of the human soul. The Arabs, robbed of their land, ended up regarding the Jewish state as a colonialist and racist state.[83] In tandem with this, an anti-Arab racism started to rise in Israel.

In June 1982, the Israeli Army invaded Lebanon, and in September of the same year, protected by the army, the Christian Falangist militia led by Elie Hobeika, in an attempt to avenge other massacres as well as the murder of Bachir Gemayel, the leader of the militia of the Lebanese forces, entered the Palestinian camps of Sabra and Chatila to murder women, children, and old men in cold blood.

This Israeli invasion had nothing to do with any alleged genocide of the Lebanese-Palestinian people, or with the destruction of the Warsaw ghetto, as was claimed by many of those who sought to 'Nazify' their enemies. But the attitude of the Israeli Army at the time of the massacres triggered a wave of protest in Israel. A commission of inquiry under Judge Itzhak Kahane showed that, if the killings had indeed been carried out by the Falangists alone, the conduct of the Israeli military campaign was flawed.

Thus, Ariel Sharon saw his personal responsibility under fire for 'his non-action', and he was forced to resign. This episode in a perpetual war aggravated the difficulties in which Israel found itself and had a knock-on effect on the Jews of the diaspora and their allies, who found themselves obliged either to relativize the significance of the event, and to give even more unconditional support to Israeli policy by wilful blindness, or to adopt an increasingly critical attitude, at the cost of being described as bad Jews or, even worse, '*alterjuifs*', to the delight of the real anti-Semites of the period, the Holocaust deniers.

With Sabra and Chatila, 'the innocence of Israel was dead'.[84]

6

A Great and Destructive Madness

Between 1950 and 1966 in France, with the exception of a few groups of neo-Nazis and those nostalgic for the Vichy regime, nobody could imagine anybody ever denying the existence of the genocide of the Jews, and nobody dared to call himself or herself 'anti-Semitic' in public. Anti-Semitism, no longer the expression of a policy supported by particular party or an authorized opinion, had become an individual way of thinking – or not thinking – about the Jewish question: it was, first and foremost, a matter for the unconscious, and was thus all the more pathological, shameful, and emotional in that it was repressed, finding utterance in slips of the tongue, denials, or linguistic oddities. There is evidence of this in a moving account given by Jacques Derrida. Born in Algeria, he had experienced a childhood haunted by the humiliation of being a Jew, especially in 1942 when, after the abolition of the Crémieux decree,[1] he was expelled from his lycée. In 1952, at the age of twenty-two, now living in France, he was invited to stay with the very traditional family of Claude Bonnefoy and was forced to confront, during an apparently civilized conversation, an anti-Semitic allusion.

A few days later, Derrida wrote a letter to his friend in which he noted the differences between the anti-Semitism he had known in Algeria and the anti-Semitism which predominated in metropolitan France:

> I'm Jewish [. . .]. I had no right to conceal the fact – even though it was an artificial question for me [. . .]. A few years ago, I was very 'sensitized' to this topic, and any allusion of an anti-Jewish type would

have made me furious. At that time I was capable of reacting violently. [. . .] All this has calmed down in me somewhat. In France I have known people who remained quite untouched by any trace of anti-Semitism. I learned that in this area, intelligence and decency were possible, and that this saying (unfortunately common in Jewish circles) – 'everything that is not Jewish is anti-Jewish' – was not true. It has become less of a burning issue for me, it has retreated into the background. Other non-Jewish friends have taught me to link anti-Semitism to a whole set of defining factors. [. . .] Anti-Semitism in Algeria seems more immovable, more concrete, more terrible. In France, anti-Semitism is part, or claims to be part, of a doctrine, of a set of abstract ideas. It remains dangerous, like everything which is abstract, but less tangible in human relationships. Basically speaking, French anti-Semites are anti-Semitic only with Jews they do not know. When an anti-Semite is intelligent, he does not believe in his anti-Semitism.[2]

If, according to Derrida, intelligent, anti-Semitic French people did not believe in their anti-Semitism at a time when the genocide of the Jews had still not been identified as such, anti-Semitism was still present in France, silently and unconsciously, fourteen years later, when the question of the specific extermination of the Jews was just starting to be studied.

In December 1966, a survey by the French Institute of Public Opinion on the Jewish question indicated that 19 per cent of Jews 'were not French like other French people', especially the communists (where the figure rose to 28 per cent). Around 10 per cent of French openly admitted their antipathy towards Jews, and only 9 per cent said they were anti-Semitic. But 50 per cent stated that they would not vote for a Jewish candidate standing for the office of president of the Republic, 31 per cent thought that there were 'too many Jews in politics', and 81 per cent highlighted the place occupied by Jews in business. Finally, one French person in every hundred described the genocide of the Jews as an 'ultimately salutary measure', while a third of them thought that there had been around 5 or 6 million dead.[3]

During the academic year 1966–7, at the age of twenty-two – and thirty-five years before I could compare my own experience to that of Derrida – I was appointed to a teaching job at the Hydrocarbon Centre in Boumerdés, in Algeria, with the task of reorganizing French studies for pupils barely younger than myself who were preparing, under the aegis of Soviet teachers, to become technicians and engineers specializing in the oil business. These young people had experienced the violence of war. Some had seen their parents tortured or executed by French soldiers; others had witnessed massacres perpetrated during the war of the Wilayahs.* Having been victims, some of them turned into aggressors: for instance, they had raped my predecessor, a woman teacher who dared, so they said, to describe the destiny of George Sand and to sing the praises of free love.

All these pupils wished to receive a traditional education based on the syllabuses of French lycées. When I decided to add to the list of authors deemed worthy of study in France the names of several French-speaking Algerian writers – Mohamed Dib or Kateb Yacine – they expressed their displeasure. They actually demanded to be taught nothing but the culture of the former colonizing power, even though they loathed this power. I rejected their demand and decided to add to my list the name of Frantz Fanon. Forced to read *The wretched of the earth*, most of them pointed out to me that he was a 'negro'. This was a harsh experience for me, especially because I felt that I was the heir of Sartre and of those who had given discreet practical help to the Resistance. I had come to Algeria with quite a Manichean vision of the post-colonial situation, convinced that it was my job to make up for the misdeeds of colonization by providing my pupils with a good education. After somewhat protracted negotiations, my pupils accepted my syllabus, on condition, they said, that they would have the right to recite alexandrines. They loved the tragedies of Corneille and Racine, and they were very keen on the theatre. So I had thought of getting them to study the plays of Jean Genet – especially *The Screens*.[4] But I gave up the idea.

During the Six-Day War, to my great surprise, the walls of several classrooms – including mine – were covered with swastikas. Most of the French teachers, who were at that time called 'red feet' [*pieds rouges*] because they had actively supported Algerian independence before moving to the country as teachers, refused to see this action as a demonstration of anti-Semitism. Several of them were fascinated by the Chinese Cultural Revolution and often went to the Chinese Embassy in Algeria, where they could watch propaganda films on the life and work of Mao Zedong. It was on this occasion that I attended a screening of *The East is Red*, a dreadful film which immediately put me off any idea of supporting Maoism. At this political juncture, hostility towards Israel was so intense and guilt towards previously colonized populations so obsessive that nobody dared to tackle the question of the swastikas. I remember one conversation with a teacher, a man who had deserted from the French Army.[5] He explained to me

---

* These were military districts under the Army of National Liberation in Algeria: there are serious disputes over their boundaries – Trans.

that a symbol did not have the same meaning in different contexts. Thus, cultural relativism could be used to justify the way a swastika could become the legitimate expression of the revolt of a people crushed by American–Israeli imperialism. There was nothing here, I was informed, that had anything to do with Nazism or anti-Semitism.

There were lively discussions between those who, like me – unfortunately there were very few of us – obstinately refused to continue teaching in rooms scrawled over with such revolting symbols and those who were unwilling to suspend their activities just a few weeks before the end of the school year.[6]

Eventually, I decided to ask my pupils to clean the walls as soon as possible. They accused me of being a Zionist enemy who hated them. Admittedly, I could accept the idea that young Algerians might consider the Israelis as their enemies, but I could not understand why, in order to designate them, they needed to resort to the major signifier of the extermination of the Jews of Europe. And, to make sure that they really understood what I was trying to tell them, I taught them about the Second World War and the death camps. I included several details that reminded them of the traumatic events of their own childhoods. They solemnly cleaned the walls, claiming that they had known nothing about all this. And, of course, they asked me if, like them, and as a Jewish woman, I had lost any relatives in the disaster.

So they thought that I was Jewish because I was fighting anti-Semitism. I was indeed Jewish, but not in the way they imagined. I was Jewish in the sense of Jewishness and not of Judaism: a materialist, without any real religion, I felt just as much an heir to Catholicism (a religion of art and desire admired by my father) and to Protestantism (a religion of free will professed by my mother, whose father belonged to the upper echelons of Protestant society) as I did to Judaism (the religion of the book, of knowledge and of intelligence). To this mixture I added the Greek gods, my favourites, since they were the gods of history, of tragedy, of philosophy, and of cunning. As the product of a family of assimilated republican Jews, who had been supporters of de Gaulle's Resistance from the outset, I was forever as a child – quite unlike my schoolmates, the children of deportees who never said a word – listening to people talking about the extermination, about Roman and Christian anti-Judaism, emancipation, anti-Semitism, and the Dreyfus Affair.[7]

None of those around me had been exterminated, and none had worn the yellow star. As early as 1938, my parents had been resolutely opposed to the Munich Agreement and perfectly lucid about

Hitler's criminal intentions. So they had taken every possible precaution to obtain false certificates of baptism and papers of every kind to conceal their origins and resist the occupiers more effectively. For several years, in France, I had never dreamt of defining myself as Jewish or non-Jewish, and I needed this experience in Algeria to become aware, not of the concrete existence of anti-Semitism but of its structural – and thus interminable – presence at the heart of human subjectivity.

In short, these young Algerians had taught me that, by taking Israelis for Jews, they had identified with Nazis and thus with anti-Semites even though they knew nothing about the Shoah. Anti-Semitism was written into their unconscious, and this anti-Semitism was aimed at 'the Jew' in the generic sense of the term, and not at the territorial enemy. I remember telling them that the fight against anti-Semitism could not just be a matter for the Jews, for any man worthy of the name. And I pointed out that it was not as a Jewish woman that I had made my gesture: anyone could and should have behaved in the same way.

Faced with the cultural relativism professed by an anti-colonialist militant, who dared to see these swastikas as the sign of a justified revolt against imperialism, and being in contact as I was with young people who were the heirs of colonial horror but able to become aware of their history through discovering a history which was not theirs, I became certain that one should never yield when it came to the symbolic function.[8] From this sprang my conviction that, in history, the notions of 'context', of 'mentality', or of 'contextualization' cannot be used indiscriminately. While it is obvious that Christian anti-Judaism cannot be interpreted as a form of anti-Semitism *avant la lettre*, because it needs to be seen within the context of a particular period, it is also obvious that it would abusing the notion of context to accept that anti-Zionism could be associated with the external signs of Nazism on the pretext that, within the 'context of the Arab world', a swastika or *The Protocols of the Elders of Zion* did not have the same meaning as in the Western world. In actual fact, and in the form of a 'context', this experience showed rather that, after the Six-Day War, anti-Zionism also threatened to be the channel for an anti-Semitism that dared not speak its name. We should also remember that, in the Israeli–Palestinian conflict, the process of Nazifying the enemy had widened after 1945.

In the course of this experience, I also realized that there were two ways of criticizing Israel. The first consisted in questioning the principle of its existence, the second, its policies. Now, to question the

existence of Israel stems from an attitude of denial which can author-
ize a shift from anti-Zionism to anti-Semitism, and thereby debars
any political critique. Attacking France's colonialist policies never led
to questioning its very existence.[9]

This new awareness of mine was not unrelated to my later admiration for the work of Claude Lévi-Strauss and, more generally, what
was called structuralism, which – in its modern, postmodern, and
deconstructive variants – seemed to me the best rampart (after
Sartre's venture) against every form of barbarism founded on psychologism, sociologism, behaviourism, scientism, and other so-called
cognitive, naturalist, or affective approaches to human existence.

If it is true, as Aimé Césaire states, that Hitler is the 'white man's
demon', since he applied to Europe barbarian procedures that had,
before him, affected only negroes, Arabs, or Asians, it is just as much
the case that, if we are not careful, the formerly colonized peoples,
just as much as their former colonizers, can be haunted by the demon
of Hitler – that is, by anti-Semitism.[10] It then hardly matters that this
demon was invented in Europe in the nineteenth century: wherever
it may be, it needs to be fought.

From the 1980s onwards, an increasing number of studies on the
Shoah were produced. However, the more the history of the extermination was studied (at the same time as the twofold approach to the
Jewish question and the colonial question was being given fresh
impetus), the more a new form of anti-Semitism – Holocaust denial
– started to develop, undermining the achievements of historiography.
But, simultaneously, on both sides of the Atlantic, a new type of
argument was now deployed, identifying any criticism of Israeli
policy and any anti-Zionism as a form of anti-Semitism. Hannah
Arendt had already been a victim of this, and others after her would
be targeted, earning themselves the label 'new anti-Semites' as a result
of their support for the Palestinian cause or their attachment to
Marxism, anti-colonialism, and then anti-globalization.[11] Admittedly,
as we have said, the discourse of anti-Semitism can also be transmitted by anti-Zionism – even more when this anti-Zionism merges with
a radical Islamism. But, for there to be a real identity between anti-
Zionism and anti-Semitism, the critique must be uttered in a discourse that appropriates the signifiers of a hatred of Jews. An
imputation of anti-Semitism loses all meaning if it is not based on
solid arguments. In other words, if anti-Semitism is everywhere, it is
no longer anywhere in particular and, if all anti-Zionism is equated
with anti-Semitism, we risk confusing someone who opposes a certain
policy with a Jew-hater, thereby suggesting that supporting Israel or

its policies is the same as combating anti-Semitism. In this area, an apologia is as useless as anathema. To pour scorn on the State of Israel because it is merely an artificial creation invented by the West to perpetuate the spirit of colonialism is just as pointless as seeing it as the sole possible horizon for the Jews of the diaspora: a sort of miraculous land, embodying the struggle against the barbarity of the Third World.[12]

The PLO leaders were aware of these contradictions: in 1969, in their third charter, they defined the objectives of their struggle in these terms: 'Fatah does not struggle against the Jews as an ethnic or religious community, but against Israel considered as the expression of a colonization based on a theocratic, racist and expansionist system.'[13] Admittedly, seeing Israel as a racist and colonialist state was debatable, as I have had occasion to say, but Jews in the generic sense were not being targeted by this text, which had the merit of distinguishing between anti-Semitism, the struggle against Israel, and the struggle against Zionism.

After the Second World War, anti-Semitism in Europe had become a matter for the unconscious: Holocaust denial[14] was a perpetuation of it in the form of a madness that aimed not merely at exterminating the Jews a second time, by trying to murder their memory,[15] but at denying that the State of Israel had any legitimacy at all (though, as we know, this state rests on fragile and debatable foundations). Later on, in spite of what was stated in the different charters of the PLO, there was a gradual merging of the Holocaust denial that had emerged from the European far right and the anti-Zionism of the Arab world. The Jews, it was said on both sides, had lied so as to make the West seem guilty and to make possible the creation of a 'criminal' state of which the Palestinians were the victims. And just as, at the end of the nineteenth century, colonialism had been the vector of anti-Semitism, anti-Zionism now performed the same role: it was as if anti-Semitism were so indestructible that it could be used in the service of two such contradictory causes.

The singular history of Holocaust denial began in 1948 with Maurice Bardèche, the brother-in-law of Robert Brasillach, an anti-Semite, an anti-communist Vichy supporter and an anti-Zionist. In its initial form, this discourse put forward a representation of history that consisted not merely in turning its signifiers and its causal patterns upside down, in a process of denial identical with that used by the perpetrators of genocide, but in introducing the idea of a conspiracy into this reversal. In other words, instead of relating the facts as they had actually occurred, the Holocaust deniers always began by explaining them in a form akin to a mania of interpretation. For instance, the liberation of France in 1944 was presented by Bardèche as a disastrous moment in the country's history. He claimed that, while Pétain's aim was to protect the Jews from a persecution for which they themselves were responsible, the Allies plunged the West into chaos: they shaved women's heads, committed rapes, and massacred the German civilian populations in the most appalling bombardments. After savagely murdering the vanquished, they sought to pass judgement on them, and at Nuremberg they invented a vile procedure that drew on mendacious testimony. They thus gave birth to the myth of the Holocaust – a thoroughgoing imposture intended to disguise the reality of the Jews' new domination of the world.[16]

Bardèche's ideas were merely a classic continuation of those prevalent under the Vichy regime, later taken up by far-right movements (even when these were at odds with one another).

This whole set of ideas would not have met with the same historiographical impact had they not been endorsed – and even fostered – by another discourse: the strange thinking produced by Paul Rassinier, a socialist and anarchist Resistance fighter deported and tortured in Buchenwald in 1943, who, over the years, soured by the failures of a grey, vengeful life, joined Bardèche and also accepted the idea that the history written by the victors was merely an imposture, a falsification of reality. Not only did Rassinier claim that the behaviour of the communists in the camps had been more actively murderous than that of the Nazis, but he also maintained that nobody had ever been able to prove that there had been any gas chambers.[17] From that moment, this reversal of the truth spread and the method of the Holocaust deniers gained in focus. All real eye-witnesses reports were presented as fables – produced by the Jews as well as by the Nazis – while the scholarly 'assessments' tried to demonstrate, with all the evidence needed to 'prove' it, that it was physically impossible to have gassed the Jews at all.[18] As Vidal-Naquet later wrote:

> To work at the level of the mass media, they had to ally themselves theoretically and practically with the only groups for whom such a position had ideological interest: the anti-Semitic far right (of either fundamentalist Catholic or paleo- or neo-Nazi stripe) and the fraction of the Arab Islamic world struggling – for good or bad reasons – against Israel.[19]

From 1965 onwards, after the death of Rassinier, the movement grew when Pierre Guillaume, a former militant in Socialisme ou Barbarie,* a 'perverse and megalomaniacal' personality,[20] created the

* Socialism or Barbarism: a group of intellectuals and workers, of libertarian socialist tendencies, that included many prominent left-wingers in France (1948–65) – Trans.

bookshop La Vieille Taupe [The Old Mole]:[21] until it closed in 1972, this was to be the main meeting place for an ultra-left sect including, notably, Serge Thion, a specialist in South-East Asia and a sociologist committed to anti-colonialist struggles. Like Guillaume, he went on to join the ranks of the far right after being struck off in 2000 from his position as a researcher at the CNRS.[22] As for Gabriel Cohn-Bendit, a libertarian militant, he very rapidly disowned his earlier opinions.[23]

When Robert Faurisson entered on the scene, Holocaust denial entered a new phase.[24]

Faurisson was a pupil of Jean Beaufret; he was trained in literary criticism and, while still young, cultivated the habit of coming out with Hitlerian remarks or organizing punitive expeditions against his classmates. Right from the start, he had been obsessed by the idea of a Jewish plot and by the censorship imposed by publishers who refused to reissue Céline's pamphlets. Hungry for fame, and convinced that all literary avant-gardes were essentially phoney, he had embarked on his career with what was apparently a psychoanalytic interpretation of Arthur Rimbaud's great 'vowel' sonnet: this analysis was published in the review *Bizarre*, edited by Jean-Jacques Pauvert. He next attacked Lautréamont (who, he claimed, had never existed), and then took it into his head to prove, with a sheaf of evidence, that Anne Frank's diary was a complete fabrication – as, indeed, were all the eye-witness accounts produced by the Nazis on the extermination camps. In 1978, he managed to interest the big media channels in his claim that the gas chambers had never existed.

One year later, when a really bad American TV series, *Holocaust*, was screened, much of the French press – out of a sense of so-called objectivity based on the old principle of balance – tended to contrast those who thought that the genocide had really occurred and those who denied it. But Pierre Vidal-Naquet put a stop to this ridiculous attempt, declaring that, while a historian worthy of that name had a duty to unmask the fakers, he should in no case agree to hold any dialogue with them, but rather keep them at a distance from the community of scholars.

This was not the opinion of Noam Chomsky, a respected linguist already world-famous for his recasting of the theory of language and his definitive rejection of the structuralist theories of his master, Roman Jakobson, the most eminent linguist of the twentieth century – who never shared his pupil's view on these matters. The so-called generative theory put forward by Chomsky was a nihilistic revolution based on the idea that there might be a communicative universality of language. The aim of his theory was to develop the grammar of a language as the explicit model for this language by separating the 'grammatical' sequences from the so-called agrammatical series. To carry out this liquidation of any meaning to language as the bearer of an unconscious, he needed to reintroduce into linguistics an ideal of communication which Saussure had rejected: a notion of the intuitive subject taken from the most behaviourist – and thus the most simplistic – psychology.

In order to account for the phenomenon of language, the new linguistics was based on a naturalization of the human mind, constructing a grammar of competence associated with a grammar of performance that involved two models: that of emission (speaker) and that of reception (listener). This epistemological move led to the complete ossification of linguistics, which became subsumed into neuropsychology. As Tzvetan Todorov wrote:

> The first structuralists were immersed in the plurality of languages, and could cite examples from Sanskrit, Chinese, Persian, German, or Russian. Chomsky, on the other hand, was the total and complete negation of all that, because he always worked in and on English, his native language. Even if he was a good specialist in what he did, his influence was disastrous because it led to an altogether striking sterilization of linguistics.[25]

At the request of Serge Thion, Chomsky gave his support to Faurisson in a text which was used as a preface (and thus an endorsement) of a new book published by the latter, which denied the Holocaust and accused the Jews of having invented their own extermination. Chomsky, the son of an eminent professor of Hebrew, was admittedly courageous in his denunciation of the damage wrought by colonialism and American imperialism, in a context where anti-Zionism and anti-Semitism were melded in a particularly noxious brew. However, having been the inventor of a theory of cognition which emptied human subjectivity of any form of meaningful relation with language, he equated political analysis with ethics and rejected anything that might resemble a symbolic order. He also refused to arrange the great systems of governance invented by human beings into any kind of hierarchy.

So, placing Nazism, communism, and capitalism on the same level, Chomsky drew no real distinction between the first system, based on the industrial production of corpses, the second, which consisted in a perversion of the ideal of emancipation, and the third, centred on profit and the commodification of subjects.[26] He therefore attacked this last, which he deemed to be more murderous than the two others because it was the system adopted by democracies whose duty it was to be 'moral'.

This art of deductive comparison had indeed led Chomsky to denounce the 'bloodbaths' produced by Western countries against the oppressed peoples of the entire planet and to compare them to those of the *Gulag Archipelago*,[27] so as to relativize the devastating effects of the genocide perpetrated in Cambodia by the Khmer Rouge.[28] Likewise, again drawing on his theory of language, he continually compared – on the basis of flawed correlations – things which cannot (and should never be) compared; he then expressed surprise at the criticisms that were addressed to him, in which he saw a 'conspiracy', one that was, as often as not, French.

In 1983, Chomsky referred to his own political commitment, explaining that he found his country's policies terrifying – though he immediately added that all the policies carried out by all the other countries in the world seemed just as alarming. And, without even realizing how absurd his comments were, he said: 'Let's suppose for example that in 1943 a German journalist had written some articles on the atrocities committed by the British, the Americans, or the Jews, even if what he wrote had been correct, this would not have caused us much alarm.'[29]

It was in the name of freedom of expression, and to protect Faurisson from any potential 'persecutions' from the French state, which was in his view an enemy of freedom, that Chomsky endorsed Holocaust denial, though he also admitted that he had not read the book he was supporting[30] – a book in which, to say it yet again, the author claimed that the gas chambers did not exist because they do not exist. This was proved, he said, by the fact that the deportees had all returned from the camps (*sic*) and that the evidence produced by Nazis – such as the SS doctor Paul Kremer – had been entirely concocted by the Allies, as had Anne Frank's *Diary*, the autobiography of Rudolf Höss, and Kurt Gerstein's report.[31]

Quite naturally, Faurisson took a malign pleasure in pointing out all the mistakes made by the frenzied proponents of a revision of the history of the Jewish question that consisted in making the texts of the past say absolutely anything. And so he gleefully denounced the stupidity of a regional representative of the LICRA [International League Against Racism and Anti-Semitism] who had protested to the French government following a television broadcast of *The Merchant of Venice*. 'Not only is this play of a kind to encourage anti-Semitic hatred', the LICRA representative claimed, 'but the director, Jean Le Poulain, in his production and in his way of playing the role of Shylock, emphasized the anti-Semitic character of this play which was broadcast at peak watching times.' In reply, Le Poulain, accused of anti-Semitism, threatened to take the LICRA to court, pointing out that he had played Shylock in such a way as to bring out the solitude and despair of an abandoned man, rejected by racism and hatred.[32]

It is well known that, in *The Merchant of Venice*, written between 1594 and 1597 at a time when Queen Elizabeth I had re-established a certain tolerance towards the Marrano Jews who had taken refuge in England, Shakespeare depicted, in the context of a Venice torn by conflicts and tensions between communities, a life-and-death struggle between Christians and Jews that ended with the defeat of Shylock, a sublime and fierce moneylender who had demanded from his alter ego, the melancholy Christian Antonio, that his debt be repaid in the form of a pound of flesh. But this defeat, which showed the cruelty of Christian anti-Judaism, was also the triumph of reason over vengeance and of love over greed.

An ambiguous and tortured hero, Shylock embodied the position of the European Jew at the end of the sixteenth century forced into a dual identity as persecutor and persecuted: a character who was proud of his faith and contemptuous of that of his oppressors, and who, in his laments, gave a human face to Jewish otherness, caught between a quest for identity and the desire for emancipation:

Hath not a Jew eyes? Hath not a Jew hands, organs, dimensions, senses, affections, passions? Fed with the same food, hurt with the same weapons, subject to the same diseases, heal'd by the same means, warm'd and cool'd by the same winter and summer, as a Christian is? If you prick us, do we not bleed? If you tickle us, do we not laugh? If you poison us, do we not die? And if you wrong us, shall we not revenge? If we are like you in the rest, we will resemble you in that. If a Jew wrong a Christian, what is his humility? Revenge.[33]

Faurisson was playing on the blindness of those who denounced an imaginary anti-Semitism, accusing them of seeking to 'set up a thought police'.

As for Chomsky's bizarre idea that, in the 1970s, France had re-established a censorship worthy of the *ancien régime*, one might be tempted to interpret it as a temporary aberration. But this was not the case: Chomsky never regretted his gesture on this occasion, and even made so bold as to claim that he himself was a victim of the French intellectual scene, while adopting a posture close to Faurisson's – and accusing the State of Israel of being a Holocaust denier.[34]

Without being an example of Jewish self-hatred, Chomsky was indifferent to any of his contemporaries' reflections on this question.

He felt a deep respect for his father, who had taught him Hebrew, but he felt that his studies were rather superficial.[35] He loved his mother, and felt thoroughly Jewish. But he could not forgive his country for being responsible for dropping the atom bomb on Hiroshima, an event that had had a traumatic impact on him when he was a teenager: he likewise hated Europe for having been the place where the genocide of the Jews had occurred. He thus despised everything from that accursed part of the world and preferred to devote his attention to other continents. He felt that the philosophers of the Frankfurt School were ridiculous, and he regarded psychoanalysis as bunkum, Freud as a charlatan, and Hollywood movies as trash. Furthermore, from the 1970s onwards, he continued to cast scorn not only on surrealism, Dadaism, structuralism, existentialism, and phenomenology, but on the whole set of French thinkers who had been given such a triumphal reception in the literature departments of American universities.[36] He could not find words harsh enough to denounce their 'imposture' and was quite convinced that French academia was populated by pre-Darwinian ignoramuses who knew nothing of their own history or of German philosophy.[37] Vidal-Naquet wrote: '[R]egarding himself as untouchable, invulnerable to criticism, unaware of what Nazism in Europe was like, draped in an imperial pride and an American chauvinism worthy of those "new mandarins" whom he used to denounce, Chomsky accuses all those who hold a different opinion from his own of being assassins of freedom.'[38]

Convinced that he had put his finger on the 'great censorship' of the French government and revealed the absence of civic rights in this country, Chomsky attacked 'French intellectual life', its media (especially those on the left), its reviews, and one of its greatest historians – Pierre Vidal-Naquet – and claimed, in the preface to the book that he had not read, that Faurisson was completely worthy of being discussed by the community of French scholars:

> As I have said, I do not know his work very well. But from what I have read, mainly because of the nature of the attacks made on him, I can find no evidence that would support such conclusions. Nor can I find any credible evidence in the documents about him that I have read, whether in published texts or in private correspondence. As far as I can judge, Faurisson is a sort of apolitical liberal.

A little further on, he cast doubt on Faurisson's anti-Semitism. And in the same text Chomsky, who still continued to criticize the absence of civic rights in his own country,[39] sang the praises of the First

Amendment to the Constitution, because it made it impossible to take anyone to court for denying the Holocaust: 'In the United States, Arthur Butz (whom one might regard as the American Faurisson) has not been subjected to the kind of merciless attack levelled against Faurisson. When the "no holocaust" historians hold a large international meeting in the United States, as they did some months ago, there is nothing like the hysteria that we find in France over the Faurisson affair.'[40]

In order to understand such an exaggerated attitude, which consisted in claiming that Faurisson was not just a victim of the French intelligentsia but also a more significant author than most French thinkers of the twentieth century, we need to read the comments on the whole affair made by Chomsky's best disciple, the Belgian physicist Jean Bricmont, the co-author, with Alan Sokal, of a work on the so-called impostures of French intellectuals.[41]

In a 2008 article in which he tried to sum up the polemic 'objectively', Bricmont also gave a positive assessment of Faurisson's position, emphasizing that 'his inquiry was more historical than sociological or philosophical'. And he accused Vidal-Naquet of having by his attacks helped to spread Faurisson's ideas while contributing to the exclusion from the French scene the arguments of a 'Jewish American anarchist' who was in a better position than any French person to embody republican ideals. He added:

> Using this term [i.e., 'investigation'] implies no judgement on the value of this investigation. As a physicist, I often receive crazy letters or papers written by 'independent' researchers on questions of physics. Reading these texts, I have no way of guessing at the intentions of their authors, but I cannot see why I should not speak about work in physics with regard to them, even if they have no particular value.[42]

In other words, following the procedure of denial and the method of baseless comparisons, Bricmont was claiming that the question of the existence or non-existence of the genocide of the Jews was indeed part of a scientific debate – and that no Holocaust denier should therefore be excluded from the field of historiography.

Bricmont had already addressed this subject in 2000, in his preface to a book by Norman Finkelstein, in which the author noted the desire to include in the field of historiography one of the most redoubtable Holocaust deniers in the English-speaking world.[43]

As we can see, in 2008 the disciple was expressing the same opinions as his master and explaining why he had written this preface to Faurisson's book. In Chomsky's view, a Holocaust denier was just a historian like other historians. And he needed to be taken seriously. Chomsky had, in contributing this preface, sought to rehabilitate Holocaust denial. Of course, we cannot fail to be glad that he lost this battle, but we have a right to ponder why exactly this 'Jewish American anarchist' should always have expressed such hatred for the intellectuals of Europe, whether Jewish or not, and for all democratic states – even exploiting, in Faurisson's interest, the Palestinians' struggle to have their national rights recognized.

The Jews of the United States had of course always defined themselves, even after the Shoah, as Jewish Americans rather than as American Jews. As they identified with the American nation (they were more assimilated than the Jews of France), they did not often make their *aliyah*. They did, on the other hand, set themselves up as the State of Israel's best defenders, while there were fundamental divergences between the conservatives and the liberals, the émigré Jews (or children of émigrés) and the Jews who had been born on American soil.[44] Thus, only the religiously Orthodox Jews returned to the Promised Land, convinced that the whole of Palestine belonged to them – according to God's law. Hence the process of unrestrained colonization that could not be stemmed – one that would later be imitated by other fanatics from the former communist countries.

Chomsky's attitude to all this was paradoxical. He did not feel the least kinship as a Jew with the European diaspora, which he hated, and he accused the American Jews, on the right and the left, of being madly and ridiculously in love with the people of Israel.[45] In 1967, after the Six-Day War, he had referred to the Vietnam War, saying – as if he were proposing some new, revolutionary idea – that 'resorting to violence [is] illegitimate except when [it] is legitimized by the need to eliminate a greater evil.' And against Hannah Arendt, whom he reproached for her 'absolutization of democracy', he stated that China was the only country in which true freedom reigned.[46] A nihilist and a relativist, fascinated by all the 'other worlds' outside the Judaeo-Christian West, he sometimes proclaimed himself to be a Maoist and a Marxist, sometimes an anti-Maoist and an anti-Marxist, and felt not the slightest sympathy, even a critical one, for the State of Israel, since the complex question of the relations between Judaism, Jewishness, Zionism, anti-Semitism, and anti-Zionism had no real meaning in his view. Chomsky was fundamentally anti-everything, and only the endlessly moralizing protest against everything and its opposite met with favour in the eyes of this logician of meaninglessness.

So sometimes he claimed that Hamas was more open to negotiations than the United States and Israel, and sometimes he claimed the contrary. Sometimes he stated that the Palestinians should move beyond their rejection of America, and sometimes he advised them never to yield on a single point. He continually showed himself to be as favourable to a two-nation state as to the creation of two states. Finally, he never voiced his support for a viable solution to the Israeli–Palestinian question. In his view, Israel was sometimes a country ruled by apartheid, sometimes a mere 'pawn' being exploited by the United States, sometimes a land of welcome where he could democratically debate with his friends on the far left the massacres committed, in the name of democracy, by the Americans and the Israelis.

At bottom, the Jewish question was of no interest to Chomsky, except when it came to supporting Faurisson so as to demonstrate that France – and, with France, the so-called Europe of the Enlightenment – was simultaneously anti-American, reactionary, anti-Semitic, and anti-democratic, since it lay behind three scourges: the Gulag, the Shoah, and capitalism.

From the 1990s, as the quest for peace faltered in the Middle East, in spite of the Oslo Agreements and the productive discussions between Yasser Arafat and Yitzhak Rabin,[47] Holocaust denial was being given an increasingly sympathetic hearing in the Arab-Islamic world, thanks to the rise of radical Islam in the region, as Hamas gradually supplanted the PLO and Fatah.[48] Hence the success[49] of the book *The founding myths of modern Israel* by Roger Garaudy, a former deportee and ex-Stalinist who had converted to Islam.

The author set out to denounce the 'heresy of political Zionism which consists in replacing the *God* of Israel with the State of Israel, the unsinkable nuclear aircraft carrier of the temporary masters of the world: the United States.'[50] The work was stuffed with more or less truncated quotations whose subtext was that the author was a victim of the West, in favour of any non-fundamentalist religion, an heir to Gaullism, and a critic of the great conspiracy by which the de-Judaized Jews of the diaspora and their Zionist accomplices had managed to persuade people that the gas chambers had actually existed. In this way, Holocaust denial, allied with anti-Zionism and Islamism, became a political force. Indeed, in France, Faurisson allied himself with this combination, to the extent of becoming a farcical figure in its shenanigans, together with the comedian Dieudonné Mbala Mbala and other refugees from the far right and the extreme left.[51]

Holocaust denial stems from the will to genocide, insofar as its discourse has the sole purpose of denying the extermination of the Jews – in other words, effacing the trace of this extermination. It is thus an attempt to carry out, in discourse, the effacement of the massacre. Thus it is consubstantial with genocide itself, since it makes it possible for the crime to be perpetuated and, indeed, turned into a perfect crime – without trace, and without memory. And it was with this same desire for negation that the Nazi bosses decided to conceal their crime by organizing their suicide. Unlike the Japanese generals who killed themselves openly, following the feudal ritual of *seppuku*, so that the people might be born again after the defeat for which they felt responsible, Hitler and his colleagues arranged, after the great scene in the bunker, for their bodies – and thus all trace of their suicide – to disappear. In this way they perverted the act of suicide, stopping it from seeming like a sacrifice.

While Holocaust denial is the continuation of genocide by other means, one can see why certain states – Germany, Austria, and so on – decided to bring in a law to condemn anyone who denies this genocide and thus incites others to perpetuate it without limit.

The Gayssot law,[52] made part of the French penal code in 1990, and very different in its object from the Pleven law of 1972 on incitement to racial hatred, also aimed to solve the problem of anti-Semitism judicially, but it risked the legislator seeing himself invested with the responsibility of deciding on a question which lay in the field not of law but of intellectual labour. And, while this law made it possible to bring to trial and sentence the authors of books or remarks denying the Holocaust, we should note that such authors – Robert Faurisson and Paul Rassinier – had already been sentenced for moral crimes in virtue of article 1382 of the Civil Code.[53]

Like several other intellectuals and lawyers, I am opposed to this law, which indeed lies behind several nefarious laws on memory.[54] Of course, it has meant that the spread of books denying the Holocaust has been stopped in France. But, by turning Holocaust denial into a criminal offence, it has restricted the freedom of those who seek the combat it in writing, and who always in turn run the risk of being taken to court for tolerating Holocaust denial. In this area, we might say, the more extended the freedom of expression becomes, the more effective the fight against vile opinions can be. In countries where such measures do not exist, the situation is not very different from that in France. No propaganda on behalf of Holocaust denial has ever managed to gain the least legitimacy in any university: Holocaust deniers meet separately, like a sect, whether or not they are welcomed by regimes that officially support Holocaust denial.[55] And, in this respect, neither Chomsky nor Bricmont have carried the day.

Freedom to express such opinions exists to different degrees in states ruled by law, but every state has created laws which restrict this freedom – much more in Europe, that centre for the extermination of the Jews, than across the Atlantic.[56] But, if we are to imagine that this freedom might exist unconditionally, the law must not replace the freedom of the pen, which remains the best resort, the most unlimited and the most rational, against the expression of Holocaust denial and the anti-Semitic opinions that underpin it.

Other forms of denial reared their heads as Holocaust denial grew in strength, and they even became more common in French public life – witness the remarks uttered by Raymond Barre in an interview for France Culture with Raphaël Enthoven, broadcast on 1 March 2007.

A centrist politician, universally respected, prime minister in a right-wing French government between 1976 and 1981, there was nothing of the demented Holocaust denier about Raymond Barre – nor did he have anything in common with a young Algerian traumatized by the violence of war. Born in 1924, he came from a family of Catholic tradespeople who had settled in Saint-Denis de la Réunion, where he had spent his childhood. He was jovial, cultivated, intelligent, and plump: nothing in his attitude could have led anyone to suppose that he might be haunted, without even being conscious of it, by a form of anti-Semitic passion. He was normality itself. And yet, on 3 October 1980, when there was a bloody attack on a synagogue[57] in the rue Copernic, Paris, he made a stupefying announcement, whose meaning escaped nobody in France, the most Freudian country in the world: 'This hateful attack', he said, 'was meant to strike Israelites going to the synagogue, and it struck innocent French people crossing the rue Copernic.'[58]

For twenty-seven years, people forgot the savage undertone of this sentence, which had erupted into the speech of a first minister disturbed by the horror of an act of terrorism. The political class had decided he had made an innocent slip, without any major consequences. And this is precisely why, on 1 March 2007, Raphaël Enthoven asked Barre, who was to die a few months later, to go back over this event. He was thunderstruck to hear the old man, usually so sensible, singing the praises of Maurice Papon, who had been sentenced for crimes against humanity in 1998, and Bruno Gollnisch, a member of the National Front, a town councillor who had also been sentenced for remarks denying the Holocaust by virtue of the Gayssot law.

As for the affair of the rue Copernic, not only did Raymond Barre not regret his comments: he reaffirmed them.

QUESTION: Do you regret making that remark?
ANSWER: No, I remember very well the atmosphere in which I said it. Don't forget that, in the same declaration, I say that the Jewish community cannot be separated from the French

Q:
A:

Q:
A:

Q:
A:

Q:
A:

community. When you quote, you quote, in full. And the campaign that had been waged by the Jewish lobby[59] most linked to the left stemmed from the fact that we were in the middle of an election campaign, and I wasn't intimidated by it; they can continue to repeat it.

But why *innocent French people*?

Yes, after all it was French people who were walking along the street and who were caught out because someone wants to blow up a synagogue. Now those who wanted to attack Jews, they could have blown up the synagogue and the Jews. But that's just what they didn't do! They carried out a blind attack and there are three non-Jewish French people. And this doesn't mean that the Jews aren't French.

Yes, but *innocent*?

Because what was characteristic of those who carried out the attack was to punish guilty Jews.

In their view!

In their view, yes, of course! In my view, the French weren't involved in this business at all. In any case, none of my Jewish friends – and I have quite a few – have criticized me over this. You know, I have to tell you that, when it comes to this affair, I consider that the Jewish lobby – not just as far as I am concerned – is able to mount operations that are unworthy, and I really have to say this publicly.[60]

Convinced that he was being persecuted by some lobby – which obviously existed only in his imagination – Raymond Barre turned out, on this occasion, to be unable to grasp the significance of his own words. He affirmed his good faith as sincerely as one can possibly do so. And yet, rising up from the depths of the unconscious, his repressed passion revealed itself uninhibitedly in the syntagm: 'French – innocent; Jewish – guilty'.[61]

No writer, even one with a gift for Jewish humour at its best, could have made up such a dialogue. This is a classic case of what textual analysis can show.

Before this, in the spring of 2000, another affair had divided not the political world, but the intellectual community, revealing not just the passions surrounding the Israeli–Palestinian conflict but the deep crisis which that community has to face over the fourfold question of Jewish identity, the question for origins and roots, the obsession for lists (inherited from Drumont), and, finally, the definition of a new form of anti-Semitism, unnameable, elusive, denied, repressed – one that brings the denunciation of genocide and the loss of the sovereign grandeur of eternal France (its beautiful language and its fine republican educational system, with its school smocks and its Latin) together with an open hatred for communists (seen as 'Moscow's eyes'), social democracy, progressives in general, anti-racists, Arabs, cross-breeding, the thugs who rule the suburbs, and petty bourgeois vulgarity.

Renaud Camus, an open homosexual, frequently identified with the baron de Charlus, the Goncourt brothers, Gobineau, and Charles Maurras, was the author of some forty or so books that were the preserve of connoisseurs. He was a past master of the art of writing a long-term diary in which he could express directly, without any censorship, his angers, his whims, his intimate feelings, and his sexual practices. He could thus express, under cover of a naïve common sense tinged with a quite aristocratic and faux-childlike perversity, a series of remarks that he presented as considered aesthetic judgements.

In *La campagne de France*,[62] for example, Camus defended the 'pure-blooded French' against immigrants, and listed all the 'Jewish' journalists working for France Culture, while still claiming how deeply he was repelled by Nazism and the Shoah:

> The Jewish collaborators of Panorama[63] on France Culture do overdo it: on the one hand, there are about four out of every five in every broadcast, or four out of six, or five out of seven, which on a national and almost official station constitutes the clear over-representation of a given ethnic or religious group; on the other hand, they ensure that at least one broadcast a week is devoted to Jewish culture, to the Jewish religion, to Jewish writers, to the State of Israel and its politics, etc.

And, further on:

> Small shopkeepers in the suburbs have to undergo, fifteen or twenty times in succession, armed attacks on the part of young men who are always of the same ethnic origin. If they point this detail out, and say they mistrust teenagers or young men of that origin, they get called racists. And if the media consent to publish these facts, they make it their duty not to say anything about the origin of the aggressors.[64]

These declarations, of course, had nothing to do with Raymond Barre's later remarks. Quite the opposite: Camus's comments were far from off the cuff. He sincerely thought that there were *too many Jews* among the presenters of France Culture, and he was convinced that the media concealed the fact that young suburban Arabs were attacking shopkeepers.

And it is this conviction that we need to examine. Anyone who knew the programme *Panorama* will see that Camus' argument does not stand up. The presenters were mad about literature and loved debating ideas: they were always quarrelling between themselves, not brandishing their Jewishness or any so-called Jewish culture, but dissecting, programme after programme, works about which they totally disagreed: Blanchot, Bataille, the New Novel, the avant-garde, feminism, surrealism, *Tel Quel*, Foucault, sexuality, Otto Rank, Freud, Philip Roth, Claude Simon, Philippe Sollers, Lévinas, Derrida, Althusser, Reich, Marcuse, Adorno, Arendt, Heidegger, Benjamin, etc. In any case, they were in the habit of tearing strips off their guests. I remember, for example, spending about an hour in the company of that fine team in 1993, when my book on Lacan provoked the mother of all verbal fist-fights. At the end of the broadcast, one of the journalists, feeling quite ill, even had to lie down on the floor, begging for mercy. Other authors were attacked as I was, with just the same zest, and forced to defend themselves the best they could.

The fact that Renaud Camus could imagine that such a broadcast was dominated by the Jews, and even indulge in a nauseating piece of totting up the figures, clearly meant that, in his view, only Jews, foreign to the literature of the 'pure-blooded French', could reign over a public radio station without being censored. This meant he could suggest that France Culture was a Jewish radio station – one that concealed the crimes committed by Arabs in the suburbs.

The publication of this book, followed by its withdrawal and then its reappearance in bookshops,[65] triggered a real storm in French, Canadian, and American intellectual circles,[66] as hundreds of debates and articles show. Supported by the literary right and far left, by several journalists in *Libération* and *Marianne*, and by conservative and *souverainiste* scholars and philosophers, or those of a libertarian and apolitical stamp, Camus was attacked by a different wing of the French intelligentsia – Lacanian, Foucauldian, Althusserian, Sartrean, etc., and by the entire journalist staff of *Le Monde*.

Jacques Derrida, Jean-Claude Milner, Bernard-Henri Lévy, Serge Klarsfeld, Jean-Pierre Vernant, and Philippe Sollers were among the first to sign a petition launched by Claude Lanzmann, who described as 'criminal'[67] the passages in *La campagne de France* devoted to listing the Jewish presenters.[68] Hence the fury of Camus' two principal defenders: Pierre-André Taguieff and Alain Finkielkraut.

Forever on the alert to signs of anti-Semitism in the work of Spinoza, Voltaire, Marx, Deleuze, Genet, and Nietzsche, and among communists, Maoists, Trotskyists, Arabs, Muslims, and Jews in favour of a Palestinian state, Taguieff emphasized how these remarks stemmed from a certain 'naïvety' on the part of the author.[69] As for Finkielkraut, seduced by Maurras-inspired aestheticism, he declared, *as a Jew*, that 'the different degrees of belonging to a nation', together with Camus' refusal to 'ignore the element of heritage in one's identity, and his desperate attachment to what little remains of "knowledge through time", assume a meaning different from the essentialist, racist, criminal meaning that people have hastily seen fit to attribute to it.'[70]

This whole affair was, at bottom, simply the revelation of an old anti-Semitism in the world of literature of which Holocaust denial was the vile face. This reappearance of Drumont's legacy in France occurred at a time when, on the political level, the old populism was appearing in a new guise with the rise of the National Front.

In 1985, Marc-Édouard Nabe[71] – who claimed to be influenced by Léon Bloy, whereas he was much more of a direct heir to Drumont – had rehabilitated the writers of the collaboration, asserting that Céline's anti-Semitic pamphlets were superior in literary value to his novels and that, instead of reading and admiring *Journey to the end of the night*, it would be better to republish them. Striking the posture of the most persecuted person in France, and thinking himself, no doubt, to be its greatest writer, he spent fifteen years denouncing Jews, homosexuals, Africans (whom he compared to 'degenerate monkeys'), transsexuals, whites, Arabs, the intellectual scene, and so on.[72]

But the most interesting feature of the whole affair was that, in 1999, in a text where the word 'Jew' did not even appear, Nabe endorsed the notorious idea that the Jews are responsible, through Freud, Marx, and Einstein, for the destruction of humanity, and even more for the invention of a factory for producing human corpses:

Take Freud, the ignoble Freud, for example. The one who fascinates you. The re-booter of adipose Oedipuses, the de-dreamer of the scared, the third thief in that scary trio of villains on the pile of crimes from which we have been somnambulistically walking for nearly a hundred years! Marx–Einstein–Freud: the accursed tripod is so implanted in our intimate cakes that these days you can no longer evaluate its poisonous strength without breaking out into a sweat. All the shit has emerged from these three anuses, let's make no mistake about it: the total turd, the twelve inches of brown! One day, perhaps, people will be able to imagine what the twentieth century might have been without these Marx Brothers of depression. The bomb, the complex, the social: why dream of anything better to destroy a universe?[73]

Ten years later, Nabe came full circle: he made a declaration about Barack Obama which clearly showed that, in his case, as with all his fellows, the mainspring is the same:

> Throughout his campaign, Obama repeated his unwavering support for Israel. He wants an Israeli Jerusalem, and troop reinforcements on the holy territory occupied by those filthy Palestinians . . . Everything for Israel! 78% of Yankee Jews voted for him. You can trust them: they wouldn't have elected a Negro if they hadn't been sure he was their man. [. . .] Electing a Black man really means that the Yanks were knackered . . . Obama wasn't elected because he was Black, but because the Whites in power realized that, by putting a Black at their head, America would be able to return to the first rank by wiping out its dastardly deeds. Its image had been so blackened by its crimes that they really needed a Black man to clean it up. Obama is washing America whiter than white.[74]

Here, we realize that it is because America is dominated by the Jews that its citizens elected not a real black man, but a 'whitened negro', a half-caste, the only man able to make America Jewish again so that Zionism could profit.

While Holocaust denial was becoming a matter for historians from across the world, and also enjoying wide publicity in the Arab world, several Zionists discovered that Zionism was no longer an answer to the Jewish question. Thus was born post-Zionism, based on postmodernism.

Refusing to accept the grand narratives of origins – the law of return, Israeli-centric commitments, etc. – some Israeli Jewish intellectuals decided to become increasingly critical of the nationalism of their rulers. They knew that, one day or another, it would be necessary to ask whether a state could be described as Jewish while still being secular – in other words, similar to other democratic states – and thus, by definition, irreducible to Jewishness, even if this were completely detached from Judaism. This tendency was supported by the brilliant Israeli school of historiography that was known as the 'new historians'.[75] When Pierre Vidal-Naquet died in the summer of 2006, several of these historians paid homage together with Stéphane Hessel, a former member of the Resistance and co-writer of the Universal Declaration of 1948, and two great representatives of the Palestinian cause: Leila Shahid and Elias Sambar.[76]

In France, just when Faurisson's Holocaust denial was in the news and denunciations of the 'new anti-Semitism' were flying thick and fast, a new form of revisionism was invented that I have already mentioned. This consisted in regarding as anti-Semitic any questioning of Israeli policy and any attempt to raise the Jewish question other than in support of an idealized Zionism, as if the State of Israel had become, with the memory of the Shoah, the only possible marker of identity for the Jews of the diaspora: an injunction to fusion.[77]

Thus the sociologist Shmuel Trigano, together with Muriel Darmon, forged the neologism '*alterjuif*' ('other-Jew') to refer to the bad Jew, the black sheep, the lost sheep, to whom he refused any possibility of belonging to Jewish identity, to Jewish history, to the Jewish people: foreclosed Jews, as it were, unworthy, irredeemable, who needed to be banished from the world of Jewishness. The aim of this label was clearly to stigmatize all who criticized Israeli policy so as to identify them with those who both denied Israel any right to existence and denied the reality of the genocide. Among the '*alterjuifs*', Trigano also included people who had nothing to do with one another: French Jews of the right, the left, the centre, journalists, writers, press barons, philosophers, intellectuals, and, finally, 'post-Zionist' Israeli historians, even though the widely diverging range of opinions they covered no longer needed to be demonstrated. They were all accused of demonizing Israel. In short, Trigano, like Renaud Camus, Nabe, and many others, seemed unaware of the fact that counting up Jews – and thus 'drawing up lists' – made them direct heirs to the tradition of Drumont.[78]

Among those most stigmatized was the sociologist Edgar Morin, who, in 2002, together with Danielle Sallenave and Sami Naïr, had written an article against Israeli policy in which they emphasized that 'it was difficult to imagine that Jews of Israel, descendants of the victims of an apartheid called "the ghetto", could ghettoize Palestinians.' They quoted Victor Hugo: 'In yesterday's oppressed, tomorrow's oppressor'. And they continued: 'It is the awareness of having been a victim that allows Israel to become an oppressor of the Palestinian people. The word "Shoah", which marks out the singularity of the Jewish fate of victimhood and makes all others seem commonplace (those of the Gulag, the gypsies, the enslaved blacks, and the Indians of America), becomes the legitimization of a colonialism, an apartheid, and a ghettoization of the Palestinians.'[79]

Admittedly, the text was rather exaggerated in places, even if the reference to Hugo was correct. It also made the mistake of attacking the 'Jews of Israel' as a whole rather than the policy of the state, forgetting that this policy was often criticized by Israeli Jews. But it did not deserve such hatred. And, above all, it did not contain any anti-Semitic remark. However, the authors were taken to court for 'racial defamation' by two associations: France–Israel and Avocats sans frontières.*

So Jews denounced Jews, to the glee of anti-Semites and other Holocaust deniers who could not fail to approve of this thought police, this new witch hunt.

In the same vein, in 2007 there was published a strange *Dictionary of Anti-Semitism* aimed at revising so-called orthodox historiography and finally naming the real anti-Semites who populate our planet. The author, Paul Éric Blanrue, was a journalist and the founder of a 'Cercle de zététique':[80] his purpose was to unmask networks, plots, impostures, or allegedly 'dangerous' liaisons which might corrupt political power.[81] Thus he drew up a 'list' of over five hundred allegedly anti-Semitic personalities, whose names had according to him been concealed by official history. He focused mainly on writing long entries on actors and thinkers of every time and country – who were not in the slightest anti-Semitic – and also on writers accused of having depicted dubious characters in their novels. In this list, together with Hitler, Goebbels, Céline, and Rebatet, you could find the names of Moses, Tacitus, Beaumarchais, Shakespeare, Cervantes, Goethe, Spinoza, Diderot, Voltaire, Sade, Dumas, Baudelaire, Marx, Freud, Proust, Deleuze, Lévi-Strauss, Gandhi, Clemenceau, Philip Roth, Salvador Allende, and even the French writer Pierre Assouline, who stood accused of writing in his biography of Marcel Dassault that the latter used to say 'With money, you can do anything.'[82]

In his preface, just as 'zetetic' in tone, Yann Moix, a writer and journalist, denounced the guilty authors in his turn: 'I am extremely proud: my favourite author, Charles Péguy, does not appear in this *Anthology*. When you see how many people do appear in these pages who have, either throughout their lives or just once, made some vile remark about Jews, the example is rare, singular and exceptional enough to be pointed out.'[83]

After appointing himself the destroyer in chief of so-called anti-Semites, Blanrue shifted to a virulent anti-Zionism. In 2009, eager to unmask those who were responsible for the great 'overturning of the Republic' to the benefit of lobbies of American and Israeli Jews, he voiced his support for the ideas of Thierry Meyssan, who had distinguished himself by the publication of a best-seller, *L'effroyable imposture*,[84] which denied that the Pentagon had been attacked by terrorists on 11 September 2001.

And so, castigating the Jews and their nefarious influence, Blanrue claimed to be part of the same trend as two American academics,

---

* Lawyers without Borders – a French human rights organization – Trans.

John Mearheimer and Stephen Walt, who had demonstrated the role played by the pro-Israeli lobby in the development of neo-conservative American policy. However, they had both been upbraided by Chomsky, who criticized them for not going far enough in their analysis of Zionist influence in the United States . . . After imagining that France was in thrall to a veritable intellectual dictatorship, the linguist had also become convinced that no sector of American civil society was now safe from the grip of Zionism.[85]

In actual fact, Blanrue was now out-Chomskying Chomsky, claiming as he did that there was an anti-Western Jewish discourse at work, which was merely the mirror image of the alleged anti-Semitic discourse that he had ascribed to almost all the thinkers, writers, and political figures of world culture – from Moses to Roth, via Freud, de Gaulle and Shakespeare.

Admittedly, works such as this never obtain any academic recognition, any more than do those produced by Holocaust deniers. And the press as a whole, as well as publishers and publicists, tends to err on the side of caution. The fact remains that, between 2001 and 2009, in a period when – after the destruction of the World Trade Center – interpretive mania had replaced any critical analysis, this 'zetetic' impulse echoed the eccentric notions of certain authors who were perfectly well integrated into the scholarly community. By dint of seeing anti-Semitism where it did not actually exist, you always end up, after some perverse twists and turns, projecting onto the Jews the imaginary conspiracies and discourses that you had thought you could detect in those you had labelled as ignoble.

As Sartre said in 1946: 'Anti-Semitism is a passion. [. . .] It precedes the facts that are supposed to call it forth; it seeks them out to nourish itself upon them.' It was not just a joy in hating: 'It is *fun* to be an anti-Semite.'[86]

I would be tempted to say that this passion does not need any object in order to exist, as it is so instinctive and imbued with the desire to inflict a radical death on oneself and on the other. Among the Jews themselves, it finds expression sometimes in the attempt to abolish a Jewishness that is deemed to be shameful and sometimes, conversely, in an arrogant vaunting of the Jewish condition. And when the situation is propitious and the passion gives birth to a political movement, the worst can ensue.

Because this passion is a pure enjoyment [*jouissance*], it desires nothing but itself, and it is fascinating because it can procure for an informer who has nothing to denounce the pleasure of enjoying his own mania for accusation. Thus, if you indulge in this passion, you always risk producing a discourse on the Jewish question which is similar to the very discourse you claim to be criticizing.

In other words, as Pierre Vidal-Naquet has brought out very clearly with regard to Holocaust denial, it is always possible to put forward plausible interpretations of texts, narratives, or critical inquiries – able to seduce readers by their logic – that are nonetheless yet pure inventions, completely lacking any validity. The details in these fictions are not always false, and they are sometimes based on authentic sources or can draw on real references, but, once the whole argument has been constructed, they nonetheless comprise a formidable system of lies.

As a worldwide phenomenon, then, Holocaust denial in France will have taken, with Faurisson and other *fous littéraires*, a turn that has been as crazy as it has been destructive. But it is also in France that Holocaust denial was combated with a vigour to be found nowhere else. For, as Hölderlin put it: 'Where there is danger, there also grows that which saves.'

7

Inquisitorial Figures

As I have said, I had always felt that a certain hatred of the idea of revolution – the Revolution of 1789 – was comparable with a certain form of hatred of Jews.[1] Indeed, throughout the nineteenth century, counter-revolutionary discourse always ran alongside the theme of the Jewish and masonic conspiracy.[2] And, when anti-Semitism became first a political and then a literary movement, it attacked both the Jews and those who had emancipated them.

From the 1930s, with the rise of Nazism and fascism in Europe, the Jews were again subjected to discrimination. In France, under the Vichy regime, they were handed over to the Nazi occupiers by the French police, while intellectuals became either collaborationists and anti-Semites (Louis-Ferdinand Céline, Robert Brasillach, Pierre Drieu la Rochelle, etc.) or communist, Gaullist, and socialist members of the Resistance (Louis Aragon, Paul Éluard, Jean Paulhan, Jean Cavaillès, Georges Canguilhem, Marc Bloch, etc.). Others remained critical (Jean-Paul Sartre, André Gide, André Malraux, etc.) but did not become committed members, either physically or in their writing, of the Resistance.

In France, then, we have seen – from 1894 onwards, and in the most unexpected transformations – a replay of the inaugural scene of Dreyfusism and anti-Dreyfusism. It was, after all, the Dreyfus Affair which gave birth to Zionism, since Herzl and Nordau, its two founding fathers, both of them journalists and writers, frequented the circles of the Parisian literary intelligentsia.

Fernand Braudel remarked on the strangeness of this structural division, so characteristic of the French exception. The unity of

France, he said, is never assured. So it must always rebuild itself, otherwise it runs the risk of falling apart. Thus the history of the country is that of an inner battle, forever being refought: Protestants against Catholics, revolutionaries against monarchists, Communards against Versaillais, colonialists against anti-colonialists.[3]

And without the French Revolution, which emancipated the Jews, turning them for the first time anywhere in the world into citizens endowed with equal rights, the Dreyfus Affair would never have taken place and thus contributed, as it did, to the emergence in France of a self-aware intellectual class – Zola against Barrès, Clemenceau against Drumont – and we would never have witnessed such a fierce and bloody battle as that which set the Resistance against collaboration, de Gaulle against Pétain, communists against fascists.

In other words, the French exception means not only that France is capable of the best as well as the worst – Valmy and Vichy – but that, in France, the status with which language – its lexicon, its individual words – is endowed is of vital importance. In France, every combat is also a matter of the pen, and this is why anti-Semitism is the business of literature and philosophy: there is a language of anti-Semitism and a structure to its discourse. And this is also why Holocaust denial in France, in its craziest and most self-publicizing version, was – as we have seen – produced by a professor of literature whose main interest had been the interpretation of texts by Rimbaud and Lautréamont.

Far from viewing their language as an instrument of communication, the French elites – both progressive and conservative – have always made it a value, making its written form the symbol of a homogeneous nation and then of the Republic. Hence the importance granted not only to the French Academy, whose role is to make laws about 'speaking properly' and 'writing well', but also to writers and intellectuals. And it was this primacy of language in France which Chomsky came up against when he attempted to defend the freedom of expression of Faurisson without having ever looked closely at his writings, or when he tried to set a logic of meaninglessness against the formal power of Saussurean linguistics.

So it comes as no surprise to realize that this struggle to the death should have repeated itself during the events of May 1968, when the idea of revolution was again on the agenda. Nor is it surprising that, after such an important turning point in the second half of the twentieth century, it was played out as a farce, given that the search for truth, against the background of the Israeli–Palestinian conflict, was replaced by insults, verbal harassment, inquisition, and hatred, as the discourse of anti-Semitism replaced any reflection on the Jewish question. In short, there was an upsurge of pure passion.

And since France is also – for reasons I have just set out – the only country where Freudianism was viewed on the one hand as a revolution in mind and language, thanks to surrealism and Lacan's renewal of Freud's teaching, and on the other, in reaction to this, as an orthodox practice meant to set itself against any form of 'Oedipal' revolt,[4] it seems quite logical that the first book that violently opposed the May events was written by two ultra-conservative psychoanalysts – Bela Grunberger and Janine Chasseguet-Smirgel – who in 1969 saw it as their task to denounce as 'bad Jews' not only the rebellious students, but all the young people of France who had preferred Lacan's teaching to the more orthodox – and perfectly respectable – teaching delivered by the Société psychanalytique de Paris (SPP).

Under the pseudonym 'André Stéphane', the two authors attacked the student revolt in a work called *L'univers contestationnaire: les nouveaux chrétiens* [*The world of rebellion: the new Christians*]. This was an incredibly violent pamphlet, which set out to explain not merely that rebellion would give birth to an experience akin to that of the concentration camps – both Nazi and Stalinist – but that it was the expression of a new anti-Judaic and thus anti-Semitic Christianity, characterized by a regression to the anal stage.

In short, the two incumbents of the SPP, obsessed by the anus, bowel movements, and other faecal matter, set themselves up as inquisitors into the schemes of young people who, in their view, had become terrorists and – as good Christian Hitlerians – were intent on nothing other than avenging the Arabs of Palestine who had been humiliated in the Six-Day War by the glorious Israeli Army.

In one fell swoop, the authors lambasted the whole 'modernity' of a period that had, in their view, lost any sense of duty, of obedience, of the family, and of fatherhood. Of course, Jacques Lacan, a non-Jewish thinker from a Christian background, was designated as mainly responsible for the state of deliquescence into which French society had lapsed – he and his sidekick in anti-Semitism, Karl Marx. As for all those who had taken part in this 'anal' revolution, they were presented – from Jean-Luc Godard to Maurice Clavel, via Herbert Marcuse – as the perverse practitioners of primary masochism.

But Chasseguet-Smirgel and Grunberger did not just denounce the alleged stupidity of French philosophical thinking – from Sartre to Foucault – they also denied the existence of any link between Judaism and Christianity, thus turning Christianity not into a fully fledged religion, but into a sort of sect that had emerged from a schism and become the prototype of all so-called anti-Jewish dissident movements, including Jungianism and Lacanianism: the former because it had been created by a Protestant, the latter because it had been created by a Catholic.

But what were they to do with Freud's Jewish dissidents: Adler, Ferenczi, Rank, Reich, etc.? What were they to do with Spinoza and the founders of Ego Psychology? The authors abstained from giving any answer to this question. And, without noticing that Marcuse was Jewish, they chucked the revisionism of the rebels into the wastepaper bin of Christian schisms. And they used the same argument to come up with a weird interpretation of what they saw as the structure of 'rebellious Christianity', pointing out that Christians must be less gifted than Jews when it came to curing their neurosis, as their religion, founded on the 'schism' of the son, prohibited them from resolving their Oedipal conflict. Because of their beliefs, they were thus guilty twice over: guilty for their anality, the consequence of their spirit of rebellion, and guilty for their anti-Semitism, which was the product of their Christianity. So they needed to be compared – for having dared to erect barricades in the Latin Quarter – with those who had 'profaned Jewish cemeteries'.[5]

Several pages were devoted to Daniel Cohn-Bendit, the undisputed leader, in the eyes of the authors, of the 'world of rebellion'. Admittedly, the two psychoanalysts did note that the young man was a Jew. But, eager to demonstrate that any revolt stemmed from the great Christian schism, they explained that Cohn-Bendit was an anarchist before he was a Jew.[6]

At this point in their argument, the authors came up with an interpretation of the discourse of May '68 that was later to be rehearsed several times, in different guises. Noting that Cohn-Bendit had opted to take German nationality, they stated that this made him more German than Jewish.[7] Thus, they claimed, the demonstrators who had invented the slogan 'We are all German Jews' did not identify in the least with the Jewishness of their leader. In their unconscious, the May rebels were basically protesting against the father – protesting, that is, against the Jew as the prototype of the religion of the father. This meant they were anti-Semitic.

This was how the book rejected the main symbolic value of May '68. The demonstrators had sidestepped the word 'anarchy' and had highlighted the word 'Jewishness' – a word that was absent from the discourse of Georges Marchais. They had thus identified with a Jewishness of exile while claiming that a German was not the same as a Nazi. Against all forms of Germanophobia and anti-Semitism, they had proclaimed – over and above the memory of the Shoah – the need for France and Germany to be reconciled: they wished to be European, anti-nationalist, anti-chauvinist, international. This was their 'revolt against the father': not a drift into anarchism, terrorism, anti-Semitism, Stalinism, or Nazism, but more simply the expression of an aspiration to a less rigid society, less mandarin and more open to the individual freedoms of women, homosexuals, children, the mad, the marginal, etc.

This work, unique in the annals of the French history of psychoanalysis, was criticized by the majority of psychoanalysts of all tendencies, including those in the SPP. This was precisely why the authors had resorted to a pseudonym.[8] From the moment it was published, it aroused such indignation that it was in certain quarters renamed 'the stupid, stationary world' [*l'univers con et stationnaire*]. In *Le Nouvel Observateur*, Anne-Lise Stern published a letter with the title 'Un lapsus de SS' ['An SS slip of the tongue']: 'How am I to express my revulsion, my disgust, my sense of powerlessness [. . .]? Many psychoanalytic colleagues, including some important figures, share these feelings but hold back from expressing them – for excellent reasons. I cannot, I must not.' And, at the end of her letter, she drew a triangle followed by her concentration camp number.[9] As for Michel de Certeau, the Jesuit and historian, he declared:

> An extraordinary psychoanalytical patois is throwing the cloak of Molière over the wisdom of Prudhomme [i.e., giving a comical rhetorical twist to pompous platitudes – Trans.]. This results in a book where the solemn demeanour of the actors is the mainspring of the comedy. It is just that the bleedings and the enemas [of Molière's ignorant, jargon-spouting doctors – Trans.] are replaced by anality and the avoidance of the father [. . .]. What a fine thing it is to be a psychoanalyst.[10]

Such a book ought logically to have fallen into oblivion. But this did not happen. The force of this great discourse of hatred continued, over the decades, to come crashing down on the student revolt and even more on the famous slogan about 'German Jews', which was soon identified as a discourse of 'anti-globalization', 'Islamicist', 'anti-*souverainiste*', and anti-patriotic, inimical to the French nation.[11] With the support of the review *Contrepoint*,[12] the book was hailed as a masterpiece by Alain Besançon, Jean-François Revel, and many others. And when it was republished, in 2004, the authors added a preface explaining that they had been pioneers in denouncing the abasement of the patriarchal family and in criticizing the Lacanians and other thinkers of the 1970s who had supported the students. They also emphasized that they had now decided to attack Islam rather than Christianity, so as to show how the religion of Muhammad had become – more than Christianity – the spearhead of anti-Judaism, and thus of anti-Semitism. So they were happy to register the support they had won from certain thinkers on the conservative right: Trigano, Taguieff, etc.[13]

Only the conviction of the racial superiority of Jews over non-Jews can help explain why Freudian Jews, proud of their identity, could have adopted – in the name of Freudianism and Jewish identity – the emblems of anti-Semitism and anti-Freudianism. As Anna Freud was to do in 1977, but by other means, they turned psychoanalysis into a 'Jewish science', reserved for 'good Jews': they thus failed to understand not only the question of Jewishness in Freud and his work but all the work produced by historians of Viennese Jewishness.[14]

Central Europe, destroyed by Nazism, played no part in the thinking of the two authors: they seem to have forgotten that Freud was Jewish, that his work had sprung from the deconstruction of the patriarchal order, and that his conception of Jewishness, as expressed in *Moses*, was the complete opposite of this interpretative rigmarole based on anality and the sexual enjoyment of faeces.

So this discourse was no different from that of the anti-Semites, who were also convinced that the Jews were, by definition, lured by the gold hidden inside the intestines and tempted by enemas. Indeed, in the work of these two writers, Christians occupied the place ascribed to Jews by anti-Semites. And this is why, in the preface to the new edition, and in spite of the softening of the anti-Christian remarks, the theme of the Jesuit plot was still in evidence: Michel de Certeau was indeed referred to, pejoratively, as 'the reverend father',[15] because he had dared to write that, in 1968, the people had captured the right to speak just as in 1789 the people had captured the Bastille.

When I met Janine Chasseguet-Smirgel for the first time, in 1985, to gather information for my *Jacques Lacan & Co.*, I was struck by the way she accused Lacan and the Lacanians of having turned psychoanalysis away from its Jewish essence. And when I pointed out that that it was Lacan, and not the Freudians of the IPA, who had made the Jewish question a real priority in his school, she met my remark with disapproval. And since she was convinced that there must be something of a Jewish fellow feeling between herself and me, she remarked that Jews were now in a minority in the French psychoanalytic community, forgetting that they had in fact always been so – and that the problem did not lie there.[16] She then suggested that I count the number of Jews in her own society so as to prove that she was right. Among them, she even separated out the 'good' Jews from the 'bad' Jews – the second were the ones who had been Christianized by Lacan – and between the Ashkenazim and the Sephardim, the former being more noble in her view than the latter (who were like Arabs).

We had several meetings. Then, as I happened to remark, at a public gathering, that it was the duty of every historian not to ignore the question of the collaboration between certain Freudians and the Nazis – any more than the conflict between Jones, Freud, and Eitingon – she replied: 'Anyone who criticizes Jones criticizes Freud, and anyone who criticizes Freud is an anti-Semite.' I was dumbfounded, and walked out of the room there and then, but not before I had pointed out that it would be a long time before psychoanalysts would finally be able to analyse the history of their movement.

This was the first time anyone had accused me of being anti-Semitic[17] or had tried to intimidate me by showing me the face of an inquisitorial Jewishness. It gave me the feeling that it would henceforth be possible to use this vengeful fabrication and throw the 6 million Jews exterminated by the Nazis into absolutely anyone's face – including the faces of other Jews. Resorting to the figure of the inquisitorial Jew quite simply threatened to make the figure of the Jew of the Shoah freeze in terror.

This transformation was a consequence of the widening gap between the Jews of the diaspora and the territorial Jews. The former, admittedly, did not constitute a homogeneous population, but the State of Israel had become an unavoidable reference point for their sense of identity. Thus they felt obliged to 'choose their camp', either cursing or extolling Israel. Some were hostile, questioning either its policies or its very legitimacy, while others identified closely with the Promised Land. As for the territorial Jews, united in one nation, they were so different from one another, thanks to their many different origins and the opposition between secular and religious, that it was difficult for them to live together. While they had long since ceased to question the legitimacy of their state, they were nonetheless divided over the policy to be adopted in the face of permanent war. The Jewish question, having first been raised by anti-Semitism, was now kept open by the conflict between Israel and the Arab world.

I was aware of this split and the disasters to which it led: I had realized that several French intellectuals of my generation, who have sometimes remained my friends, were being dragged either into a denial of their youthful rebellion (and thus into an unconditional support for Israeli nationalism) or into an anti-Israeli radicalization close to that of Chomsky: they would even go so far as to decide that Islamism might be the path to a new liberation. By criticizing the Enlightenment and rebuking Western democracies for trampling all over human rights, they had started to confuse the communist ideal with religious obscurantism. The first group claimed to detect in any criticism of Zionism an anti-Semitism even more dangerous than that of Drumont and the Nazis, while the latter were forever denouncing the first group as 'philo-Semites', and considered Israel to be *sui generis*, a colonialist, genocidal, racist state – thereby forgetting that state's own internal divisions.

So the time of the prosecutors had arrived, together with that of the Holocaust deniers and those who hated the French Revolution. As a result, an attempt to track down anti-Semitism spread in a very curious way across literature, film, the human sciences, psychoanalysis, and philosophy. It had little in common, by this stage, with the necessary struggle against anti-Semitism, since those who claimed to be its proponents could no longer distinguish between those who were anti-Semitic and those who were not.

The events of May '68 were an opportunity for young intellectuals, who drew inspiration as much from the structuralist revolution as from a commitment to anti-colonialism, communism, feminism, Maoism, situationism, or libertarianism, to make their entry on the political scene, reactivating interpretive quarrels which had already filled various reviews in the wake of the Liberation, mainly *Critique* and *Les Temps modernes*.

What is modernity in literature? What is commitment? Can one read, assess, and interpret the works of anti-Semitic writers and thinkers who had denounced the Jews, been in favour of Nazism, and supported collaboration? Should Céline's *Journey to the end of the night* be read in the light of his pamphlets? Or should his novels be lauded while ignoring the other part of his oeuvre – the obscene, repellent part which was still continuously present in the texts he wrote after the genocide? Anti-Semitism may be a passion or a madness, but this is no excuse. A madness must be listened to or treated; an anti-Semitic madness must be combated.

Céline returned from his sojourn in Sigmaringen madder than ever. He continued to poison French intellectual life until his death, publishing texts that were increasingly feeble from the literary point of view, and had little in common with the baroque, despairing flamboyance of the two great novels he had written before the pamphlets:[18] 'Well then, I mean to say, Augsburg (Auschwitz!)', he wrote in 1952, 'that was more than a pile of pimples! That was total slash-and-burn! All those skins for the AA (SS) lamps! Roasted lampshades and book-bindings, kazoos, Valkyries, Sabbaths of water-nymphs and gas chambers! Nothing to do with *moi*! Not my backside, nor Augsburg! I didn't declare war!'[19] In actual fact, by tracking down the Jewish microbe and denouncing it wherever he found it, Céline had drowned his literary genius in anti-Semitism – with the result that the novels he wrote after Auschwitz were hardly any different in form from his pamphlets: they were quite simply mad, and this madness found expression in the language of anti-Semitism. After Auschwitz, Céline merely continued to corrupt his own writing, which had already been destroyed by his pamphlets.

I would like to contrast Céline's abjection with a narrative that is one of a kind: *Ô vous frères humains*, written by Albert Cohen in the wake of the genocide. In this story, without mentioning Auschwitz, Cohen tells of the humiliation suffered by a Jewish child in Marseilles in 1905 when, on his tenth birthday, he is insulted by an anti-Dreyfusard *Camelot*.*

Referring to François Villon's poem,** Cohen here drew on Sartre's idea that a Jew is defined by the hatred he arouses in others. But, instead of adopting a phenomenological position, Cohen used the same language as Céline and Drumont – in the way that a Shylock who had survived the catastrophe might have done – to intimate the terrible pain of the Jewish condition in the face of an anti-Semitism that is forever being rekindled. The Jew of the Shoah is contrasted with the inquisitorial Jew:

> Death to the Jews Death to the Jews Filthy Jews Filthy Jews. These were the words of the fine inscription seeing which I knew my life was lost [. . .]. The filthy Jew was in pain, the filthy Jew's mouth was hanging half open in misfortune [. . .]. It was the pain of a filthy Jew and even a Yid or an Ikey. [. . .] Anti-Semites, you kind souls, I am seeking for neighbourly love, tell me, do you happen to know where neighbourly love might be?[20]

These were the questions that preoccupied the years 1945–60, which were then taken up, albeit in a different way, in May 1968 and until 1980, by French intellectuals – the ones whom Chomsky so hated.

This questioning, focused as it was on the memory of the extermination, was structured by two celebrated sequences. First, how can one write after Auschwitz, how can one find suitable words?[21] Second, how can one reinvent a cinematographic art that is able to relate such

---

* The *Camelots du Roi* were French royalist thugs associated with the Action Française – Trans.

** Villon's 'Ballade des pendus' ['Ballad of the hanged men'], an epitaph for himself and his fellow thieves, begins with 'Frères humains, qui après nous vivez / N'ayez les coeurs contre nous endurcis' ['Brother humans, who live after us / Do not harden your hearts against us']; the title of Cohen's book reprises Villon's first line – Trans.

an event without succumbing to the superficial reconstitution of facts that it is impossible to represent?

While it was Sartre's great merit to have defined in magnificent style the anti-Semitic passion in relation with the question of Jewish identity, it was Alain Resnais who first[22] directed a documentary on the extermination that showed the horror raw: piles of corpses, skeletons, survivors half alive and half dead – in short, something like the *real* of the genocide.[23] Sartre discussed the Jew, the Jews, the Jewish question, and anti-Semitism without describing the extermination and with reference to Drumont, while Resnais displayed the extermination in black and white, without naming either the Jews or anti-Semitism: in this way, the genocide of the Jews became the putting to death of man himself in his greatest universality.[24]

In the text by Jean Cayrol that accompanied the images of *Night and Fog*,[25] the word 'Jew' appeared just once. So Resnais showed what Sartre did not name, and vice versa.

Separated by a few years, the philosopher's text and the film director's documentary formed an unbreakable whole. But *Night and Fog* also raised, for the first time, a question that turned out to be decisive for the directors of the New Wave: François Truffaut, Jacques Rivette, and Jean-Luc Godard. The question of how to write after Auschwitz and how to think of Auschwitz had already been asked, so it was legitimate to ask a quite different question: on what conditions could one film Auschwitz? And it was in this context that Luc Moullet, drawing on Fuller, uttered these words: 'Ethics is a matter of the tracking shot.'[26]

In his wake, in 1961, Rivette wrote a celebrated article that launched the great debate on the ethical conditions of a new cinema. In it, he violently attacked Gillo Pontecorvo's *Kapo*, the first Western film in which – in fictional form – the system of the concentration camps was depicted. Obviously, he did not criticize the upstanding left-wing Italian director for choosing this subject. Quite the contrary: he thought that *everything* could be filmed or reconstituted, and that no limit should be imposed on the art of the cinema in this respect. But he did attack the director's aesthetic choice, the form he had decided to give his film: in it, death was presented quite attractively, directly, with realism, emotion, and fine feelings, as in any television series. The director was thus asking the spectator to act as a witness for what Rivette called an 'abjection' – in other words, an absence of cinematographic ethics which made the film as a whole obscene:

> Many people, on the right and on the left, have quoted – more often than not without any real thought – a remark of Moullet [. . .]. They

have claimed to see this as the height of formalism . . . But look, for instance, at the scene in *Kapo* where Riva commits suicide by throwing himself on the electrified barbed wire. The man who decides at that moment to do a forward tracking shot to reframe the corpse in a low angle shot, taking care to include the lifted hand in a corner of his final shot – that man deserves nothing but the most profound contempt.[27]

Actually, Godard had reversed Moullet's words, claiming not that ethics is a matter of tracking shots but that 'the tracking shot is a matter of ethics'. For a whole generation of cinephiles, to which I belong (as do Serge Daney and many of my friends), this command bore within it an ideal of subversion that I later encountered in a commitment to structuralism, once I had confronted the question of my Jewishness at the time of the Algerian episode of the swastikas. For if looking at cinema can act as a vector for ethics, and not vice versa, this means that, after Auschwitz, one cannot aestheticize abjection with impunity. Thus, every cinematographic gesture needed to be associated with an ethic, a way of thinking the world and representation that avoided relapsing into obscenity.[28]

May 1968, indeed, was a time when, for many young intellectuals of my generation, the question of supporting a revolutionary ideal involved the investigation of language and form rather than any directly political commitment. And this is why, for us, signifiers played such a crucial role. The slogan 'We are all German Jews' was a replay of our support for the Godardian idea that the tracking shot is a matter of ethics and that the heritage of Auschwitz could not be thought of without inventing a new way of calling oneself Jewish, whether one was actually Jewish or not. We needed to support an Enlightenment Jewishness, not only against anti-Semites who were forced to disguise their feelings or repress their anti-Semitism, but also against the new figure of the inquisitorial Jew, whether or not this was embodied by a real Jew.

In this respect, *L'univers concentrationnaire* deserved nothing other than the adjective applied by Rivette to *Kapo*. But there is a strange paradox in the way this work was written by practitioners of the unconscious who turned psychoanalysis into a 'Jewish science' in the name of Freud, and that it was then used as the emblem of a whole throng of inquisitors who, under cover of restoring the 'Law of the Father', launched into a fierce denunciation of the most decisive elements which the Viennese Jewish community had contributed to the contemporary world.

Other questions also arose – questions that had first been tackled in the aftermath of the Second World War. Was it imaginable, after the extermination, that the anti-Semitic texts of Drumont, Rebatet, Brasillach, and many others should continue to be published? But, above all, what was to be done with the work of Martin Heidegger? Could *Being and Time*[29] still be read while ignoring the support given to Hitler and National Socialism by this great philosopher, whose work, filled with disguised references to National Socialism, had been of crucial importance to the history of European culture ever since the interwar period?[30] This work was so very rich that it could quite easily be read without these references ever becoming a source of embarrassment for those who were not concerned with a thorough-going exegesis, or even a misplaced interpretation. In other words, the philosophy was great and the philosopher was a scoundrel, as Sartre had emphasized:

> Heidegger was a philosopher before he was a Nazi [. . .]. 'Heidegger', you say, 'is a member of the National Socialist Party, so his philosophy must be Nazi.' That's not the point. Heidegger has no character, that's the truth of the matter. Will you therefore deduce that his philosophy is an apologia for cowardice? [. . .] That's not the point. Don't you know that men sometimes fail to live up to their works?[31]

But it was not enough to say that the man did not live up to his works. It was necessary to go further than Sartre and state that, the more important the thought was, the more one needed to compare and contrast it with the ignominy of his political commitments.[32] This is why Heidegger's anti-Semitism and his support for Hitlerism – never confessed, never regretted – became, in the French intellectual and political field, the object of a recurring set of questions – so obsessive as to be quite crazy.

Two statements made in 1949 were endlessly discussed – the only two which Heidegger ever made about the genocide of the Jews. The first suggested that the gas chambers were the same kind of thing as the atomic bomb and the industrialization of agriculture: 'Agriculture these days is a motorized food industry, in its essence the same thing as the manufacture of corpses in the gas chambers and the annihilation camps, the same thing as the blockading and reduction of countries to famine, the same thing as the manufacture of hydrogen bombs.' The second distinguished between two ways of dying, the one supported by the essence of being, the other by the manufacture of annihilation: 'Hundreds of thousands die en masse. Do they die? They perish. They are killed. Do they die? They become reserve items in a stock of corpse manufacture. Do they die? They are discreetly liquidated in annihilation camps. And, without that – millions are today perishing of hunger in China.'[33]

Since 1945, via several polemics, Heidegger – condemned in Germany for his support of Nazism, his work rejected by Adorno[34] – had become a major reference figure for French philosophy. Jean Beaufret, a former member of the French Resistance, had managed to convince himself that this philosopher, by whose work he was dazzled, had never been a Nazi,[35] which did not prevent the vast majority of commentators – Emmanuel Lévinas, Jacques Derrida, Élisabeth de Fontenay, Alain Finkielkraut, and many others – from taking this question seriously. In successive waves, every ten years or so, Heidegger's political commitment was the subject of many debates within academia, while the man responsible for the French transla-tion of his works, François Fédier, Beaufret's heir, presented the Master as an irreproachable god who was under attack on all sides for his genius.

In actual fact, Heidegger was the only philosopher in the century of the Shoah of whom one can say with certainly that he was a 'case'. There could be no doubt about his anti-Semitism, his support for National Socialism had been deliberate, at least between 1932 and 1935, and his expressions of regret were barely credible.[36]

Hitler's seizure of power had been a moment of blinding realiza-tion for Heidegger: he had seen it as a political aestheticization of his own thought. And since, in his view, the German language alone was able to rediscover the original and originary truth of the pre-Socratic Greek language, this meant that Nazism – founded on the idea that the Aryans were a chosen race – could provide man with a doctrine of salvation that would enable him to transform the world. And this idea underlay his view that it was necessary to carry out a demolition (*Abbau*) and destruction (*Destruktion*) of the sovereign power of Western metaphysics, since this had disguised the true, mythical (and pre-Socratic) origin of man's being-there. But this doctrine could, if one ignored the philosopher's Nazi beliefs, be interpreted as a revolution in thought which, in its critique of the Cartesian cogito, continued the work of his master, Husserl. In short, there was nothing to say that this work could be reduced to Heidegger's political commitments. In its apoliticism, its atemporality, its rejection of all historicity (replaced by a 'historial-ity'), the work appeared as 'foreclosed' from the discourse and the actions of its author. Thus Heidegger's oeuvre could function as a doctrine that stood apart from the political activities of the man who had produced it. And this meant that all interpretations were open.

And even the two statements referring to the camps could be read *also* as a critique of Nazism: the one indicated that the factories of annihilation were the product of science and technology and that the phenomenon could be perpetuated outside Germany – in all democratic regimes, for example. The other meant – why not? – that the Nazis had prevented those whom they exterminated from dying their own deaths. The problem is that the word 'Jew' was missing from both texts, that, in them, science and technology – and not the perverse way they were used – were condemned for their destructive essence, that genocide was relativized, and that modern democracies, founded on human rights, were in Heidegger's writing merely disguised dictatorships, haunted by the death drive.

In 1987, four months after Klaus Barbie had been sentenced for crimes against humanity, and at a time when the debate on Holocaust denial was at its peak, the polemic surrounding Heidegger's Nazism took a different turn in France with the publication of a book that met with a meteoric success, *Heidegger and Nazism*,[37] written by a Chilean philosopher, Victor Farías, who had been a faithful disciple of the master before denying him after his death. Where three generations of philosophers had appropriated the work, via many sophisticated debates, turning it into something that it was not – so much so, in fact, that the interpretative readings had become almost as rich as the original – an unknown scholar from the Latin American world was now reversing the trend by contributing some important new information.[38] But he drew from this an argument for turning Heidegger's whole oeuvre into an apologia for Nazism, which led to a debate among specialists being transformed into a matter for public opinion. All the media – television, radio, press – asked French intellectuals to give their views: for or against Heidegger.

Since it was now open knowledge that this philosopher, lauded by so many prestigious thinkers, had been a Hitlerian even before the appearance of Nazism – in other words, as early as 1911 – because he had been born, said Farías, in a town where 'Catholics and Old Catholics' confronted one another, because at that time he had suffered from 'cardiac ailments with no physiological cause' (sic),[39] and because it was an established fact that his oeuvre was the equivalent of *Mein Kampf*, the question now arose whether they and their work were also Hitlerians. And if it was open knowledge that all French Heideggerians of all tendencies whatsoever were the accomplices of a Nazi, they could quite legitimately be suspected of anti-Semitism.

Written by the philosopher Christian Jambet,[40] the preface had little to do with the book's contents: 'If the core of Hitlerism is the "final solution", if the extermination camps, and their gas chambers, are the substance of Nazism, what is the meaning of the biography of a man who gave his assent to that?'[41] Jambet, who loathed Heidegger's philosophy, was nonetheless saying largely the same as Philippe Lacoue-Labarthe, who belonged to the Heideggerian tradition and had just devoted a study to the question. But he formulated it in the 'Heideggerian' way, insisting that, in 'the apocalypse of Auschwitz, it is neither more nor less than the West in its essence that has been revealed – and which has not ceased to reveal itself since then.' And he added: 'And it is the thought of this event that Heidegger failed to provide.'[42]

Jacques Derrida was the one most affected by this affair.[43] He had also at that time published his own reflections on the 'question': 'I shall speak of ghost, of flame, and of ashes. And of what, for Heidegger, *avoiding* means.'[44] Derrida was then better known in the United States than in France, but nonetheless he embodied throughout the world, especially since the deaths of Sartre and Foucault, the critical tradition of the French Enlightenment, drawing on deconstruction[45] and on the idea that the best way to receive the inheritance of a way of thinking was to be unfaithful to it: neither liquidation, nor hagiography; neither anathema, nor apologia.

And it was precisely in this way that, while being an unfaithful reader of Heidegger's thinking, Derrida felt Jewish, like Freud and Arendt, but also convinced that he was haunted by 'what was left of Judaism throughout the world'. The Jewish signifier was in his view all the more present in his life and thought since it seemed absent from his work. As early as 1967, Derrida had distanced himself from Beaufret, as he did not approve of the way the latter's thought was developing, and he viewed himself, given his Algerian origins, as a 'little black and very Arab Jew'.[46] He admired Nelson Mandela, who had, he said, managed to turn the English democratic model against the proponents of apartheid,[47] and he attacked all forms of imperialism, of the tyranny of the One.

Without questioning the legitimacy of the State of Israel, Derrida unhesitatingly voiced his disagreement with the policies of its successive governments, and was even sometimes criticized for being a 'bad Jew'.[48] In a word, he dreamt of a Europe in which it would be possible to criticize Israeli policy without being taxed with anti-Semitism, in which one could support the aspirations of the Palestinians to 'recover their land without thereby approving of the suicide attacks and the anti-Semitic propaganda which tends – too often – in the Arab world, to give new credence to the monstrous *Protocols of the Elders of Zion*.'[49]

Furthermore, he continued to state that the West needed to integrate with Greek thought a reflection on the three monotheisms – a
way of emphasizing, with Lévinas and against Heidegger, the extent
to which the return to the Greeks was effectuated through a return
to Jerusalem[50] – but also through the deconstruction of the phallo-
centrism characteristic of these three monotheisms, which shared, in
their very essence, an exclusion of woman as 'difference' and '*dif-
férance*'. In 2001, he told me:

> Orthodox Jews, and hardly the least refined among them, will tell you
> that if circumcision is abandoned, Judaism risks losing something
> essential. More generally if circumcision is abandoned (literal or figural
> circumcision, but everything is played out around the letter, in Judaism
> as well as in Islam), one is on the road to an abandonment of phal-
> locentrism. This would apply *a fortiori* to excision. This abandonment
> also applies to Christianity, since these three religions are powerfully,
> although differently, phallocentric. In any case, phallocentrism and
> circumcision link Islam and Judaism. I have often stressed the pro-
> found irreducibility of the Judeo-Islamic couple, or even its often
> denied privilege, in comparison to the confusedly accredited couple
> Judeo-Christian.[51]

Caught up in the furious debate, Derrida defended his views in the
French media: this made him even better known. He insisted especially that scandals such as this one ran the risk of leading to the
banning from academia of any form of real discussion of Heidegger's
work and the reduction of the latter to *Mein Kampf*: libraries might
gradually be denuded not just of the books written by the German
philosopher, but of those by his commentators too.[52] A year previously, in a scurrilous piece which had met with a certain success, he
had been described as a nihilistic, anti-democratic deconstructor of
the same ilk as Lacan, Bourdieu, and Foucault.[53]

This media storm was nothing compared to the one Derrida had
to face at the same time in the United States. Hated as much by
conservatives (who deemed him to be nihilistic, anti-democratic, anti-
American, and hostile to Israel) as by the positivist and analytical
schools (who regarded him as a '*littérateur*'), he was also rejected by
Chomsky and his supporters, who saw him as an imposter who was
in any case much too favourable to Western democracy and 'American imperialism'. Thus he was violently attacked by the American
press in the wake of the posthumous revelations about the past of
his friend Paul de Man.

Born in Belgium in 1919, de Man had emigrated across the Atlantic in the aftermath of the Second World War. He taught European

literature in various universities, and in 1966, at the famous symposium at Johns Hopkins University in Baltimore,[54] he had been the first to introduce structuralism into that country: this had made him some firm enemies and led to accusations of formalism, nihilism, and apoliticism. For his part, he criticized academic and psychological approaches for denying the autonomy of literary form and considered the departments of English language and literature to be hidebound. He and Derrida shared a close friendship.

Now, in the summer of 1987, a Belgian researcher, Ortwin de Graef, discovered two hundred newspaper columns on literature written by the young de Man between 1940 and 1942 and published in the Walloon press: most of them were less than a page long, and twenty-five others were more substantial. At that period, King Leopold III had agreed to submit to the Nazi occupiers while considering himself to be a prisoner in his own country. As for his advisor Henri de Man, Paul's uncle, a former leader of the Belgian Workers' Party who believed that Marxism needed to be superseded, he was convinced that National Socialism had now triumphed for a long time to come in Europe. And he had a far from negligible influence on his nephew.[55]

Among the texts exhumed in 1987, only one, 'The Jews in present-day literature', is really anti-Semitic. In it, Paul de Man criticized 'vulgar anti-Semitism', which in his view tended to hunt for traces of an 'en-Jewished' or 'polluted' literature. But he found it consoling that Western intellectuals had managed to preserve themselves from 'Jewish influence'. And he added: 'One thus sees that a solution of the Jewish problem that would aim at the creation of a Jewish colony isolated from Europe would not, for the literary life of the West, entail deplorable consequences. The latter would lose, in all, a few personalities of mediocre value and would continue, as in the past, to develop according to its great evolutive laws.'[56] So de Man was attempting to draw a distinction between a good anti-Semite and a bad one – in words that were terrible and unforgivable, said Derrida, as he struggled to grasp the meaning of his friend's moves.

All his life long, de Man had concealed from his friends his activities as a literary columnist with a collaborationist newspaper in occupied Belgium, and he had died without ever explaining his actions. In 1987, his enemies were not inclined to reach a fair judgement on the mistake he had made forty-five years earlier, and they described him as a collaborationist, a Nazi, and an anti-Semite, if only to put deconstruction on trial (i.e., *Destruktion* in Heidegger's sense of the word).

No sooner had this past been revealed than the deconstructors, with Derrida at their head, were accused of being complicit with a Nazi and of seeking to destroy the teaching of the humanities in the departments of Romance languages and literature in the universities of America, so as to ensure their own 'falsifying' hegemony over the entire continent. Jeffrey Mehlman, a past master, as we have seen, in this type of campaign, stated that 'deconstruction, in its entirety, was a huge plan to amnesty the collaborators'.[57] In other words, in the eyes of his detractors, de Man was simply a sort of Rebatet who, after emigrating, had concealed a dark past and plotted against America.

As for Chomsky, convinced as ever that French intellectuals were persecuting Faurisson, he took advantage of this polemic to explain to Edward Said, a connoisseur of Foucault, Barthes, Freud, and European thought, that he needed to tear himself away from this nefarious structuralist-deconstructionist ideology: 'I liked Derrida', Said remarked, 'and we had good personal relations [. . .]. But he became a "Derridean" [. . .]. There is in his works – and I can remember discussing this with Chomsky – a whiff of more ambiguity and complacency than there is any serious attempt to commit himself politically on certain current problems, whether Vietnam or Palestine, or imperialism. There was always a sense that he was being evasive.'[58]

Called a Nazi for his Heideggerianism, then accused of having had a dubious friendship for a former collaborationist, Derrida retorted by insisting that this kind of retrospective trial was very close to being an exploitation of the Shoah and the Jewish question.[59] But he was forced to realize, as Hannah Arendt had done before him, that every newspaper article was simply repeating another one, that the media machine was merciless. Admittedly, the rumour that deconstruction-ism was a Nazi plot hatched against the West, with the complicity of Heidegger, soon crumbled, and the whole affair eventually helped to give Derrida's political commitments a greater dynamism. But it still did not come to an end and was indeed rekindled in France in 2005, in the work of Emmanuel Faye, a Germanist and professor of philosophy.

While producing a more serious and erudite study of Heidegger's Nazism than that of Farías, the author had no compunction about stating not only that it should be forbidden to teach such writings anywhere in the world, but that the term 'deconstruction' had been born from Heidegger's term *Destruktion*: 'Such a work cannot continue to be placed in the philosophy section of libraries, its place is rather in the historical archives of Nazism and Hitlerism.'

Furthermore: 'This is the provenance of "deconstruction", which, translating Heidegger's *Abbau* and *Destruktion*, departed France in conquest of the "humanities departments" of American universities, at first with the critical support of Paul de Man. That endeavour made it possible for Heidegger to expand to the United States and subsequently to the entire world . . .'[60]

What is most surprising about the whole business is the way nobody seemed to take any serious interest in Farías: he was garlanded with praise, but he was never invited to express his views in the media. And yet, haunted in his turn by a great conspiracy fantasy, he decided, after the affair, to undertake a huge desacralization of the so-called official history of his country, so as to provide the proof that Salvador Allende, who had died on 11 September 1973 after launching an attack on the military junta led by Augusto Pinochet, was in actual fact merely a proponent of the 'Final Solution', an anti-Semite, a homophobe, and a despiser of 'inferior races' – in short, a Nazi in socialist guise. But how was he to prove that such a fable could have any close or distant resemblance to the truth?

In answer to this question, Farías decided to exhume the works written by Allende as a young man when, already active on the left, he had in 1933 presented to his teachers at the University of Santiago a dissertation on the question of mental health and delinquency. In this text, Allende set out theories that had been adopted in Europe at the end of the nineteenth century. And it was the Italian school from which he drew most of his references, especially Lombroso, who had inspired Max Nordau, and who had written that the criminality 'specific to the Jews was usury, calumny and falsity, combined with a notorious absence of murders and crimes of passion'. Quoting these words and ascribing them to Allende, Farías insisted that the latter had remained a lifelong Nazi. In this way he endeavoured to dethrone one of the most popular figures – with Che Guevara – of Latin American anti-fascism. In between the lines of his essay, one could sense the presence of a crazed conviction. Just as he was calling a martyr a 'Nazi', he had likewise reduced to a Nazi tract the entire oeuvre of a philosopher whose cowardice and anti-Semitism had proved to be a major problem for every philosopher in the second half of the twentieth century. But history had preserved only the accusation brought against Heidegger: nobody, or almost nobody, had noticed the link between the two affairs.[61]

If a quarrel over a work of this sort had managed to cause so much heart-searching in the French intellectual and media world, and if the posthumous trial of Paul de Man had so easily turned into a trial of deconstruction, this was clear confirmation of the fact that, from the 1980s onwards, a long-term neo-conservative revolution was under way.

This revolution drew succour from the collapse of communism, an event that filled with glee the new prosecutors of thought, eager to exploit, as against the tradition of the Enlightenment, the tense relation between Israel and the diaspora. It was just as if, in response to the madness of the Holocaust deniers, the rejection of the revolutionary spirit, and, finally, the crisis of Zionism, there was a need to revise the whole basis of European culture to unearth anti-Semitism where it did not exist – on the left, if possible – so as to disguise it more effectively where it presented itself in new or masked forms.

Hannah Arendt had already been suspected of sympathy for the killers, and an explanation was now about to be provided as to how almost all Enlightenment thinkers, as well as their heirs, were nothing other than anti-Semites – from Spinoza, Voltaire, Marx and Freud, to Lacan, Derrida, Blanchot, Gide, Lévi-Strauss, Sartre, and Deleuze.

In 1982, Jeffrey Mehlman, a brilliant American academic, a peerless translator, undisputedly a leading figure in the study of French literature, deconstruction, and French theory, took it into his head to apply the structural method of psychoanalytical deciphering of textuality to authors whom he had loved so much that he now hated them. This conversion from idolatry to anathema had coincided, he later said, with a sort of self-analysis that had led him, between 1974 and 1980, to discover that he was not the person he had thought he was.[62] And from then on he continued to brandish, against French intellectual power, the weapons of the inquisitorial Jew: for him, the task was now not just to detect in the slightest dubious term the shameful trace of a repressed anti-Semitism, but also to invent anti-Semitism where it had no right to be – or never to pardon the errors of those who had committed them and confessed to them.

In this way, in a review article, and then in a book with the title *Legacies of anti-Semitism in France*,[63] Mehlman attacked authors as different as Jean Giraudoux, André Gide, Maurice Blanchot, and Jacques Lacan. Unhesitatingly identifying with Gershom Scholem, he embarked on an operation of catching people 'in flagrante delicto',[64] aimed at completely overturning the way anti-Semitism was represented in the French humanities. So he was not making any secret of his intentions. Leaving to one side the vociferations of Céline and other collaborationists, which he thought were ultimately not so dangerous, he sought to show that, under the surface, in the writings of its most prestigious writers, playwrights, and thinkers, the France of Drumont and Vichy was present where nobody expected it. And his choice of writers was far from innocuous.

Giraudoux embodied a major renewal in the art of the theatre of which the Théâtre-Français had been the symbol for over a century. As for Gide, the founder of *La Nouvelle Revue française*, the prince of the Gallimard publishing house and winner of the Nobel Prize for Literature, he was in person the symbol of the literary France that was the heir of Zola and Voltaire – so much so that, when he arrived in Paris in June 1940, Otto Abetz declared that the city was dominated by three powers: the *NRF*, freemasonry, and the big banks.

While Gide and Giraudoux had been chosen by Mehlman for their popularity, their classicism, and their academicism, Blanchot and Lacan had been selected for the opposite reason. They represented *the other France*, the France of modernity, formalism, subversion, and structure: they were the successors to Mallarmé, Rimbaud, and surrealism.

As he explored the work of these four authors, aiming to prove that they had been the biggest anti-Semites of the twentieth century, Mehlman was changing into a new Robert Paxton, whose task it was to reveal to readers in the 1980s not only that the France of Vichy was still sticking to their skins without their realizing it but, even worse, that the tribunals set up to purge collaborators had chosen the wrong target: the 'real' anti-Semites had managed to evade any judgement, and they were haunting the shelves of the libraries of France and Navarre,* like Shakespearean ghosts rising from the depths of a guilty conscience. But Mehlman was obviously forgetting that, at this date, as I have mentioned, there were ever more studies on the question of collaboration, genocide, and Jewish identity coming out in France.

A writer and diplomat born in 1882, Giraudoux had refused under the Popular Front to take over the Comédie-Française, but he had agreed to being made a commander in the order of the Légion d'honneur. He had then become politically active, and at the outbreak of the Second World War he became president of a higher council for information. A Germanophile, but an anti-Nazi as well, he was neither a supporter of Pétain nor a member of the Resistance, and he died in September 1944 before he could explain his attitude. His work is clearly marred by anti-Semitism: in particular, there was the racist book published in 1939, in which Giraudoux extolled a policy

---

* An allusion to the old title of the French kings: '*roi de France et de Navarre*' – Trans.

of controlled emigration, meant to preserve France from too much interbreeding with other races – including the Jews. He wrote:

> There have entered among us, through a process of infiltration the secret of which I have tried in vain to discover, some hundred thousand Askenasis [*sic*] who have escaped from Polish and Romanian ghettoes whose spiritual rules – but not their particularism – they reject [. . .]. Wherever they pass, they bring the not-quite-right, the underhand activity, extortion and corruption, and they are a permanent threat to the spirit of precision, good faith and perfection that used to be the spirit of French craftsmanship. A horde which ensures it falls short of its national rights and can thus outface all expulsions, and which its precarious and abnormal physical constitution brings in its thousands into our hospitals, on which it is a heavy burden.[65]

Encouraged by this 'argument', Giraudoux called for a Ministry of Race, so as to ensure the well-being of France: 'We fully agree with Hitler in proclaiming that a policy attains its higher form only if it is racial.'[66]

This is an unambiguous text: Mehlman was able to rub his hands. He had caught a *real* anti-Semite and he was not going to let him go. And so, on the basis of a reading of a volume of essays in literature published in 1941, he would turn the playwright into the new theorist of the infernal couple of Semites and Aryans, showing that his theatre was nothing other than a transposition of the exterminating policies of Vichy. Even the character in *La folle de Chaillot* was annexed to serve this interpretation. Faced with a vile audience of creditors, crooks, and people on the make, was the crazed Countess perhaps the incarnation of a Europe gone mad – a Europe which Giraudoux was still, posthumously, extolling, since he gave his heroine the mission of ejecting from the world stage the kings of finance – in other words, the Jews? Not only did Mehlman ascribe to a fictional character anti-Semitic remarks which did not exist in the text, but it was of little importance to him to know that this play had been premiered by the Louis Jouvet company on 22 December 1945, on behalf of and in memory of the deportees. The essential thing, in his eyes, was always to reveal the other side of the coin, including in fictional texts which shed no particular new light on the matter. Since the France of the Liberation was secretly perpetuating the policies of Vichy, this meant that the crazed Countess was posthumously expressing Giraudoux's own repressed anti-Semitism.

As for André Gide, he had never written the least anti-Semitic text. And yet, on a closer look, he still turned out to be at fault, in Mehlman's view, since, in his journal dated 27 January 1914, he had spoken of the 'Jewish race' and 'Jewish literature'. Forgetting that the use of this word was common at the time, Mehlman did not hesitate to turn the founder of the *Nouvelle Revue française* into an heir to Drumont.

In Lacan's case, the accusation of anti-Semitism took a comical turn – and with good reason. Knowing the work as he did, Mehlman had still not managed to unearth, in the past of the renewer of psychoanalysis, the least 'fault' that would have enabled the American to exercise his inquisitorial talents. Convinced that he needed to unearth evidence of it at all costs, even when it was not there, he claimed to show that Lacan's whole work was infested by a repressed anti-Semitism. And, on the basis of this 'thesis', he quoted an innocuous passage in the *Seminar* of 1964, in which Lacan, referring to 'Kant with Sade', placed his own return to Freud under the sign of a period 'after Auschwitz' and an acknowledgement of the figure of the Jew of the Shoah. In fact, Mehlman had focused on just one statement in this *Seminar*. Here it is:

> Did I perhaps represent Freud to you last time as some such figure as Abraham, Isaac and Jacob? In his *Salut par les Juifs*, Léon Bloy depicts them as three equally old men who are there, according to one of the forms of Israel's vocation, squatting around some piece of canvas on the ground, engrossed in that eternal occupation of dealing in second-hand goods. They are sorting out the various objects on the canvas. Some things they put on one side, others on the other. On one side, Freud put the partial drives and on the other, love. He says – *They're not the same.*[67]

Accusing Bloy of being Drumont's accomplice – in other words, *just like Drumont* – Mehlman set out to demonstrate, on the basis of an interpretation of *it's not the same thing*, that Lacan's return to Freud was nothing other than the obliteration of any trace of a return to Bloy. Lacan was fundamentally a supporter of Bloy – in other words, of Drumont – and his Freudianism was the 'suture of this mistake' – and thus a form of anti-Semitism.[68] When I met Jeffrey Mehlman after he had translated my *Jacques Lacan & Co.* into English, I told him what I thought of his way of reading Lacan's work. He subsequently abandoned Lacan for pastures new. However, the rumour of an anti-Semitic and Vichyist Lacan was repeated by other writers, for instance in the new edition of *L'univers contestationnaire*. This soon sold out.

But the person whom Mehlman forgave for nothing was Maurice Blanchot, the writer he had admired the most when he was still in thrall to his idealization of French intellectual power. When, in 1974,

he suffered a terrible shock in learning from Sternhall's book something that everyone else already knew – that Blanchot had been a
fascist in his youth – he continued to pursue him with his vengeance,
going so far as to state that Blanchot's support for Israel and his overt
interest in Jewish mysticism sprang from 'philo-Semitism' – in other
words, from a disguised anti-Semitism. And yet, to say it yet again,
Blanchot had confessed to his 'error' ['*faute*'] in December 1992, in
a letter addressed to Roger Laporte.[69] On that occasion, he had stated
that the 'very name of Maurras was the expression of a dishonour'.
This was all that Mehlman needed to accuse Blanchot of denouncing
Maurras so as to denounce himself. Not only was Blanchot unforgivable, but so was his unconscious.

And so, for thirty years, with the support of a small section of the
French intelligentsia,[70] who opposed the more enlightened members
of the Jewish community,[71] this excellent American academic continued to depict Blanchot's work as a monument of anti-Semitism. And,
through Blanchot, Mehlman was also attacking Derrida, since
at the time of the de Man affair he had stated that deconstruction
was being used to repress Europe's Nazi past. And yet, Derrida
did not share his friend Blanchot's positions: neither on Israel, nor
on the impossibility of writing after Auschwitz, nor even on the way
the break represented by the genocide of the Jews had been
turned into an absolute. This mattered little: both of them would
henceforth, in Mehlman's view, be implicated in Nazism and
anti-Semitism.

In a few years, after 1990, Blanchot, the great interpreter of what
it means to be a Jew after the Shoah, the friend of Derrida, of Lévinas,
and of Israel, became, in the eyes of his inquisitors, a destructive
writer who, through the omnipotence of his invisibility and his metamorphoses, had infested French literature and philosophy – much
more than had Céline, whose pamphlets (rather than his *Journey*)
were endlessly being extolled.

Might one go so far as to say that this Blanchot, disfigured by his
detractors, had to some extent become the equivalent of that Jew
who, in Drumont's opinion, was the bane of France? To those who,
with their Freudian interpretations, continually brandished the 6
million dead in Blanchot's face, this remark of Lévinas's could have
been made: 'Judaism brings this magnificent message. Remorse – the
painful expression of the radical impotence to repair the irreparable
– announces the repentance which generates the pardon that repairs.
Man finds in the present something that can modify, wipe out the
past. Time loses its very irreversibility. It collapses in exhaustion at
man's feet, like a wounded beast. And he frees it.'[72]

If Blanchot was dragged through the mud all his life long for a youthful error for which he had atoned countless times, and if Paul de Man was condemned for never having confessed to his error, Jean Genet was the posthumous victim of a trial for anti-Semitism based on quite different reasons: his unconditional support for the Palestinian people.

The transformation of Genet into an anti-Semitic writer, and even a Nazi officer, actively collaborating between 1940 and 1944, and then in terrorism during the last fifteen years of his life (1970–86), started in the United States,[73] twelve years after the death of Sartre; the latter had been the first philosopher to devote a monumental study[74] to this poet and playwright whose youthful years had been like those of a character from *Les Misérables*. The process continued in France, after 2001, with the publication of two works by Éric Marty,[75] a semiologist and specialist in Barthes who adopted a Lacanian approach to literary texts. He turned Genet into a sort of Gestapo member, one who abolished the difference between the sexes and the generations, was incapable of accepting the 'Law of the Father', was afflicted by a negative 'mimetic rivalry', and whose homosexuality was simply the manifestation of a barely repressed anti-Semitism: he was a pederast, a pervert, and therefore a Nazi.

The aim of this series of interventions was political. The author chose the 'Genet case' to focus on first and foremost so that he could liken the French press to a 'Doctor Mabuse' figure that had organized a plot against Israel, secondly so that he could deny any responsibility (even passive) on the part of Ariel Sharon for the massacre of the camps in Sabra and Chatila in Lebanon in 1982, and thirdly to accuse the Palestinians of inventing a 'metaphysics of exile' (*Naqba*) out of hatred for the Jews and the Israelis.[76] Here, the author was in agreement with the authors of *L'univers contestationnaire*,[77] while his style made him more akin to Jeffrey Mehlman.

Yet again, an emblematic figure from the literary world was summoned to appeal before a tribunal that was purging suspects at a time when, twenty years after his death, his work and his various political activities had been discussed in many scholarly works without the least whiff of hagiography.[78] Could Genet, one of the greatest playwrights of the second half of the twentieth century, have been such a Nazi, anti-Semite, and terrorist that he needed to be put to death so as to ensure the survival of the State of Israel?

Not only had a parliamentary commission, in Israel itself, indicated Ariel Sharon's responsibility in the massacre in Lebanon, but the reality of the *Naqba* was no longer denied by a single serious commentator. As for the accusation laid against the French press, it came from a conspiracy-theory mentality which I have already had occasion to discuss.

In the wake of this publication, another scholar, Ivan Jablonka,[79] who drew on the traditions of the *Annales* school and the dispassionate rigour of the positivist trend, set out to write what would at last be a 'demystificatory biography' of Genet to show not just that the man had been a Hitlerian, whose childhood had been 'pampered', but that his work as a playwright had been completely Nazi. This, he explained, had escaped the notice of all Genet's commentators: Sartre, Derrida, Foucault, Bataille, and so on. It was time, he wrote, to point out that this pathological liar was merely a collaborationist, of the same kind as Rebatet, Brasillach, and Céline. Had he not had the gall to evade deportation at a time when thousands of Jews were being exterminated, two great French poets – Max Jacob and Robert Desnos – among them? Yet again, the media played a significant role in this debate, at the end of which, we should point out, Jablonka's ideas were discounted.[80]

Throughout the first part of his life, Genet's existence was like that of the 'infamous men' whose history Foucault planned one day to write, insisting that they incarnated the accursed share of human societies. Their lives are unmentionable, he said – a reverse mirror image of the lives of illustrious men. And when they did acquire any notoriety, it was most often through the power of a criminality that was deemed to be bestial or monstrous.[81]

Born in 1910, abandoned by his mother and deprived of any knowledge of his origins, Genet was placed as a ward of public assistance in a foster family in the Morvan region. When he left school, he could best hope for a job as a servant or a farm labourer. While still very young, feeling himself to have an exceptional destiny ahead of him, he started to loathe the French state while feeling an overwhelming and passionate love for the French language. This language was his sole parent, mother and father combined, masculine and feminine in one. Woods, books, culture, art, beauty, the names of flowers – rose and broom* – became for him both a genealogical inheritance and a territory of exile, enabling him to indulge in transgressive fantasies that drew him headlong towards creatures who were as humiliated as he was, but also more dangerous, either as victims or as killers: prostitutes, transvestites, sodomites, criminals, tramps, mercenaries. In his narratives and in his dramatic works, he gave them common names 'with a capital letter'[82] – Mimosa, Querelle

---

* Genet often played on the resemblance of his name to the French word '*genêt*', meaning the plant broom – Trans.

[Quarrel], Divine, Yeux-Verts [Green-Eyes], Divers [Diverse], Notre-Dame-des-Fleurs [Our Lady of the Flowers] – so that they would have the right to a sacred name before giving up the ghost or climbing the scaffold.

Unable to adapt to the conditions of existence that had been assigned to him, Genet started to run away: at the age of fifteen, he encountered child neuropsychiatry at a time in its history when it was expanding rapidly. Assessed by a psychiatrist from the school of Georges Heuyer, who classified him in the category of the weak-minded and unstable, he followed a psychotherapeutic 'treatment' at the Patronage de l'Enfance in the Centre Henri-Rolet, which merely made things worse. After several periods living rough, and a three-month internment at La Roquette prison, he was placed in the *colonie pénitentiare agricole* at La Mettray, one of the 'prison hulks for children' that were later abolished at the Liberation.[83]

Genet signed up in France's army in the Middle East and discovered the Arab world, which was then experiencing a nationalist awakening, as well as the rigours of colonialism (of which he was himself one of the agents) and the texts of Lawrence of Arabia, for whom he felt an ambivalent fascination. Between 1933 and 1940, he led a wandering life, committing petty thefts, and making his way through Europe as it was being subjected to Nazi rule. The little thief of fabrics and books was regarded as a criminal, a deserter, and a dangerous vagabond, just as mass murder and persecution was being organized legally by increasingly murderous states and in countries torn apart by war. Thus Genet viewed himself as the victim of an injustice when, on his return to France, he was yet again sentenced to prison for stealing a dozen handkerchiefs from La Samaritaine and a complete edition of Proust from a bookshop.

Genet was glad that France, in which the only thing he liked was the language, was now under Nazi dominance. And since the state which had judged him to be a criminal had become much more criminal than he, he was finally able to metamorphose into another man. It was his meeting with Jean Cocteau that allowed him to gain the status of a writer, and it was writing that saved him from a wretched existence.

On 19 June 1943, as millions of Jews were being exterminated throughout Eastern Europe and the collaborationist press was denouncing them more and more violently each day, Genet, whose only thoughts were for his own freedom, was again brought face to face with psychiatry in the person of Henri Claude,[84] a great mental health specialist at the Sainte-Anne hospital. In his wisdom – or profound stupidity – Claude assigned the poet to the category of 'moral madness', suggesting that his aspirations to a literary life were barely credible even though he could boast of having weighty protectors in the Parisian intellectual world: he was neither demented nor perverted, said Claude, but afflicted by a 'moral blindness' that made him live in obscurity, far from the realities of life. And he added that the 'moral madmen' of his type constituted a danger for society and that justice was duty-bound to be severe, so as to place him beyond any ability to cause harm.[85]

Sent back for trial and sentenced to three months in gaol, Genet reoffended, stealing an edition of *Le Grand Meaulnes*; on 25 December, as his first major book was being published,[86] he was transferred to the camp at Les Tourelles, then run by the French militia under the control of the German police. Here were gathered, before being deported, political prisoners and people sentenced for common law offences – the latter despised by the former. Ready to do anything, even to sign up in the Wehrmacht to strengthen the Atlantic Wall, Genet appealed to his friend François Sentein, a fascist writer, who passed on his appeal to Joseph Darnand, who on 14 March 1944 ordered him to be freed.[87]

From this date, Genet stopped stealing. A month later, he met Sartre, Simone de Beauvoir, and then Marguerite Duras, Juan Goytisolo, and many other writers committed to the left or the far left. They formed a real family for him, the literary family of which he had dreamt to be a part by stealing books and turning his mother tongue into his sole parent. When he was pardoned in 1948 by French President Vincent Auriol, he moved from the state of unwilling pariah to that of voluntary pariah.

As he became a part of the literary order by composing a baroque and pornographic work haunted by the thrill of evil, the cult of the sacred, and focused on a master–slave dialectic that was simply a parody of Hegel's, since it led to no solution, Genet was still the person he had always been: an outlaw of thought and norm, filled with a visceral loathing for the rich, the bourgeoisie, and democracy, and finding it quite intolerable to be honourable, celebrated, and admired – and soon wealthy and known throughout the world. In this way, he sublimated his murderous drives through his writing.

Protected by Sartre, supported by the Gallimard publishing house, courted by the best playwrights of the time, Genet inflicted physical hardships on himself that he had not experienced as a child: he had no fixed abode, he neglected his body, he dressed in rags (or, occasionally, with great elegance), he chose his lovers from circus performers and outsiders – Arabs, if possible. And, more than anything, he loved to shock his entourage by continuing to say that he was a thief, a delinquent, and a traitor, even though this was no longer true. Through perpetual metamorphoses, he pretended to be someone he was not (or was no longer), but he remained hateful, insomniac, often melancholy, and forever in search of a declared enemy. Thus he was a permanent scandal for his own friends but above all for the French right and its authors. It showed the greatness of Gaullism, especially (of course) of André Malraux, that it granted him the right to express himself without ever banning him. Having dreamt of freedom under Nazism, he never ceased, once he had found it under a democratic regime, to aspire to all the forms of imprisonment and discipline of which he had been the victim. Hence his liking for the murderers, saints, and warriors of the mediaeval period: there was, in his view, nothing more sublime than imagining a barbarous coupling between Gilles de Rais and Joan of Arc.

As a voluntary pariah, Genet did not share the destiny of the *poètes maudits* and sodomites of the end of the nineteenth century – Rimbaud, Verlaine, and Wilde – even though he was their heir. Nor did he share the fate of Sade, the prince of perverts, who had been imprisoned for almost thirty years under three different political regimes. Things had changed. Willingly or not, Genet was, in spite of himself, a post-Auschwitz writer, a writer of the Shoah. And this is why, throughout the latter half of his life, he was obsessed, if not by the Jewish question, at least by the question of the extermination of the Jews – in other words, by Hitler, the figure of absolute evil. But Hitler interested him only as a singular personage on whom he could project his erotic fantasies. By destroying France, Hitler had certainly 'avenged' Genet for the real and imaginary humiliations that the French republican institution had inflicted upon him, and Genet therefore lavished strange 'gratifications' on him, turning him into a castrated sodomite disguised as a ghost or sullied with the menstrual blood of Joan of Arc on her stake.[88] Genet went further: he reduced Hitler to a moustache, dyed by l'Oréal, its black, stiff hairs conveying murderous words: strangulation, rage, foam, despotism, cruelties, asps, parades, prisons, daggers.[89]

But Genet also knew the cost of this vengeance, and, despite being incapable of feeling the least compassion for the survivors of the camps, he was forever haunted by the real of the extermination: barbed wire fences, crematorium ovens, fingernails and toenails pulled out, skin dried and tattooed to make lampshades. He loathed mass crimes: the only criminals he admired were the solitary ones, the aristocrats of evil.

Genet had moved in fascist circles during the Occupation, but he had never supported Hitler's ideals, or denounced anyone, or incited anyone to murder Jews. He never wrote the least anti-Semitic text, never engaged in collaborationist activities, never adopted the language of anti-Semitism, and never, in later years, gave the least support to radical Islamists or to Holocaust deniers. In any case, political commitment was not his line. Genet was incapable of following a party line: he could not be assimilated, he always wore a mask, he was in constant metamorphosis. But the Jews remained an enigma for him, since, through the curse weighing on them, which was in his view the sign that that they had been chosen by God, they had managed to vanquish absolute evil. They were even the only people to have performed such a miracle for centuries: they had contrived to mobilize hatred to ensure their own survival.[90]

However, far from loving the Jews, Genet envied their torment, and this in turn was a way of viewing them as rivals. And this is why, in the wake of the Allied victory, he addressed to the survivors of the Shoah a baroque hymn imbued with a macabre and venomous obscenity:

> We will have been so badly mistreated in prison, in such a cowardly way, that I envy you in your tortures [. . .]. A mere flick of the fingers from their gendarmes was vivified by the burning blood of the heroes of the North, this flick grew into a plant of wondrous beauty, tact and skill, a rose whose twisted, curled petals, showing the red and the pink beneath an infernal sun, are named with terrible names: Majdanek, Belsen, Auschwitz, Mauthausen, Dora. I raise my hat. But we shall remain your remorse.[91]

From 1970, in the last years of his life, having ceased to write, Genet gave his support to the American Black Panthers, to the members of the Red Army Faction in Germany,[92] and finally to the *fedayin* of Al Fatah. The first two groups were mainly in state prisons, while the last had been deprived of their land. When he defended the first group, Genet drew inspiration from Zola's *J'accuse*, and, when he composed a text in support of the second group, he accused the state of the Federal Republic of Germany of having repressed its Nazi past.[93] So he caused a scandal when he created the impression that he was lauding the virtues of the Soviet Union. And when he went to Chatila to describe the carnage, he was finally able to give voice to the loathing that he felt, not for the Jews as such, but for Israel as a state. He described the carnage in identical terms to those he had used to evoke the extermination, and he added some words – later cut – reproaching the Jews for having survived the curse laid on them, only to become, in the State of Israel, a people of colonizers.[94]

In 1976, Genet explained the strange way he had eroticized Hitler. Insisting that his admiration had 'emptied', he added that the empty space left had not been filled by anything else: 'I was avenged [. . .] but I also know that it was a conflict within the white world that far transcended me [. . .]. Then, I could not fail to see myself in the oppressed people of colour and in the oppressed who had rebelled against the whites.'[95]

And in his last book, *Prisoner of Love*,[96] published posthumously, Genet took sides with the Palestinians, among whom he had lived on several occasions, but only since he viewed them as the victims of a colonial state, insisting that, if one day they did obtain land of their own, he would be their declared enemy. He stayed with Leila Shahid and adopted, in his own language, the ideas put forward both by Edward Said and by the new Israeli historians, who argued that the Palestinians had become the 'victims of the victims': 'The classic victims of years of anti-Semitic persecutions and the Holocaust', Saod would state, 'have become in their own homes the tormentors of other people who have thus become the victims of the victims.'[97] In addition, as Tom Seguev said: 'Free men, the Arabs, headed into exile like wretched refugees, and the Jews seized the houses of the exiled to start their new lives as free men.'[98]

As he wrote this – occasionally quite mad – testament, in which he claimed that the Palestinians had led to a disintegration of his own vocabulary, Genet summoned up Hitler's ghost one last time, saying he was giving him the kiss one gives a leper, and redeeming him from his crime in burning the Jews.[99] His words were obscure, intolerable, and provocative, but they seemed to have been written by a Sadian moribund who had guessed that, one day, his fiercest enemies would set out to depict him as a Nazi, a member of the Gestapo, and an anti-Semite: the last thrill of pleasure for a perverse writer who condemned murderous states for their perverse inversion of the Law. But he also imagined that he might have been an 'elderly rabbi brought up in the Talmudic faith', the heir of the people of origins and seeking his ancestors among the furriers: 'I'd have curls down to my chest. I'm sorry to have missed that.'[100] And, to go with this effeminate rabbi he dreamt of being so that he could beget a son who would be a future agent of Mossad, he invented another couple, formed by his friend Hamza and his mother, comparing them to a *Pietà*. A strange rehash of a family! As the son of his mother tongue and the father of a work in a state of perpetual disintegration, Genet lived, in the period just before his death, as the captive of a darkling trio in which the three monotheisms entwined: Mary, Mother of God, the ringletted Rabbi of Yahweh, and the Jesus of the Fatah. So he was quite unable to turn his last work into the manifesto that his Palestinian friends, first and foremost Yasser Arafat, had hoped for.

Was he anti-Semitic? Sartre had given an answer to his question very early on:

> Genet is anti-Semitic. Or rather he plays at being so. As one can imagine, it is hard for him to support most of the theses of anti-Semitism. Deny the Jews political rights? But he doesn't give a rap about politics. Exclude them from the professions, forbid them to engage in business? That would amount to saying that he is unwilling to rob them, since businessmen are his victims. [. . .] Does he therefore want to kill them by the million? But massacres don't interest Genet; the murders of which he dreams are individual ones [. . .]. Israel can sleep in peace.'[101]

Indeed, Genet *played* at being anti-Semitic: and it is probably better for Israel to have a declared enemy of the calibre of a Genet than inquisitorial false friends.

In this testament, Genet also dealt with an essential question that had evaded the notice of his accusers.[102] The fate of the Jewish victims, he said, is sealed with that of the Palestinians, victims of the victims. And, to indicate the existence of this bond even more clearly, he brought together two slogans and six words that were as impossible to unite as they were to keep separate: Palestine will conquer/ Israel will live.[103]

In the poetic language he had made his own, Genet, an expert in Herzl's venture and a close reader of the Bible, thus interpreted the Israeli–Palestinian conflict not just as a metaphor of the struggle at night between Jacob and the Angel, but as the infinite repetition of the struggle to the death that had given birth to Zionism: 'A land without people for a people without land'. And he drew the angry conclusion that the Jews would always win thanks to their mastery of language. The true victor would always be the one who could win not through physical strength but through the powers of the mind. If, in one case, a people without a state was condemned to conquer in order to exist, and if, in the other, a people whose state was never able to give itself a name was sure of its victory thanks to the sovereignty of its word, this meant that the Jews were promised an eternal survival, endlessly punctuated by the terror of their potential disappearance or their fossilization. This was exactly what Freud had said.

An anarchist, materialist, atheist, anti-Zionist, homosexual, and pervert, Genet was thus defending the Palestinian cause in the same way as Chomsky, in terms that mean we cannot follow him. But, far from hating European or American language and culture, and rather than representing himself as the grand master of the sovereign power of meaninglessness, he attached his own fate as an old victim, fascinated by the murderers, to the fate of the three monotheisms, and even more to that of the first people, simultaneously chosen and accursed.

What Jews? What state? What catastrophe? What people?

In 1993, in a novel of great audacity, *Operation Shylock*, Philip Roth – who had also (like Genet, Freud, and Derrida) been called an anti-Semite – tried to reply to this question in fiction, by depicting the great Jewish obsession with identity, chosenness, dispersion, and catastrophe. So he invented a double of himself, named Moshe Pipik, a Jungian and a post-Zionist. To solve the new Jewish question bound up with the disastrous split between Israel and the diaspora, Pipik, the crazy double, forever seeking a land and an usurpation, set out to create a movement similar to the old form of Zionism: diasporism. Borrowing an identity from the real Roth, a Freudian writer, a neurotic, without a land of his own, and a friend of the Israeli writer Aharon Appelfeld, a survivor of the Shoah,[104] he proposed bringing back to Europe all the Ashkenazi Jews of Israel. They could then regenerate this old continent, which had lost its soul by trying to exterminate them all. Through this return to the Promised Land, the genius of Jewish history would be given a new lease on life: Hasidism, Jewishness, Haskalah, Zionism, socialism, communism, psychoanalysis, the works of Heine, Marx, Freud, Spinoza, Rosa Luxembourg, Proust, and Kafka.

Instead of celebrating 'next year in Jerusalem' every year, these new Jews would finally be able to celebrate the memory of their liberating departure and give the Arabs back their land, also leaving there the Sephardi Jews, who had long since been settled there, as well as the fanatics, racists, and fundamentalists: 'last year in Jerusalem', they would say, aware that they had finally won a historic victory over Hitler and Auschwitz. It is better to lose a state, Roth suggests, than to lose your soul at the risk of unleashing a nuclear war.[105]

We can imagine a sequel to this confession of the great Jewish writer of the diaspora at the end of the twentieth century. But it would be less droll and more tragic. It would tell the story of the spread, in Israeli public opinion, of the extravagant ideas of Yoram Hazony, ideas that run completely counter to those of the Freudian narrator and his fake Jungian double.

Born to Israeli parents who emigrated to the United States in 1965, Hazony had settled in Israel twenty years later, thereby coming full circle, like so many American Jews. Linked to the review *Commentary*, and heavily influenced by the teaching of Rabbi Meir Kahane,[106] who propounded a racist policy favourable to a Greater Israel and the expulsion of all Palestinians from the country, he founded the Shalem Centre in 1994, with other like-minded intellectuals, and launched a huge programme of investigation into Jewish history and Israeli political institutions.

Hazony became the leading light of a neo-Zionist movement, hostile both to the Israeli left and to the new post-Zionist historians and the best Israeli writers – Amos Oz, David Grossman, etc. At the end of 2000 – at the time of the Second Intifada[107] – he published a very anti-diasporic work in which he reinterpreted the history of Zionism since Theodor Herzl so as to promote a radical re-Judaization of the State of Israel: education was to refocused on Jewish values, Jewish patriotism was to be fostered, the Haskalah and the Enlightenment were to be consigned to oblivion, and a strong emphasis would be laid on the characteristics proper to the Jewish people and the 'Jewish soul'. In short, this strange return to Herzl bore a close resemblance to a return to Drumont, whom Herzl had challenged with the idea of a return to Zion.

Hazony violently attacked Aharon Appelfeld, Philip Roth's friend, accusing him of questioning in his autobiography the discipline imposed on him by the Tzahal during his military service. Hazony also denounced the conspiracy hatched by bad Jews,[108] secular and universalist, against the existence of Israel *as a Jewish state*. And he finally suggested solving the question of the nature of this state, which had been a controversial issue for sixty years, by suppressing the democratic principle from its foundations. In his view, this word – democracy – had become harmful in the face of the rise of the dual peril orchestrated, on the one hand, by de-Judaized Jews and, on the other, by the Arabs. According to Hazony, the State of Israel should no longer be Israeli, but Jewish, the preserve of Jewish citizens alone, albeit on condition that they agree to re-Judaize themselves and identify with a Jewish nation – a gentle euphemism for the 'Jewish race'.

The problem is that this idea, aiming at a transformation of the State of Israel, either into a theocracy like an Islamic Republic or into a dictatorship founded on racism and apartheid, or both at once, was adopted by its conservative leaders when faced with a Palestinian Authority that was itself outflanked by Hamas. Yet again, a racialist doctrine invented by academics, which should have been argued over by scholars, ended up serving the interests of a policy based on perpetual war.

Freud had imagined this nightmare when he had feared that racist Jews and anti-Semitic Arabs might clash in the Promised Land, between the Wailing Wall and the Dome of the Rock.

And since, at the dawn of the twenty-first century, this nightmare has become a reality, this means that the Israelis are now faced with a real choice: either turn their state into an even more secular and more egalitarian democracy, continuing to call it 'Israel', while admitting that a state where there is the rule of law can only be non-Jewish if it is to be truly democratic; or affirm the Jewish character of their state, thereby accepting that it will cease to be Israeli and democratic, becoming instead religious and racist.

In the first case, they would remain Jews, in the sense of Judaism or Jewishness, while being Israeli citizens, just as much as are non-Jews: one group of people living among another, capable of granting land to a people that had been robbed of it. In the second case, they would cease to be Israeli citizens, accepting that they are Jews in the sense of nation, ethnic group, race, and a vengeful and murderous God. They would then be sure that they had lost the essential feature in what comprises the universality of the Jewish people and its capacity to resist all catastrophes: a unique ability to transmit to mankind the idea that no person can be reduced to his or her community, roots, and territory.

For such is the history of Jacob, the biblical patriarch, the prophet of Islam, who gave his name to Israel: wounded by God, victor over God and himself, chosen by God to be a man among other men.

Notes

Introduction

1 Stéphane Amar, 'Cette maison est à nous, ce pays appartient au peuple d'Israël', *Libération*, 6 December 2008.

2 Islam is the third monotheistic religion, founded in the seventh century by Muhammad. It derives from Judaism and acknowledges the authority of its prophets, of Abraham and Moses, so it is labelled an Abrahamic religion. Judaism is a religion of Halakha, Islam a religion of sharia: in both cases, the law handed down by God regulates the believer's life: law, worship, ethics, and social behaviour. The word 'Muslim' designates those who profess Islam. The word 'Islamic' refers to Islam as a religion. Islamism is a political doctrine that sprang up in the twentieth century, and so-called radical Islamism is a more intense form of Islamism that aims to establish, in the name of God's law, a theologico-political regime to take over from pre-existing secular states. But Islam, like other religions, also refers to a whole culture. 'Fundamentalism', in Christianity, designates the strict adherence to a doctrine. (In French there are two terms, *'intégrisme'* and *'fondamentalisme'*, the former referring to Protestantism, the latter to Catholicism, but they have both been extended to Judaism and to Islam.)

3 In French, the word *'Juif'* is written with a capital letter to designate Jews in the sense of *'Judéité'* (who together comprise a people) while *'juif'* in lower case designates Jews in the sense of *'Judaïté'*(those who practise the Jewish religion, or Judaism, similar to Christians or Muslims).

4 The neologism 'Islamophobia' designates a defamation of Islam and is seen as a form of racism, while the Universal Declaration of Human Rights, in which no breach of God's rights is admissible in law, regards

this type of remark as a case of blasphemy. Islamophobia, Judaeophobia, Christianophobia, and their opposites, Judaeophilia, Islamophilia, Christianophilia, and philosemitism are ambiguous neologisms – to be used with caution.

5 Cf. 'Les racines de l'antisémitisme arabe', press cuttings, *Courrier international*, February–March–April 2009, special number, pp. 12 and 13. And remarks made in 2009 against Zionism and its 'accomplices' by the Egyptian *ulema* Alla Said and then broadcast on the Al-Rahma television channel, 2 January 2009.

6 The *Protocols* are a document fabricated in 1903 by an agent of the Russian secret police, Matvei Golovinski (1865–1920), and designed to prove the existence of an alleged plot fomented by a group of Jewish sages bent on exterminating Christianity. See Roger Garaudy, *The mythical foundations of Israeli policy* (London: Studies Forum International, 1997): this is available online at: https://ia700308.us.archive .org/19/items/TheFoundingMythsOfIsraeliPolitics/RGfounding.pdf (accessed 8 January 2013). (There is only one French edition of *Mein Kampf*, published in 1934.)

7 PLO: Palestine Liberation Organization, whose (secular) charter, enacted in 1964, was declared 'null and void' in 1989 by Yasser Arafat, who in 1959 had founded Fatah, the main organization for national resistance to the State of Israel. In this declaration, Arafat recognized the existence of this state. Hamas: Islamic resistance movement, an offshoot of the Palestinian branch of the Muslim Brotherhood (who deny the right of the State of Israel to exist).

8 The founding text of the Charter of Hamas: it can be found online at, e.g., www.thejerusalemfund.org/www.thejerusalemfund.org/carryover/ documents/charter.html (accessed 16 September 2012). See also Charles Enderlin, *Le grand aveuglement: Israël et l'irrésistible ascension de l'islam radical* (Paris: Albin Michel, 2009).

9 Torrents of insults of this kind, with the inventing of neologisms playing a key part, are poured forth on the Internet the whole time.

Chapter 1   Our First Parents

1 Jacobus de Voragine (1230–1298) was the author of a famous collection of legends and lives of saints, *The Golden Legend*. The story of Judas is told in the life of St Matthias: see http://saints.sqpn.com/ the-golden-legend-the-life-of-saint-matthias/ (accessed 16 December 2012). Freud did not know this story; nor did Otto Rank, who does not mention it in *The myth of the birth of the hero: a psychological exploration of myth*, trans. Gregory C. Richter and E. James Lieberman (Baltimore and London: Johns Hopkins University Press, 2004).

2 The Nineteenth Ecumenical Council convened by Pope Paul III in 1545, in response to the demands of Martin Luther in the context of

the Protestant Reformation. This council marked a split between the mediaeval Church and the Church of classical times. Against the anti-Judaism of Luther, the council decreed: 'If a reason is sought why the son of God underwent such a painful passion, it will be found that it lies, apart from the hereditary sin of our first parents, in the sins and crimes that men, and not the Jews, have committed since the beginning of the world . . .' In 1959, the reference to 'perfidious Jews' was suppressed from the Friday liturgies by John XXIII.

3 Jean-Louis Schefer, *L'hostie profanée: histoire d'une fiction théologique* (Paris: POL, 2007). See also Léon Poliakov, *The history of anti-Semitism*, trans. Richard Howard et al., 4 vols (London: Routledge & Kegan Paul, 1974–85). The first expulsion of the Jews from France took place in 1306, in the reign of Philip the Fair, and the second was decreed by Charles VI in 1394: see Gilbert Dahan (ed.), *L'expulsion des Juifs de France, 1394* (Paris: Cerf, 2004).

4 In 1054 occurred the great schism within Christianity, which had originally been both catholic (universal) and orthodox (resting on a dogma). This schism marked the separation between the Western Church (Catholic and Roman) and the Eastern Church (Orthodox).

5 Ludwig Börne, *Lettres écrites de Paris pendant les années 1830 et 1831*, trans. F. Guiran (Paris: Paulin, 1832), 7 February 1832. This letter is quoted by Hannah Arendt in *The origins of totalitarianism*, new edn (New York: Harcourt Brace Jovanovich, 1973), p. 64. Ludwig Börne (1786–1837) was the assumed name of Loeb Baruch: he is considered, together with Heinrich Heine, as the representative of a radical literary movement that contributed to the 1848 revolutions. See chapter 2.

6 See Martin Goodman, *Rome and Jerusalem: the clash of ancient civilizations* (London: Penguin, 2008).

7 In Genesis, Ishmael is the first son of Abraham and Hagar, the Egyptian servant girl of his wife Sarah. Only Isaac, the son of Sarah and Abraham, would be God's chosen. Ishmael was thus excluded from the covenant, but Muslims view him as the father of the lineage of Arabs and the Arabic language and a forebear of the Prophet Muhammad.

8 As was Spinoza, but for the opposite reasons. The *herem* is a procedure of exclusion proper to the Jewish community, which the Christian tradition identified with excommunication.

9 Dulcigno is in present-day Montenegro.

10 Gershom Scholem, *Major trends in Jewish mysticism* (New York: Schocken Books, 1995), p. 350. Israel ben Eliezer, known as the Baal Shem Tov (1700–1760), was the founder of the new Hasidic Judaism (different from that of the mediaeval period), which advocated the return to a religious spirituality, with the aim of comforting the Jewish people in the face of persecutions. In this sense, it opposed the movement of Jewish Enlightenment or Haskala (see below), which tended to the de-Judaizing of the Jews. The two movements shared the idea of a potential 'regeneration' of the Jews. See also the *Geschichte der*

Juden by Heinrich Graetz (1811–1891), the complete text of which is available on the Internet in English as *History of the Jews*: http:// archive.org/details/historyofje02grae.

11 Jacques Le Goff, *Héros du Moyen Âge, le Saint et le Roi* (Paris: Gallimard, 2004), pp. 865–6.

12 The decrees on purity of blood, which later became laws, were struck down in 1865, with a brief interruption during the reign of Joseph Bonaparte (1808–12). See Yosef Hayim Yerushalmi, 'L'antisémitisme racial est-il apparu au XXe siècle? De la *Limpieza de sangre* en Espagne au nazisme: continuités et ruptures', *Esprit*, 150, March–April 1993.

13 The term 'marrano', in fact, is still used today [in French, *marrane*] to define an inner mode of resistance to an oppressive institution.

14 Members of the Mahamad, the secular authority that ruled the Jewish community in Amsterdam.

15 Henry Méchoulan, 'L'excommunication de Spinoza', *Cahiers Spinoza*, 3 (1980), p. 133.

16 Ibid., pp. 127–8: English translation in *The Jew in the Modern World: a documentary history*, ed. Paul Mendes-Flohr and Jehuda Reinharz, 2nd edn (New York: Oxford University Press, 1995), p. 57.

17 Spinoza, *Tractatus theologico-politicus*, para. 105 (Elwes translation, 1883).

18 See Daniel Lindenberg, *Figures d'Israël* (Paris: Hachette-Littératures, 1997), pp. 168–70. On prosecutors of thought, see chapter 7.

19 See Dominique Bourel, 'Humanisme juif et philosophie des Lumières: en Allemagne: Moses Mendelssohn', in *Colloque des intellectuels juifs de langue française*, 3: *L'idée d'humanité* (Paris: Albin Michel, 1994).

20 This is how Hannah Arendt interprets Mendelssohn's message in 'The Enlightenment and the Jewish question', in Arendt, *The Jewish writings*, ed. Jerome Kohn and Ron H. Feldman (New York: Schocken Books, 2007), pp. 3–18, at p. 9. Orthodox Jews would reject the very principle of this Jewish Enlightenment, advocating values that were the opposite of reform.

21 See also Michael Löwy, 'Humanisme juif et philosophie des Lumières', in *Colloque des intellectuels juifs de langue française*, 3: *L'idée d'humanité*, pp. 148–59.

22 Article 'Juif' ('Jew') in the *Encyclopédie* (1750), with an introduction by the Chevalier de Jaucourt. While the sovereigns of Christendom used the term 'first parent' to designate Judaism, Enlightenment philosophers tended to describe it instead as the 'mother religion'.

23 Ibid.

24 This is the expression used by Dominique Bourel. See also Enzo Traverso, *The Jews of Germany: from the 'Judeo-German symbiosis' to the memory of Auschwitz*, trans. Daniel Weissbort (Lincoln, and London: University of Nebraska Press, 1995), and Jacques Ehrenfreund, *Mémoire juive et nationalité allemande: les juifs berlinois à la Belle Époque* (Paris: PUF, 2000).

25 D'Holbach, *L'esprit du judaïsme ou Examen raisonné de la loi de Moïse et de son influence sur la religion chrétienne* (London: 1770).

26 Voltaire, article 'Jews', in *Philosophical Dictionary*, trans. J. Hunt and H. L. Hunt, 2 vols (Whitefish, MT: Kessinger, 2003), vol. 2, p. 68. This work was condemned by the Parlement and by Rome. See also Voltaire, *An essay on universal history: the manners and spirit of nations*, trans. Thomas Nugent (Edinburgh: William Creech, 1782), especially the Introduction.

27 Jean-Jacques Rousseau, *Emile*, trans. Allan Bloom (Harmondsworth: Penguin, 1979), p. 304.

28 Montesquieu, *The Persian Letters*, trans. Margaret Mauldon (Oxford: Oxford University Press, 2008), pp. 78–9.

29 This was the term used at the time.

30 This is contrary to what is claimed by Pierre-André Taguieff: he decontextualizes the quotations from Voltaire and neglects the *herem* of which Spinoza was the victim, thereby turning them both into Judaeophobes and thus anti-Semites (*La judéophobie des modernes: des Lumières au Jihad mondial* (Paris: Odile Jacob, 2008), p. 95). The allegation that the Enlightenment was anti-Semitic had already been made in 1968 by the conservative American rabbi Arthur Hertzberg (1921–2006), who was violently opposed to any French-style secularism. According to him, anti-Semitism was invented by the Enlightenment *philosophes* and the revolutionaries of 1789, who, while emancipating the Jews, were in fact their worst enemies since they wished to impose citizenship upon them. Thus, Hertzberg preferred Christian anti-Judaism to Enlightenment anti-Semitism. This is of no help at all in understanding the genesis of anti-Semitism. See his *The French Enlightenment and the Jews* (New York: Columbia University Press, 1968). Cardinal Jean-Marie Lustiger also shared this view: 'The Enlightenment led to Auschwitz.' For this reason, he opposed the transfer of the ashes of Abbé Grégoire [an 'enlightened' priest who promoted universal suffrage and racial equality – Trans.] to the Panthéon on 12 December 1989. And for the same reason he also attacked Nietzsche, Marx, and Freud: see Lustiger, *Le choix de Dieu: entretiens avec Jean-Louis Missika et Dominique Wolton* (Paris: Fallois, 1978).

Within the same context, we should note that it is now the Christian far right, in alliance with Jewish fundamentalists, which takes advantage of this contemporary propensity to describe Voltaire as an anti-Semite, not only so as to exonerate Pius XII from any collaboration with the Nazis but also to ascribe to Voltaire the source of Hitler's anti-Semitism. From this point of view, 'Christian anti-Judaism' could be forgiven, since the Catholic Church has uttered its *mea culpa* for the genocide of the Jews, while 'Enlightenment atheism', which prefigured communism, socialism, and thus the whole of the modern left, fully deserves to be condemned since it was – so the claim goes – responsible in advance for genocide. See Paolo Quintili, *Voltaire: il manifesto dell'antisemitismo modern, a cura del padre della tolleranza*, with a commentary by Elena Loewenthal (Milan: Claudio Gallone, 1997).

31   Theodor Lessing, *Der jüdische Selbsthass* (Munich: Matthes & Seitz, 1984).

32   See, in particular, Poliakov, *The history of anti-Semitism*, quoted in Taguieff, *La judéophobie des modernes*. See also Hertzberg, *The French Enlightenment and the Jews*; and especially Robert Misrahi, *Marx et la question juive* (Paris: Gallimard, 1972). Michael Löwy goes so far as to claim that Abbé Grégoire revealed his anti-Semitism by trying to 'regenerate' the Jews ('Humanisme juif'). But the idea that Marx was anti-Semitic developed long before all this literature: see Franz Mehring, *Karl Marx: the story of his life*, trans. Edward Fitzgerald (Brighton: Harvester Press, 1981; first published in German, 1918). Gérard Bloch questioned this approach in his French translation of this work (*Vie de Karl Marx* (Paris: PIE, 1984)), and several authors have done likewise, including Robert Mandrou, in his Introduction to the new edition of the French translation (*A propos de la question juive* (Paris: UGE, 1968)) of Marx's *On the Jewish Question*. The best commentary is that of Élisabeth de Fontenay, *Figures juives de Marx* (Paris: Galilée, 1973), which has points in common with Arendt, 'The Enlightenment and the Jewish question'. See also Zeev Sternhell, *La droite révolutionnaire 1885–1914: les origines françaises du fascisme*, new edn (Paris: Fayard, 1997; first published in 1978), and Lionel Richard, 'Anachronisme et contresens: Karl Marx, juif antisémite?', *Le Monde diplomatique*, September 2005, as well as the excellent analysis by Enzo Traverso, *The Marxists and the Jewish question: the history of a debate, 1843–1943*, trans. Bernard Gibbons (Atlantic Highlands, NJ: Humanities Press, 1993). Marx's text *On the Jewish Question* is published in Marx, *Early Writings*, trans. Tom Nairn (London: Penguin, 1992), and online (see note 40, below).

33   See François Furet, *Interpreting the French Revolution*, trans. Elborg Forster (Cambridge: Cambridge University Press; Paris: Maison des Sciences de l'Homme, 1981), and *The passing of an illusion: the idea of communism in the twentieth century*, trans. Deborah Furet (Chicago and London: University of Chicago Press, 1999). For a critique of the idea that the revolution ultimately became hateful, see Olivier Bétourné and Aglaia I. Hartig, *Penser l'histoire de la révolution: deux siècles de passion française* (Paris: La Découverte, 1989). We owe to André Glucksmann the absurd idea that Hegel, Marx, and German philosophy produced the Gulag – and also the extermination of the Jews. See his *The Master Thinkers*, trans. Brian Pearce (Brighton: Harvester Press, 1980).

34   I have tackled this question in *Philosophers in turbulent times: Canguilhem, Sartre, Foucault, Althusser, Deleuze, Derrida*, trans. William McCuaig (New York and Chichester: Columbia University Press, 2010), and *La part obscure de nous-mêmes: une histoire des pervers* (Paris: Albin Michel, 2007).

35   Misrahi, *Marx et la question juive*, pp. 223–7. Conversely, in the English- and Geman-speaking worlds, there has often been too much

of a tendency to re-Judaize Marx and turn him into a prophet of Israel, the bearer of a new type of messianism, regarding the proletariat as the chosen people and calling on the Jews to emancipate themselves from the 'capitalism golden calf'. On this point, too, see Traverso, *The Marxists and the Jewish question.*

36   See Jacques Le Rider, *Modernity and crises of identity: culture and society in fin-de-siècle Vienna*, trans. Rosemary Morris (Cambridge: Polity, 1993). The notorious quotations from Marx's correspondence were collected by Léon Poliakov and have since been quoted ad nauseam.

37   In this respect, Marx was less representative of Jewish self-hatred than the Viennese Jews of the end of the nineteenth century, born after 1850.

38   Paul Giniewski, *Simone Weil ou La haine de soi* (Paris: Berg International, 1978), p. 287.

39   Marx, letter to Arnold Ruge, 13 March 1843, available at: www .marxists.org/archive/marx/works/1843/letters/43_03_13.htm.

40   Marx, *On the Jewish Question*, available at: www.marxists.org/ archive/marx/works/1844/jewish-question.

41   Élisabeth de Fontenay provides us with a magisterial commentary on these two references by Marx to Jewish history. His words here can be found in the second section of Book 1, ch. 4: they were suppressed by the French communists to be replaced by: 'There is here no antagonism, as in the case of hoarding, between the money and commodities. The capitalist knows that all commodities, however scurvy they may look, or however badly they may smell, are in faith and in truth money, and what is more, a wonderful means whereby to make money.' See Marx, *Capital*, vol. 1, Part II, ch. 4, available online at: www.marxists. org/archive/marx/works/1867-c1/ch04.htm. See also Traverso, *The Marxists and the Jewish question.*

42   With the exception of Karl Eugen Dühring (1823–1921). After being attacked by Marx and Engels, Dühring accused the Jews of being responsible for his expulsion from the University of Berlin, and in 1880 he published one of the first anti-Semitic texts of a biological stamp. See Arendt, *The origins of totalitarianism* (New York: Harcourt Brace Jovanovich, 1973), p. 35.

43   Montesquieu, 'Mes pensées', in *Oeuvres complètes*, vol. 1 (Paris: Gallimard), p. 98. We should note that, in 1890, Friedrich Engels condemned, in the firmest way possible, any form of anti-Semitism. See Traverso, *The Marxists and the Jewish question*, p. 26.

Chapter 2   The Shadow of the Camps and the Smoke of the Ovens

1   Augustin de Barruel (1741–1820) was one of the instigators of those conspiracy theories that continued to target freemasons and Jews: see his *Mémoires pour servir l'histoire du jacobinisme* (1797–8).

2 Marx and Engels, *Manifesto of the Communist Party*, available at: www.marxists.org/archive/marx/works/1848/communist-manifesto/ ch01.htm.

3 Joseph de Maistre, *Considerations on France*, trans. and ed. Richard A. Lebrun (Cambridge: Cambridge University Press, 1994).

4 The best book on this question is by Maurice Olender, *The languages of paradise: race, religion, and philology in the nineteenth century*, trans. Arthur Goldhammer (Cambridge, MA: Harvard University Press, 1992). Olender studies the works of Johann Gottfried Herder (1744–1803), Ernest Renan (1823–1898), Friedrich Max Müller (1823–1900), Adolphe Pictet (1799–1875), Rudolf Friedrich Grau (1835–1893), and, finally, Ignaz Isaac Goldziher (1850–1921), who was the only one to criticize the foundations of the use of the infernal couple and who became one of the founding figures of the modern study of Islam. See Jean-Pierre Vernant's foreword, ibid.: 'In these two linked but asymmetrical mirror-images, these projections in which nine-teenth-century scholars attempted to discern their own image, we cannot today fail to see looming in the background the dark silhouette of the death camps and the rising smoke of the ovens' (p. xi).

5 On the metamorphoses of the question of race war, see Michel Fou-cault, *'Society must be defended': lectures at the Collège de France, 1975–6*, ed. Mauro Bertani and Alessandro Fontana, trans. David Macey (London: Penguin, 2004).

6 The term 'Semite' is derived from Sem or Shem, the name of one of Noah's three sons (the other two being Ham and Japheth), ancestor of Abraham, from whom sprang the Hebrews, Arabs, Aramaeans, Phoenicians, and Elamites. The so-called Aryan languages, derived from Sanskrit, were – on this view – originally spoken by the Latins, Slavs, Greeks, Celts, Germanic peoples, and Persians, all stemming from the Indo-European group. This confuses the Indo-Europeans, peoples of Europe and Asia, with the so-called Aryans, who existed solely in the theoretical imaginings of nineteenth-century philologists who wanted to set them up in opposition to the Semites.

7 The French term *racisme* appeared in 1894, penned by a collaborator on *La libre parole*, the journal of Édouard Drumont.

8 Renan, *Histoire générale et système comparé des langues sémitiques* (Paris: L'Imprimerie impériale, 1855). This work was republished many times. Renan was a supporter of Darwin, even though the latter's ideas, in *The Origin of Species*, were quite different from his own.

9 This is the expression used by Maurice Olender.

10 In the historical, not the biological sense of the term.

11 Renan, *Histoire générale*, book 1, p. 476.

12 Zeev Sternhell, *La droite révolutionnaire 1885–1914: les origines françaises du fascisme*, new edn (Paris: Fayard, 1997), p. 20.

13 Renan, 'Qu'est-ce qu'une nation?' (1882). Quoted in Sternhell, *La droite révolutionnaire*, pp. 19–20.

14 This was the result of the way his sister Élisabeth Förster, an anti-Semite and supporter of Hitler, falsified his work.

15 Nietzsche, *Human, all-too-human: a book for free spirits*, trans. R. J. Hollingdale (Cambridge: Cambridge University Press, 1996), p. 175.

16 Nietzsche, letter to Theodor Fritsch, 29 March 1887. Available at: www.consciencia.org/nietzsches-letters-1887. See Jacques Le Rider, *L'Allemagne au temps du réalisme: de l'espoir au désenchantement (1848–1890)* (Paris: Albin Michel, 2008), especially pp. 422–32 on Nietzsche's alleged anti-Semitism. Theodor Fritsch (1852–1933), a disciple of Wilhelm Marr and the first German translator of *The Protocols of the Elders of Zion*, wrote a review of *Beyond Good and Evil*. He declared that he had found in it an 'exaltation of the Jews' and a 'harsh condemnation of anti-Semitism', and he considered Nietzsche to be a 'superficial philosopher' who had 'no understanding of the essence of the nation'.

17 Joseph Arthur de Gobineau, *Essai sur l'origine des races humaines* (1855), vol. 1 (Paris: Gallimard), p. 306. An early translation of this was *The moral and intellectual diversity of races* (1856), republished with an editor's note by Robert Bernasconi (Bristol: Thoemmes Press, 2002).

18 This is partly the argument of Pierre-André Taguieff, who takes a stand against the presentation of Gobineau's work as a racist theory for the use of anti-fascists, and contrasts the good racialism of the count with the bad racialism of Vacher de Lapouge and the Nazis: 'After 1945', he writes, 'a reversal of this ideological evaluation could not fail to happen: anti-Gobinism was mechanically integrated into anti-fascism as one of its cultural components. Gobineau's work became a source of shame for France': Taguieff, *La couleur et le sang: doctrines racistes à la française* (Paris: Mille et une nuits, 2002), p. 58. See also the article in the French Wikipedia on Gobineau and the article by Jean Gaulmier in the *Encyclopaedia Universalis*.

19 Claude Lévi-Strauss, *Race et histoire* (Paris: Gallimard, 1987), p. 10. Lévi-Strauss never concealed his admiration for some of Gobineau's works.

20 August Bebel (1840–1913) was one of the founders of the German Social Democratic Party and is famous for his works in favour of cultural diversity.

21 See Le Rider, *L'Allemagne au temps du réalisme*, pp. 137–42.

22 There were 7,000 Jews resident in Vienna in 1857 and 175,000 in 1910.

23 Quoted by Claude Klein in his 'Essai sur le sionisme: de l'État des Juifs à l'État d'Israël', in Theodor Herzl, *L'État des Juifs* (Paris: La Découverte, 2008), p. 129.

24 In anti-Semitic discourse, the Jew is always the embodiment of a so-called perverse sexuality: so he is viewed as being as dangerous as the homosexual or the transvestite. The worst type of Jew, in the eyes of the anti-Semite, is the Jewish woman, the 'feminized' Jew, or the

intellectual Jew, incapable of so-called virile activity. The hatred of women or homosexuals is often the sign of a disguised anti-Semitism. Hence the way that Jewish self-hatred goes together with a rejection of the Jew's alleged 'feminity'.

25 Carl Schorske, *Fin-de-siècle Vienna: politics and culture* (Cambridge: Cambridge University Press, 1981). See also Le Rider, *Modernity and crises of identity: culture and society in fin-de-siècle Vienna*, trans. Rosemary Morris (Cambridge: Polity, 1993).

26 Sternhell, *La droite révolutionnaire*, p. 191.

27 Moritz Steinschneider (1816–1907), *Hebräische Bibliographie: Blätter für neuere und ältere Literatur des Judenthums*, vol. 3 (Berlin, 1860). Heymann (Hayim) Steinthal (1823–1899), 'Zur Charakteristik der Semitischen Völker', *Zeitschrift für Völkerpsychologie und Sprachwissenschaft*, 4 (1860). See also Gilles Karmazyn, 'L'"antisémitisme": une hostilité contre les Juifs. Genèse du terme et signification commune', 2002, available at: www.phdn.org/antisem/antisemitismelemot.html.

28 Édouard Drumont, *La France juive: essai d'histoire contemporaine* (Paris: Ernest Flammarion & Charles Marpon, 1886). The first edition of the book, presented in two volumes with a total of 1,200 pages, sold 65,000 copies, and the work went through 150 editions. I am here quoting the 1887 edition, illustrated with 'scenes, views, portraits, maps and plans by our best artists' (Paris: Librairie Blériot, 954 pp.). See also Grégoire Kauffmann, *Édouard Drumont* (Paris: Perrin, 2008). On French anti-Semites of left and right – Joseph Proudhon, Maurice Barrès, Jules Guérin, Alphonse Toussenel, Gustave Tridon, Georges Vacher de Lapouge, Charles Maurras, etc. – see Sternhell, *La droite révolutionnaire*.

29 Drumont, *La France juive*, p. 154.

30 Ibid., p. 95.

31 Drumont draws particularly on the ideas of Théodule Ribot (1839–1916), a French psychologist and a supporter of theories of hereditary degeneracy and the inequality of races. In a celebrated work of 1873, *Heredity* (Eng. trans., 1875), he postulated that the formation of a nation resulted from physiological and psychological laws. I have given the name 'the unconscious French-style' to a pattern of thinking that has come down from this doctrine and has been constantly adapted by anti-Freudians such as Marcel Gauchet, Jacqueline Carroy, and the authors of *The Black Book of Communism* (by Stéphane Courtois et al.; trans. Jonathan Murphy and Mark Kramer, Cambridge, MA, and London: Harvard University Press, 1999). See Élisabeth Roudinesco, *Histoire de la psychanalyse en France*, 2 vols (Paris: Fayard, 1994); new edn (Paris: Hachette, 2009). On the way Max Nordau adapted the idea of degeneracy, see below.

32 Drumont, *La France juive*, p. 157. 'Say Jew and what you really mean is Protestant', as Alphonse Toussenel put it in *les Juifs, rois de l'époque: histoire de la féodalité financière*, published the same year as *La France juive* (1886).

33   The current opponents of the spirit of the Enlightenment, who claim that the latter 'leads to Auschwitz', are merely unwittingly repeating, in an inverted form, Drumont's ideas.

34   Drumont, *La France juive*, p. 318.

35   Ibid., p. 107.

36   This idea would be repeated by the Nazi perpetrators of genocide: it was uttered in these words by Rudolf Höss, the commandant at Auschwitz. See Roudinesco, *La part obscure de nous-mêmes: une histoire des pervers* (Paris: Albin Michel, 2007), especially the chapter 'Les aveux d'Auschwitz'.

37   Drumont, *La France juive*, pp. 283 and 806.

38   Henri Meschonnic and Manaka Ôno, *Victor Hugo et la Bible* (Paris: Maisonneuve & Larose, 2001), p. 22.

39   Following the assassination of Tsar Alexander II in March 1881, the Russian Jews had been accused of plotting against the regime and subjected to persecution.

40   Victor Hugo, *Oeuvres complètes*, ed. Jean Massin (Paris: Le Club français du livre), vol. 6 (1966), p. 1232.

41   Drumont, *La France juive*, p. 913.

42   Georges Bernanos, *La grande peur des bien-pensants* (Paris: Le livre de poche, 1998; first published 1930), p. 169. This work was followed by 'A propos de l'antisémitisme de Drumont' (1939), 'Encore la question juive' (1944), and 'L'honneur est ce qui nous rassemble . . .' (1949). The theme of the Jew as a poisoner, with Mongol features, is characteristic of anti-Semitic discourse. When he wrote these lines, Bernanos was quite aware that Clemenceau had been one of the main figures to take up the cause of Dreyfus.

43   Ibid., pp. 391 and 395.

44   Quoted in Kauffmann, *Édouard Drumont*, p. 17. Bernanos ascribed this rumour to Abraham Dreyfus, a dramatist quoted in *La France juive*, and he accused the communist Paul Lafargue of having spread it, which enables him to take up (likewise without the slightest humour) the defence of a Drumont who was a 'victim of the Jews and the communists' before adding these words: 'Around 1908, the same editorial offices were filled with the rumour that Maurice Barrès was descended from Portuguese Jews': see Bernanos, *La grande peur des bien-pensants*, p. 39.

45   Léon Bloy, *Le salut par les Juifs* (Paris: Mercure de France, 1892).

46   Ibid., pp. 13–14.

47   Ibid., pp. 40–1.

48   Bernard Lazare (1865–1903): socialist and anarchist, highly anti-religious, he was the first French Dreyfusard. He later briefly moved in the circles of Theodor Herzl, while remaining a socialist Zionist of the diaspora.

49   See Christian Jambet (ed.), *Léon Bloy* (Paris: Éditions de l'Herne, 2003), and Pierre Glaudes (ed.), *Léon Bloy au tournant du siècle* (Toulouse: Presses universitaires du Mirail, 2003), especially the article by Rachel Goitein.

50 Bernard Lazare, *Histoire de l'antisémitisme: son histoire et ses causes* (1849), followed by *Contre l'antisémitisme* (1895). The two works were republished in dubious conditions, with prefaces by the Holocaust denier Pierre Guillaume (Paris: La Différence, 1982 and 1983 respectively).

51 Hannah Arendt, *Jewish Writings*, ed. Jerome Kohn and Ron H. Feldman (New York: Schocken Books, 2007), pp. 283–6.

52 Adolf Hitler, letter of 16 September 1919, quoted in Eberhard Jäkel, 'L'élimination des Juifs dans le programme de Hitler', in *L'Allemagne nazie et le génocide des Juifs* (Paris: Gallimard & Le Seuil, 1985), p. 101.

53 Emmanuel Beau de Loménie, *Drumont ou l'anticapitalisme national* (Paris: Pauvert, 1968), p. 12.

54 In a text written in 1946–7, Bernanos contented himself with referring to 'the countless Jewish graves of this war', paying homage to a Jewish friend of his son who had died fighting for France. See 'L'honneur est ce qui nous rassemble' (1949), reprinted in *La grande peur des bien-pensants*, p. 401.

55 Bernanos, 'Encore la question juive', in *La grande peur des bien-pensants*, pp. 397–9. Although he said that he felt uneasy at 'the anti-Semitism of Bernanos', Élie Wiesel declared in 1988: 'I cannot harbour ill-feeling against Bernanos, who had the courage to oppose fascism, to denounce anti-Semitism, and to say precisely the things he said and wrote about the beauty of being Jewish, the honour of being Jewish and the duty of remaining Jewish' (ibid., p. 13).

56 'In Bernanos', as Bernard Lonjon emphasizes, 'the enemy is the person who hates his neighbour whatever that neighbour may do or say': in 'La psychose de l'ennemi chez l'écrivain', *Société*, 80/2 (2003), p. 37.

57 Especially with Houston Stewart Chamberlain (1855–1927), a writer of English origin and German nationality, the son-in-law of Richard Wagner, who had a great influence in Austria. See also Schorske, *Fin-de-siècle Vienna*.

58 The term 'degeneracy' was invented in 1857 by the French psychiatrist Bénédict-Augustin Morel (1809–1873) to denote an illness that marked a deviation from an ideal primitive type. It was taken up by Max Nordau.

59 The communist new man is called upon to regenerate himself by manual work.

60 See chapter 3. I have also tackled this question in *La part obscure de nous-mêmes*.

61 The appeal was signed by Sigmund Freud and Havelock Ellis.

62 See Hannah Arendt, *Imperialism*, the second part of *Origins of totalitarianism*. See also André Pichot, *Aux origines des théories raciales: de la Bible à Darwin* (Paris: Flammarion, 2008).

63 As against the biblical precepts that defended the idea of a unity to the human race (fixist monogenism), some Enlightenment philosophers (especially Voltaire) adopted a polygenist thesis, according to which the origin of mankind was founded on the existence of a

plurality of races. To isolate peoples from one another in an arbitrary way, following the principle of a dangerous differentialism, polygenism would lead to racism – in other words, to the notion of inequality between races – while Darwin himself had maintained the monogenist idea without thinking of it in essentialist terms.

64 This racist thesis was taken up by the proponents of deep ecology, for instance Peter Singer. I present a critique of it in *La part obscure de nous-mêmes*. Haeckel was also the inventor of the word 'ecology' (1866). See also Élisabeth de Fontenay, 'Pourquoi les animaux n'auraient-ils pas droit à un droit d'animaux?', *Le Débat*, 109, March–April 2000.

65 Robert Gerwarth and Stephan Malinovski, 'L'antichambre de l'Holocauste?', *Vingtième Siècle: Revue d'histoire*, 99, July–September 2008. The two authors draw a connection between the massacres committed by the Germans in Southwest Africa, between 1904 and 1907, and the genocide of the Jews.

66 See Paul Weindling, *L'hygiène de la race*, vol. 1: *Hygiène raciale et eugénisme médical en Allemagne, 1870–1933* (Paris: La Découverte, 1998), with a preface by Benoît Massin.

67 *Hitler speaks: a series of political conversations with Hitler on his real aims* (London: Butterworth, 1939), pp. 231–8, and Norman Cohn, *Warrant for genocide: the myth of the Jewish world conspiracy and The Protocols of the Elders of Zion*, new edn (London: Serif, 1996), ch. 8.

68 The generic name of Auschwitz symbolizes the genocide of the Jews by the Nazis, i.e., in total, some 5.5 million Jews exterminated in the context of the Final Solution. Within five years, 1.3 million men, women, and children were deported to the camp at Auschwitz and 1.1 million exterminated, 90 per cent of them Jews. Placed under the control of Heinrich Himmler, Auschwitz was an industrial complex composed of three camps: Auschwitz I (the main camp), a concentration camp, opened on 20 May 1940; Auschwitz II–Birkenau, a concentration and extermination camp (gas chambers and ovens), opened on 8 October 1941; and Auschwitz III–Monowitz, a labour camp for the IG Farben factories, opened on 31 May 1942. This overall arrangement was supplemented by some fifty or so small camps scattered across the region and placed under the same administration. The name 'Auschwitz' is also the signifier of the extermination by the Nazis of Jews, gypsies, and all those who represented races deemed to be 'impure'.

Chapter 3   Promised Land, Conquered Land

1 Mount Zion is the hill on which Jerusalem is built.
2 A Yiddish term referring to a victim of permanent bad luck.

3 Adalbert von Chamisso, *The true history of Peter Schlemihl* (1814).

4 Leon Pinsker (1821–1891): Russian-Polish Jew, a proponent of the Haskala. Disturbed by the Russian pogroms of 1881, he published in Berlin a work entitled *Self-Emancipation*, which led to his becoming the intellectual guide of the group the Lovers of Zion.

5 See Georges Bensoussan, *Une histoire intellectuelle et politique du sionisme, 1860–1940* (Paris: Fayard, 2002).

6 This is the term used by Hannah Arendt in *Verborgene Tradition: Acht Essays* (Frankfurt am Main: Suhrkamp, 1976); see also 'The Jew as pariah: a hidden tradition', in *Jewish Writings*, ed. Jerome Kohn and Ron H. Feldman (New York: Schocken Books, 2007), pp. 275–97.

7 The best study of this is by Henry Laurens, *La question de Palestine*, vol. 1: *1799–1922: L'invention de la terre sainte* (Paris: Fayard, 2003); vol. 2, *1922–1947: Une mission sacrée de la civilisation* (Paris: Fayard, 2003); vol. 3, *1947–1967: L'accomplissement des prophéties* (Paris: Fayard, 2007).

8 Arendt, *Origins of Totalitarianism*, pp. xviiff.

9 Apparently by Charles Péguy.

10 Between 1870 and 1913, the French colonial empire expanded from 1 million to 13 million square kilometres, and the colonized peoples from 7 to 48 million individuals. See Olivier Lecour-Grandmaison, *La République impériale: politique et racisme d'état* (Paris: Fayard, 2009), p. 15.

11 Ibid., p. 7.

12 Ibid. Speech to the Chamber of Deputies, 28 July 1885.

13 Francis Garnier, *La Cochinchine française en 1864* (Paris: Dentu, 1864), pp. 44–5.

14 Georges Clemenceau, speech of 30 July 1885 to the Chamber of Deputies, quoted in Lecour-Grandmaison, *La République impérial*, p. 7.

15 Alsace and Lorraine became *Elsass-Lothringen* by the Treaty of Frankfurt signed between France and Germany on 10 May 1871.

16 Quoted by Sven Lindqvist, *Exterminate all the brutes*, trans. Joan Tate (London: Granta, 1997), p. 144. Friedrich Ratzel (1844–1904) was a German zoologist and geographer, the author of a work called *Anthropo-Geographie* (1891) which aimed to re-establish the human element in geography: 'Mankind is a part of the globe'. He opposed the imperialism of *Grossdeutschland* and advocated instead the creation of a *Mittelafrika*. Émile Durkheim wrote about this work in 1899.

17 Lindqvist, *Exterminate all the brutes*; Rosa Amelia Plumelle-Uribe, *La férocité blanche: des non-blancs aux non-Aryens: génocides occultés de 1492 à nos jours* (Paris: Albin Michel, 2001). On the question of the definition of genocide, see chapter 4.

18 This development was made clear at the first conference on racism, held in Durban, 1–7 September 2001, just before the destruction of the World Trade Center. It was confirmed at the second conference,

known as Durban II, held in Geneva, 20–5 April 2009. On this, see Jean Ziegler, *La haine de l'Occident* (Paris: Albine Michel, 2008).

19 See Franz Rosenzweig, *The Star of Redemption*, trans. Barbara E. Galli (Madison: University of Wisconsin Press, 2005).

20 Joseph Roth, *The Wandering Jews* (London: Granta, 2001).

21 Ernst Pawel, *The labyrinth of exile: a life of Theodor Herzl* (London: Collins-Harvill, 1990).

22 Stefan Zweig, *The world of yesterday: an autobiography* (London: Cassell, 1987). Herzl had a short life: he died in 1904, at the age of forty-four, and his wife three years later, at thirty-nine. See Viviane Forrester, *Le crime occidental* (Paris: Fayard, 2004).

23 Quoted in Pawel, *The labyrinth of exile*, pp. 197–8.

24 This illumination really did occur, contrary to Claude Klein's claim in his commentary on Herzl's book *The Jewish State* (1896). See below.

25 *Aliyah*: immigration. The word means 'going up', and it refers to going up to read the Torah in front of the faithful. The dates and numbers of immigrants are: 1882–1900: 25,000; 1905: 40,000; 1919–23: 35,000; 1924–6: 60,000; 1933–40: 200,000. Between 1940 and 1948, a sixth, clandestine *aliyah* – an *aliyah beth* – took place.

26 The term literally means 'settlement'.

27 Herzl, *The Jewish State: an attempt at a modern solution of the Jewish question* (1896). The word 'Zionism' was invented around 1890, replacing 'Palestinophilia', devised by another Viennese Jew, Nathan Birnbaum (1864–1937), who strongly opposed Herzl's ideas and became an anti-Zionist. According to Walter Laqueur, the word was invented on the evening of 23 January 1892. See his *A History of Zionism* (London: Weidenfeld & Nicolson, 1972).

28 Hannah Arendt, *Penser l'événement*, ed. Claude Habib, trans. Eric Adda et al. (Paris: Belin, 1989), p. 124.

29 Quoted in Pawel, *The labyrinth of exile*, p. 345.

30 Quoted by Claude Klein, in *The Jewish State*.

31 Ibid.

32 Theodor Herzl, *Altneuland: old-new land*, trans. Paula Arnold (Haifa: Haifa Publishing, 1960: first published in German in 1902). The German title *Altneuland* could be translated as 'Ancient new land (promised land/conquered land/colonized land)' and condensed, as did the word *Judenstaat*, all the ambiguities of Zionism: was it a land of Jews or of Hebrews? A Jewish state, a state of Jews, or a state for Jews? I will return to this in chapter 5.

33 Ahad Haam, born Asher Ginzburg (1856–1927): a Ukrainian Jew, a theorist of spiritual Zionism, opposed to Theodor Herzl, hostile to the Enlightenment and to assimilation, he settled in Palestine in 1922. He favoured the adoption of Hebrew as the national language and founded a secret brotherhood, the 'Sons of Moses'. See Laurens, *La question de Palestine*, vol. 1, pp. 115–17.

34 See Pawel, *The labyrinth of exile*, p. 472.

35 This phrase was popularized in 1901 by Israël Zangwill (1864–1926), an English writer and journalist, a feminist and Zionist, the offspring of a family of Jewish immigrants from the Russian Empire.

36 Alain Dieckhoff, 'Max Nordau, l'Occident et la question arabe', in *Max Nordau*, ed. Delphine Bechtel, Dominique Bourel, and Jacques Le Rider (Paris: Cerf, 1996), p. 289.

37 Rachîd Ridâ (1878–1924): a Syrian intellectual from the reformist Islamic tradition.

38 Caliphate: territory placed under the authority of a caliph, a descendant of Muhammad. Several caliphates followed in succession between 632 and 1924.

39 See Jean-François Legrain (ed.), *À propos du 'Traité sur le califat' de Rachîd Ridâ* (Lyons: CNRS-Maison d'Orient et de Méditerranée, 2006).

40 Sandjak: a Turkish term for an administrative division (a sort of governorate) in the Ottoman Empire.

41 This preamble has attracted a variety of interpretations. See Bensoussan, *Une histoire intellectuelle et politique du sionisme*, p. 201; and Laurens, *La question de Palestine*, vol. 1, pp. 205–6.

42 Genesis 32: 28. In Hebrew, the name 'Israel' is linked to the verb 'to fight' and means 'God will fight'.

43 Joris-Karl Huysmans, *A Rebours* (1884); Oscar Wilde, *The Picture of Dorian Gray* (1890), Marcel Proust, *Sodom and Gomorrah*, vol. 3 of *In Search of Lost Time*.

44 The theme of the Jew who is simultaneously a man and a woman and capable of every sexual inversion is one of the major elements in anti-Semitic discourse. It can be found in Drumont, especially in his portrait of Marat as a 'Jewish woman'. See Élisabeth Roudinesco, 'Antisémitisme et contre-révolution (1886–1944)', in collaboration with Henry Rousso, *L'Infini*, 27 (1989).

45 Max Nordau, *Degeneration* (Lincoln and London: University of Nebraska Press, 1993; first German edn 1892 and 1893). Born Simon Maximilien Südfeld, Nordau was, like Herzl, of Hungarian origin.

46 This was the period in which Germany saw the development of the trend of thought favourable to racial hygiene, as I discussed in chapter 2.

47 Nordau was probably the first to imagine such a change – one about which even the most progressive did not dream.

48 Reported in Gaston Méry, 'Au jour le jour: chez le docteur Max Nordau', *La libre parole*, 17 September 1997.

49 Quoted in Victor Nguyen, *Aux origines de l'Action française: intelligence et politique à l'aube du XXe siècle* (Paris: Fayard, 1991), p. 570.

50 'You know of course the root differences between the Palestine Jew and the colonist Jew: to Feisal the important point is that the former speak Arabic, and the latter German Yiddish.' Jeremy Wilson, *Lawrence of Arabia: the authorised biography* (London, Heinemann,

1989; New York, Atheneum, 1990), pp. 442–3. This letter is quoted in Laurens, *La question de Palestine*, p. 369.

51 Chaim Weizmann (1874–1952): a Russian-Polish Jew, a famous chemist, president of the Zionist Organization until 1846 and the main figure behind the alliance between Zionism and British policy-makers.

52 In Arthur Koestler's words: 'Now one nation is promising to another the land of a third nation', quoted in Bensoussan, *Une histoire intellectuelle et politique du sionisme*, p. 940.

53 There is a detailed account of this in Laurens, *La question de Palestine*, vol. 1, pp. 473–7.

54 (Gerhard) Gershom Scholem (1897–1982): born in Berlin, he moved to Palestine in 1923 and became professor at the Hebrew University of Jerusalem and a member of the Berit Shalom (1925), an association for peace and the development of relations between Jews and Arabs. He was always in favour of the creation of a single two-nation state.

55 Bensoussan, *Une histoire intellectuelle et politique du sionisme*, p. 511.

56 The Jewish population grew from 83,000 at the end of 1918 to 164,000 in 1930, then to 463,000 in 1940, and finally to 650,000 after the vote in favour of the creation of the State of Israel. During this time, the Arab population doubled, from 660,000 to 1,200,000. For an account of these events, see Laurens, *La question de Palestine*, and Bensoussan, *Une histoire intellectuelle et politique du sionisme*.

57 As a result, 1940 saw the beginning of the *alya beth* (or clandestine immigration) organized by David Ben Gurion (1886–1973): he moved to Palestine in 1906. A founding father of the Labour Party, he was the first prime minister of Israel, between 1948 and 1953, and served again between 1955 and 1963. He remains, without any doubt, the greatest statesman in the history of Israel. See Alain Dieckhoff (ed.), *L'État d'Israël* (Paris: Fayard, 2008).

58 Georges Bensoussan, *Génocide pour mémoire: des racines du désastre aux questions d'aujourd'hui* (Paris: Félin, 1989), p. 13. On 7 December 1941, 900 Jews from the town of Kolo, in Poland, had 'the privilege of being the first to be gassed as part of the Final Solution'. See Claude Lanzmann, 'Notes ante et anti-éliminationnistes', *Les Temps modernes*, 592, February–March 1997, p. 14.

Chapter 4 Universal Jew, Territorial Jew

1 Zeev Jabotinsky (1880–1940): born in Odessa, in 1923 he founded the revisionist Zionist movement, politically on the right and hostile to the socialists. To keep Arab power at bay, he advocated the creation of a 'wall of steel' – in other words, a military, fascist-style force.

2 Bensoussan, *Une histoire intellectuelle et politique du sionisme, 1860–1940* (Paris: Fayard, 2002), pp. 627–9.

3   Quoted ibid., p. 715.

4   Keren Hayesod: organization founded in 1920 with the aim of settling immigrants in Palestine.

5   See Guido Ariel Liebermann, 'Histoire de la psychanalyse en Palestine et en Israël', doctoral thesis directed by Élisabeth Roudinesco, UFR-GHSS, Université de Paris-VII Denis-Diderot, 2006. David Montague Eder (1866–1936): psychiatrist and psychoanalyst, the co-founder, with Ernest Jones, of the British psychoanalytic movement and a cousin of Israël Zangwill, a Zionist and socialist activist.

6   The original manuscript of Freud's letter, dated 26 February 1930, and the copy typed by an unknown person are in the Abraham Schwadron collection at the Hebrew University of Jerusalem. Thanks to Guido Liebermann, who passed the archive on to me, and to Michael Molnar, of the Freud Museum in London, Patrick Mahoney and Henri Rey-Flaud for their judicious advice.

7   This letter of 2 April 1930 is part of the Schwadron collection.

8   Letter from Sigmund Freud to Albert Einstein, 26 February 1930, quoted in Peter Gay, *Freud: a life for our time* (London: Papermac, 1995), p. 598 note.

9   Letter from Sigmund Freud to Leib Jaffé, 20 June 1935, quoted in Peter Gay, *A Godless Jew: Freud, atheism and the making of psychoanalysis* (New Haven, CT, and London: Yale University Press, in association with Hebrew Union College Press, 1987), p. 123.

10   Quoted in Jacquy Chemouny, *Freud et le sionisme* (Paris: Solin, 1988), pp. 127 and 266. On Freud's Jewishness, there is an extensive literature: see particularly David Bakkan, *Freud et la tradition mystique juive* (Paris: Payot, 1977: first published 1958); Marthe Robert, *From Oedipus to Moses: Freud's Jewish identity*, trans. Ralph Manheim (Garden City, NY: Anchor Books, 1976); and Gay, *A Godless Jew*.

11   On the impossible solution to this question of the Holy Places, see Charles Enderlin, *Shattered dreams: the failure of the peace process in the Middle East, 1995–2002*, trans. Susan Fairfield (New York: Other Press, 2003).

12   This anecdote is related by Jacob Weinshal, *Hans Herzl* (Tel Aviv, 1945), quoted in Le Rider, *Modernity and crises of identity: culture and society in fin-de-siècle Vienna*, trans. Rosemary Morris (Cambridge: Polity, 1993), p. 249.

13   Sigmund Freud, 'Little Hans', in *Case Histories I: 'Dora' and 'Little Hans'* (Harmondsworth: Penguin, 1977), and Jacques Le Rider, *Le cas Otto Weininger: racines de l'antiféminisme et de l'antisémitisme* (Paris: PUF, 1982).

14   Sigmund Freud, interview with Georges Sylvester Viereck, *Glimpses of the Great* (London: Duckworth, 1930), quoted in Ernest Jones, *Sigmund Freud: life and work*, 3 vols (London: Hogarth Press, 1953).

15   Sigmund Freud, 'Letter of 6 May 1926', in *The letters of Sigmund Freud, 1873–1939*, ed. Ernst L. Freud, trans. Tania and James Stern (London: Hogarth Press, 1970), p. 368, and *Moses and Monotheism:*

three essays, in *The origins of religion* (Harmondsworth: Penguin, 1985).

16 Sigmund Freud, *Totem and Taboo* (first published 1912–13).

17 Moshe Wulf (1878–1971): Jewish psychiatrist and psychoanalyst born in Odessa, the founder, with Max Eitingon (1881–1943), of the first Psychoanalytical Society of the future State of Israel. After the death of Eitingon, he trained the first generation of Israeli psychoanalysts, who later forced him out of the society he had founded.

18 Judah Leib Magnes (1877–1948): a reform rabbi from the Jewish community of San Francisco, he settled in Palestine in 1922. He was the president of the Hebrew University of Jerusalem for twenty-four years. See Liebermann, 'Histoire de la psychanalyse en Palestine et en Israël', doctoral thesis directed by Élisabeth Roudinesco, UFR-GHSS, Université de Paris-VII Denis-Diderot, 2006.

19 We owe to the philosopher Yirmiyahu Yovel one of the few Israeli contributions to the question of the dark Enlightenment in Freud. See *Spinoza and other heretics*, 2 vols (Princeton, NJ: Princeton University Press, 1989).

20 *The Complete Correspondence of Sigmund Freud and Karl Abraham, 1907–1925* (London: Karnac, 2002), p. 38.

21 Ibid., p. 72.

22 Ibid., p. 364.

23 Sigmund Freud, *Correspondence, 1873–1939*, p. 366.

24 Gay, *Freud*, p. 178.

25 *The correspondence of Sigmund Freud and Sándor Ferenczi*, vol. 1: *1908–1914* (Cambridge, MA, and London: Harvard University Press, 1993), pp. 490–1.

26 Sigmund Freud and Max Eitingon, *Correspondance 1906–1939* (Paris: Hachette, 2009), p. 785.

27 Richard F. Sterba, *Reminiscences of a Viennese psychoanalyst* (Detroit: Wayne State University Press, 1982), p. 165.

28 At the age of sixteen, in 1944, Elie Wiesel was deported to Auschwitz-Birkenau with his father, his mother, and his sister. He was the sole survivor. He was liberated from Buchenwald by the American Army.

29 Elie Wiesel, *Night*, trans. Marion Wiesel (London: Penguin, 2008), pp. 76–7. See also Betty Bernardo Fuchs, 'Judéité, errance et nomadisme: sur le devenir juif de Freud', *Essaim*, 9 (2002), pp. 15–25.

30 Freud and Eitingon, *Correspondance*, p. 842.

31 On this event, see Élisabeth Roudinesco, *Jacques Lacan* (New York: Columbia University Press, 1997).

32 Ibid.

33 Freud, *Moses and Monotheism*.

34 Ibid., p. 323.

35 Jean-François Lyotard puts forward an interpretation in which Freud turned Judaism into a 'foreclosed figure', a religion founded on a rejection of reality, while Christianity was a reprise of totemism and paganism. See Jean-François Lyotard, 'Figure forclose', *L'écrit du temps*,

5 (1984), pp. 65–105. See also Élisabeth de Fontenay, *Une tout autre histoire: questions à Jean-François Lyotard* (Paris: Fayard, 2006).

36 Freud, *Moses and Monotheism*.

37 See Yosef Hayim Yerushalmi, *Freud's Moses: analysis terminable and interminable* (New Haven, CT, and London: Yale University Press, 1991). For Jacques Derrida's response, see Jacques Derrida, *Archive fever: a Freudian impression*, trans. Eric Prenowitz (Chicago and London: University of Chicago Press, 1996). I was behind the meeting between Yerushalmi and Derrida following a conference organized at the Freud Museum of London by the Société international d'histoire de la psychiatrie et de la psychanalyse (SIHPP) in 1994, on the theme *Mémoire d'archives*. One of the best interpretations of the *Moses* is that by Jacques le Rider, *Freud, de l'Acropole au Sinaï: le retour à l'antique des Modernes viennois* (Paris: PUF, 2002). And, in a very different style, Henri Rey-Flaud, *'Et Moïse créa les Juifs . . .': le testament de Freud* (Paris: Aubier, 2006).

38 Yerushalmi, *Freud's Moses*.

39 Martin Buber, *Moses* (Oxford: Phaidon Press, 1946).

40 Geoffrey Cocks, *Psychotherapy in the Third Reich: the Göring Institute* (New York: Oxford University Press, 1985).

41 C. G. Jung, *Letters of C. G. Jung*, vol. 1: *1906–1950* (London: Routledge & Kegan Paul, 1973), p. 132.

42 C. G. Jung, 'Geleitwort', in *Zentralblatt für Psychotherapie*, 6/1 (1933), pp. 10–11. Reprinted in Jung, *Gesammelte Werke* (Olten and Freiburg-in-Breisgau: Walter, 1974), vol. 10, pp. 581–3.

43 Jung, *Letters*, vol. 1, p. 78.

44 Jung, 'An interview with Radio Berlin', 26 June 1933, in *C. G. Jung speaking: interviews and encounters* (London: Thames & Hudson, 1978), pp. 74 and 78. The German version of this text was published in 1987, and analysed by M. von der Tann in 'A Jungian perspective on the Berlin Institute for Psychotherapy: a basis for mourning', in *San Francisco Jung Institute Library Journal*, 8/4 (1989). See Andrew Samuels, 'Psychologie nationale, national-socialisme et psychologie analytique: réflexions sur Jung et l'antisémitisme' (1989), in *Revue internationale d'histoire de la psychanalyse*, 5 (1992), pp. 183–221.

45 G. Bally, 'Deutsche stämmige Therapie' [Psychotherapy of German origin], in *Neue Zürcher Zeitung*, 343, 27 February 1934.

46 Jung repeats the same idea in several letters written in 1934.

47 Carl Gustav Jung, 'Zur gegenwärtigen Lage der Psychotherapie', *Zentralblatt für Psychotherapie*, 7 (1934), 1–16. Reprinted unaltered in Jung, *Gesammelte Werke*, vol. 10, pp. 181–201; Eng. trans. in Jung, *Collected Works* (Princeton, NJ: Princeton University Press, 1970), vol. 10, as 'Psychotherapy today'.

48 Some extracts from this passage are discussed in Yerushalmi, *Freud's Moses*.

49 C. G. Jung, *L'homme à la découverte de son âme* (Paris: Albin Michel, 1987), p. 111.

50 Letter of 26 May 1934, in Jung, *Letters*, vol. 1, pp. 161–2.
51 Ibid., p. 164.
52 Ibid., pp. 206–7.
53 Jung, 'Wotan', in *Collected Works*, 2nd edn, vol. 10 (Princeton, NJ: Princeton University Press, 1970), pp. 179–93. Interview with H. R. Knickerbocker, published as 'Diagnosing the dictators – an interview with Dr. Jung', in *Cosmopolitan*, cvi (January, 1939).
54 Jung's works were added to the notorious Otto list of banned books (named after Otto Abetz, the German ambassador to the Vichy government 1940–4).
55 C. G. Jung, *Essays on contemporary events: reflections on Nazi Germany* (London: Routledge, 1989: first published 1949); see the introduction by Andrew Samuels.
56 See Gerhard Wehr, *Carl Gustav Jung: sa vie, son oeuvre, son rayonnement* (Paris: Librairie de Médicis, 1993), pp. 320–1, and Aniela Jaffé, *Aus Leben und Werkstatt von C. G. Jung: Parapsychologie, Alchemie, Nationalsozialismus – Erinnerungen aus den letzten Jahren* (Zurich: Rascher, 1968). Scholem subsequently moved away from Jung.
57 Gershom Scholem, *Fidélité et utopie: essais sur le judaïsme contemporain*, trans. Marguerite Delmotte and Bernard Dupuy (Paris: Calmann-Lévy, 1978), pp. 47–50.
58 In Greek, '*eranos*' means an improvised banquet. The meetings in question were founded in 1933 by Olga Fröbe Kapteyn and took place on the shores of Lake Maggiore, in a villa near Ascona. Their aim was to mediate between East and West so as to promote understanding between two traditions of spirituality.
59 Mircea Eliade (1907–1986): a Romanian historian of religions, known for his support for Romanian fascism in the Second World War and his hostility to the Enlightenment, Jews, freemasons, and communists.
60 In his autobiography, based on conversations with Aniela Jaffé, he passed over this period of his life in silence. See C. G. Jung, *Memories, dreams, reflections*, recorded and ed. Aniela Jaffé, trans. Richard and Clara Winston (London: Fontana, 1963). As for the imposing biography by Deirdre Bair, *Jung: a biography* (Boston: Little, Brown, 2003), it sheds no light on this affair. The author prefers to pass Jung off as a simpleton who let himself be duped by the Nazis rather than to accept a truth that all historians now acknowledge. See Élisabeth Roudinesco, 'Carl Gustav Jung: de l'archétype au nazisme. Dérives d'une psychologie de la différence', *L'Infini*, 63, autumn 1998.
61 Rudolph Loewenstein, *Christians and Jews: a psychoanalytic study*, trans. Vera Damman (New York: International Universities Press, 1951), does not tackle this question. The work was translated into French in 1952 and had a wide impact, as we shall see in later chapters. Éliane Amado-Lévy Valensi (1919–2006), a philosopher and psychoanalyst trained in France, and the daughter of a deportee, later moved

to Israel and was an activist in the promotion of an ecumenical culture (Christianity, Judaism, and Islam); she devoted a work to the *Moses* of Freud that discussed the latter's identification with the prophet: *Le Moïse de Freud ou la référence occultée* (Monaco: Éditions du Rocher, 1984).

62 Yerushalmi, *Freud's Moses*, p. 99.
63 Serge Lebovici. On the role of the latter in the Brazilian dictatorship, see Roudinesco, *Histoire de la psychanalyse en France*, 2 vols (Paris: Fayard, 1994); new edn (Paris: Hachette, 2009).
64 Original document, typewritten and entitled 'Inaugural lecture', communicated by Guido Liebermann. See also Paul Schwaber, 'Title of honor: the psychoanalytic congress in Jerusalem', *Midstream*, 24 (1978). Also quoted in Yerushalmi, *Freud's Moses*. Freud's four sisters were exterminated by the Nazis.
65 Edward Said, *Freud and the non-European*, introduction by Christopher Bollas; response by Jacqueline Rose (London: Verso, 2003). Bollas is a psychoanalyst and Rose a professor of literature at London, as well as having translated Lacan into English and introduced him to the English-speaking world; she also wrote the excellent *The Question of Zion* (Princeton, NJ: Princeton University Press, 2005).
66 Edward Said, *Orientalism*, with a new afterword (London: Penguin, 1995).

Chapter 5   Genocide between Memory and Negation

1 See Enzo Traverso, *L'histoire déchirée: essai sur Auschwitz et les intellectuels* (Paris: Cerf, 1997), pp. 191–2.
2 The two first eye-witness accounts were those of Rudolf Höss, commandant of the camp at Auschwitz, who justified the extermination by explaining that he had simply been obeying the desire of his victims, and Kurt Gerstein, who took the opposite tack and tried to inform the Allies before committing suicide in 1945: he was rehabilitated by Saul Friedländer. See Roudinesco, *La part obscure de nous-mêmes: une histoire des pervers* (Paris: Albin Michel, 2007), p. 161 and ch. 6.
3 See *Raphael Lemkin's thoughts on genocide: not guilty?*, ed. Steven L. Jacobs (Lewiston: Edwin Mellen Press, 1992).
4 In particular, the notion of a crime against humanity has been revised several times since 1945. It can be used to refer to eleven types of acts committed within the context of a general, systematic attack on a civil population:

> murder; extermination; enslavement; deportation or forcible transfer of population; imprisonment or other severe deprivation of physical liberty in violation of fundamental rules of international law; torture; rape, sexual slavery, enforced prostitution, forced pregnancy, enforced

sterilization, or any other form of sexual violence of comparable gravity; persecution against any identifiable group or collectivity on political, racial, national, ethnic, cultural, religious, gender [. . .] or other grounds [. . .]; enforced disappearance of persons; the crime of apartheid; other inhumane acts of a similar character [. . .].

5 Destruction of cemeteries, monuments, art, language, books, places of worship.
6 Pierre Vidal-Naquet, *Assassins of memory: essays on the denial of the Holocaust*, trans. and with a foreword by Jeffrey Mehlman (New York: Columbia University Press, 1992), p. 171. In a fine book with a preface by Vidal-Naquet, the American historian Arno Mayer proposed the term judeocide: *Why did the heavens not darken? The 'Final Solution' in history* (New York: Pantheon Books, 1988).
7 Hannah Arendt and Karl Jaspers, *Correspondence 1926–1969*, ed. Lotte Kohker and Hans Saner, trans. Robert Kimber and Rita Kimber (New York: Harcourt Brace Jovanovich, 1992), p. 113.
8 On this point I do not share the position of my friend Jean-Claude Milner, who claims (justifiably) that the gas chamber was invented for Jews but does not specify in enough detail *what*, in the Jews, was being targeted. See Jean-Claude Milner, *Les penchants criminels de l'Europe démocratique* (Paris: Verdier, 2003). Nor do I agree with my friend Alain Badiou when he maintains that, under the cover of the word 'Auschwitz', a wild troop of rhetoricians and propagandists have turned the extermination of the Jews into the 'basis on which they can peddle their "democratic" propaganda'. Preface to Ivan Segré, *La réaction philosémite, ou La trahison des clercs* (Paris: Lignes, 2009), p. 15.
9 In this respect I do not agree with Ivan Segré, who denies this singularity, which in his view stems from a so-called Jewish concept of the destruction of the Jews. See Ivan Segré, *Qu'appelle-t-on penser Auschwitz?* (Paris: Lignes, 2009).
10 Traverso provides a detailed list in *L'histoire déchirée*.
11 Marx Horkheimer and Theodor Adorno, *Dialectic of Enlightenment*, trans. John Cumming (London: Verso, 1979; first published in German, 1947).
12 Claude Eatherly, *Burning conscience: the case of the Hiroshima pilot Claude Eatherly, told in his letters to Günther Anders*, 2nd edn (New York: Paragon House, 1989).
13 Jean-Paul Sartre, *Anti-Semite and Jew*, trans. George J. Becker (New York: Schocken Books, 1976; first published in French, 1946).
14 Louis-Ferdinand Céline, *Journey to the end of the night*, trans. John H. P. Marks (Harmondsworth: Penguin, in association with Chatto & Windus, 1966; first published in French, 1934).
15 Louis-Ferdinand Céline, 'Sartre demi-sangsue, demi-ténia', *Magazine littéraire*, 488, July–August 2009, pp. 80–1; and 'A l'agité du bocal', *Louis Ferdinand Céline*, ed. Dominique de Roux, Michel Beaujour

and Michel Thelia (Paris: Éditions de l'Herne, 1972), Eng. trans., 'To the nutcase', available at: www.marxists.org/reference/archive/sartre/comment/celine.htm.

16 Traverso, *L'histoire déchirée*, p. 190.

17 Ibid., pp. 189–91, and Dwight Macdonald, 'The responsibility of peoples', *Politics*, 2/3 (1945), pp. 82–93.

18 Maurice Blanchot, 'La grande passion des modérés', *Combat*, 9, November 1936.

19 Robert Antelme (1917–1990): poet and member of the French Resistance, married to Marguerite Duras (between 1939 and 1942). Together with Dionys Mascolo, he was in François Mitterand's Resistance group. He was deported to Buchenwald and Dachau and wrote a major eye-witness account of the living conditions in the camps, *L'espèce humaine* (Paris: Gallimard, 1947), in which he described the experience of the inhuman in a sparse style, free of any psychologism. Blanchot drew inspiration from this in writing the final version of his novel *Thomas l'obscur*.

20 Maurice Blanchot, *Thomas l'obscur* (Paris: Gallimard, 1950; first published 1941). The last version of the book has had a hundred pages or so cut.

21 This expression is used by Christophe Bident, in *Maurice Blanchot, partenaire invisible: essai biographique* (Seyssel: Champ Vallon, 1998).

22 This was signed by, among others, Robert Antelme, Simone de Beauvoir, Jean-Paul Sartre, Pierre Vidal-Naquet, Marguerite Duras, Claude Lanzmann, Pierre Boulez, André Breton, Nathalie Sarraute, Claude Simon, and Alain Robbe-Grillet. See Maurice Blanchot, *Écrits politiques, 1953–1993* (Paris: Gallimard, 2008), pp. 49–54.

23 See Bident, *Maurice Blanchot*, p. 399. Throughout the second half of the twentieth century, Sartre was the most insulted French author in his own country and abroad, and also the most famous. He was even called an anti-Semite by a female American academic and a sexual criminal by a French woman journalist.

24 Bident, *Maurice Blanchot*, p. 77. Blanchot, always an extremist, was convinced – in spite of the more sensible views of his friends – that Gaullism was a new fascism.

25 Maurice Blanchot, *Après coup* (Paris: Minuit, 1983), Eng. trans. as 'After the fact' in Blanchot, *Vicious circles: two fictions & 'After the fact'*, trans. Paul Auster (Barrytown, NY: Station Hill Press, 1985); *The Infinite Conversation*, trans. and foreword by Susan Hanson (Minneapolis: University of Minnesota Press, 1993), p. 67.

26 Jacques Derrida, *The other heading: reflections on today's Europe*, trans. Pascale-Anne Brault and Michael B. Naas (Bloomington: Indiana University Press, 1992).

27 Maurice Blanchot, 'Ce qui m'est le plus proche', *Globe*, 30, July–August 1988, p. 56. On Blanchot's political development, see Bident, *Maurice Blanchot*. Zeev Sternhall does not refer to Blanchot's later

career but states that, between the wars, Blanchot was 'a perfect definition of the fascist spirit': *Neither right nor left: fascist ideology in
France* (Berkeley: University of California Press, 1986), p. 223.

28 It should be pointed out that Claude Lanzmann's film *Shoah* (1985),
which was quite rightly hailed by the best historians, made a very
welcome contribution to secularizing the term, releasing it from the
ghetto of the history of Judaism and reconciling memory and history:
'The word "Shoah" occurred to me one night as self-evident because,
not speaking Hebrew, I did not understand its meaning, which was
another way of not naming it.' The word has been suggested to him
by an Israeli friend, who had suggested that he make 'not a film *about*
the Shoah, but a film that *is* the Shoah' (Claude Lanzmann, *The Patagonian hare: a memoir*, trans. Frank Wynne (London: Atlantic, 2012),
pp. 506 and 411).

29 The new historians have nonetheless quarrelled fiercely among themselves, not over the reality of the Naqba, but over how to interpret it.
Some maintain that it was the product of war, others that it was pro-
grammed as a piece of 'ethnic cleansing', yet others that it is simply a
case of the policy of apartheid. These extremely violent debates
confirm, if confirmation were needed, that academic freedom exists in
Israel. See Ilan Pappé, *The making of the Arab–Israeli conflict 1947–
51* (London: I. B. Tauris, 1992), and Dominique Vidal, *Le péché
original d'Israël: l'expulsion des Palestiniens revisitée par les 'nouveaux historiens' israéliens* (Paris: Éditions de l'Atelier, 2003).

30 This is the expression used by Claude Klein, in 'La constitution, encore
la constitution', *Les temps modernes*, 651, November–December
2008, p. 164. The basic work on this question is Alain Dieckhoff (ed.).
L'État d'Israël (Paris: Fayard, 2008).

31 Pierre Vidal-Naquet, *Réflexions sur la génocide: les Juifs, la mémoire
et le présent*, 3 vols (Paris: La Découverte, 1995), p. 287.

32 Note that the total population of Jews in the world, at the beginning
the twenty-first century, has been estimated at around 14 million,
spread across twenty-eight countries. Most of them live in Israel
(5,640,000), in the United States (5,500,000), and in Europe
(1,200,000). In Europe, France is the country with the most Jews –
some 500,000. So the Jewish people does exist, but – unlike all other
peoples – its existence is more diasporic than national.

33 See Marius Schattner, *Israël, l'autre conflit* (Brussels: André Versaille,
2008).

34 See Idith Zertal, *Israel's Holocaust and the politics of nationhood*,
trans. Chaya Galai (Cambridge: Cambridge University Press, 2005),
p. 4.

35 In a remarkable work, the historian Alain Dieckhoff suggests that, on
one view, the Jews were seen as a nation 'with no material reality', as
'a defunct nation, or rather a ghostly nation': *The invention of a
nation: Zionist thought and the making of modern Israel* (London:
C. Hurst, 2001), p. 24. This idea is reminiscent of Derrida's thoughts
on Marx, in *Specters of Marx: the state of the debt, the work of*

mourning and the New International, trans. Peggy Kamuf (London: Routledge, 2006). The spectre, after all, is the apparition of a startling spiritual force that never ceases to arouse fear. It cannot be overcome.

36 Ilan Greilsammer, 'En Israël, entre Juifs', *Colloque des intellectuels juifs: comment vivre ensemble* (Paris: Albin Michel, 2001), p. 149.

37 Herzl, *Altneuland: old-new land,* trans. Paula Arnold (Haifa: Haifa Publishing, 1960, p. 110 [translation modified].

38 The concept of race was officially abandoned by UNESCO in 1950, then by the worldwide scientific community. It has been replaced by the concept of ethnicity, which also creates various problems.

39 Later, in 1971, in *Race and culture,* Claude Lévi-Strauss showed that the biological evolution of men and populations is determined mainly by their cultural organization. See Claude Lévi-Strauss, *Race et histoire* (Paris: Bibliothèque Médiations, 1969; first published 1952), *Race et culture* (Paris: Albin Michel/Unesco, 2001; first published 1971).

40 Nahum Goldman, *The Jewish paradox,* trans. Steve Cox (London: Weidenfeld & Nicolson, 1978), p. 99.

41 Siri Husseini Shahid, *Souvenir de Jérusalem* (Paris: Fayard, 2005), pp. 18–19.

42 See Élisabeth Roudinesco, *Jacques Lacan* (New York: Columbia University Press, 1997). I am grateful to Jean Bollack for shedding light on this.

43 Sigmund Freud, *Beyond the Pleasure Principle* (1920).

44 At this date, Lacan did not know about the affair of the so-called rescue of psychoanalysis in Germany.

45 Jacques Lacan, *Écrits: the first complete edition in English,* trans. Bruce Fink in collaboration with Héloïse Fink and Russell Grigg (New York; London: W. W. Norton, 2006), and *The four fundamental concepts of psycho-analysis,* ed. Jacques-Alain Milner, trans. Alan Sheridan (London: Vintage, 1998), p. 275.

46 I have shown that, although Lacan had not read Hannah Arendt's work, he shared her ideas on this point.

47 Sonderkommandos: special teams of deportees forced to take part in exterminating victims in the gas chambers and crematoria; they were then executed themselves because they had seen what nobody should see. Very few survived to bear witness, including one unforgettable survivor in Lanzmann's film. It was in connection with the Sonderkommandos that Primo Levi referred to the most perfidious act of Nazism, which consisted in forcing Jews to send other Jews to the ovens so as to demonstrate that the Jews themselves were genocidal killers, as indeed Rudolf Höss emphasized. See Shlomo Venezia, *Inside the gas chambers: eight months in the Sonderkommando of Auschwitz,* trans. Andrew Brown (Cambridge: Polity, 2009), and Roudinesco, *La part obscure de nous-mêmes,* especially the chapter 'Les aveux d'Auschwitz'.

48 Zertal, *Israel's Holocaust,* pp. 67–9.

49 Ibid., p. 90.

50 *New York Times,* 11 June 1960.

51 See Erich Fromm, *On disobedience: and other essays* (London: Rout-ledge & Kegan Paul, 1984). I have criticized this position in *La part obscure de nous-mêmes*: I will be returning to this.

52 Hannah Arendt, 'Zionism Reconsidered' (1944), in *The Jewish Writings*, ed. Jerome Kohn and Ron H. Feldman (New York: Schocken Books, 2007), pp. 343–74.

53 Pierre Bouretz, 'Hannah Arendt et le sionisme: Cassandre aux pieds d'argile', *Raisons politiques*, 16 (2004), p. 128.

54 Martin Heidegger, 'The self-affirmation of the German university', in *Review of Metaphysics*, 38 (March 1985), pp. 467–502. The French philosopher François Fédier, who has always denied that Heidegger was a Nazi, translated this text into French with the title *L'université allemande envers et contre tout elle-même* [*The German university in spite of everything itself*], suggesting that Heidegger thought that the university could resist the Führer principle, while he was in fact proposing that it be subsumed within this principle.

55 See Élisabeth Young-Bruehl, *Hannah Arendt, for love of the world* (New Haven and London: Yale University Press, 1982), pp. 301–8.

56 Martine Leibovici, *Hannah Arendt, une Juive: expérience, politique et histoire*, with a preface by Pierre Vidal-Naquet (Paris: Desclée de Brouwer, 2002).

57 Arendt, *Origins of Totalitarianism*, new edn (New York: Harcourt Brace Jovanovich, 1973), p. 202.

58 Raul Hilberg, *The destruction of the European Jews*, 3rd edn, 3 vols (New Haven, CT: Yale University Press, 2003).

59 Ibid., vol. 3, pp. 1117–18.

60 Rudolf Höss theorized this vileness by claiming that, by exterminating his victims, he was obeying their desire. See Roudinesco, *La part obscure de nous-mêmes*.

61 Annette Wieviorka, *Le procès Eichmann* (Brussels: Éditions Complexe, 1989), pp. 184–7.

62 Ian Kershaw has disproved all these ideas.

63 Victor Alexandrov, *Six millions de morts: la vie d'Adolf Eichmann* (Paris: Plon, 1960).

64 Over and above the psychological differences that characterized them – Eichmann resembled neither Höss, nor Mengele, nor Himmler, nor Göring – the Nazi leaders and perpetrators of genocide shared one feature: they absolutely refused to take into consideration the acts they had committed. It is this refusal, not their 'psychological profile', that characterizes their perversion. See Roudinesco, *La part obscure de nous-mêmes*.

65 Arendt, *Eichmann in Jerusalem: a report on the banality of evil*, rev. and enlarged edn (Harmondsworth: Penguin, 1977), p. 253.

66 Ibid., p. 231.

67 Flaubert defined stupidity as the absolute evil – the invincible enemy. He was one of the first, with Tocqueville, to see it as a perversion, identifying it with the power inflicted on people by received ideas,

public opinion, and the ideals of fake sciences. Jean-Paul Sartre partly took over this idea.

68 Especially Norman Podhoretz and the review *Commentary*.

69 This polemic is clearly set out in Pierre Bouretz, 'Hannah Arendt et le sionisme'. See also her *Origins of totalitarianism* and *Eichmann in Jerusalem*.

70 *Le nouvel observateur*, 102, 25 October–1 November 1966.

71 Pierre Vidal-Naquet, 'La banalité du mal', *Le Monde*, 13 January 1967. On this point, see also Vidal-Naquet's preface to Leibovici, *Hannah Arendt*.

72 Gershom Scholem, *Walter Benjamin und sein Engel: vierzehn Aufsätze und kleine Beiträge*, ed. Rolf Tiedemann (Frankfurt am Main: Suhrkamp, 1992); Jean-Michel Palmier, *Le chiffonier, l'ange et le petit bossu* (Paris: Klincksieck, 2006).

73 Scholem, *Fidélité et utopie: essais sur le judaïsme contemporain*, trans. Marguerite Delmotte and Bernard Dupuy (Paris: Calmann-Lévy, 1978), pp. 54–6.

74 'Galutic existence': from the Hebrew word *galut*, meaning exile. The expression 'non-Jewish Jew' comes from Isaac Deutscher.

75 This question is in itself unacceptable, and Eichmann's trial has helped to make it even more unacceptable. Elie Wiesel was the first to show this. See his *Night*, trans. Marion Wiesel (London: Penguin, 2008).

76 Scholem, *Fidélité et utopie*, pp. 215–21.

77 Ibid., p. 224.

78 Thanks in particular to Claude Lefort, André Enegren, Jacques Taminiaux, Myriam Revault d'Allonnes, the review *Esprit*, and subsequently Martine Leibovici and Pierre Bouretz. French-speakers have Olivier Bétourné to thank for bringing together, for the first time, the three volumes of her main work *The origins of totalitarianism* (as *Les origines du totalitarisme*), which had previously been issued by three different publishers. He also helped me discover her work, in 1986. See also Françoise Collin, *L'homme est-il devenu superflu?* (Paris: Odile Jacob, 1999).

79 *Les historiens devant l'histoire: les documents de la controverse sur la singularité de l'extermination des juifs par le régime nazi* (Paris: Cerf, 1988); and, for a critique of these positions and François Furet's failure to take Hannah Arendt's work into proper account, see Olivier Bétourné and Aglaia I. Hartig, *Penser l'histoire de la Révolution: deux siècles de passion française* (Paris: La Découverte, 1989). By 'revising' the history of the Revolution against the grain of its real dialectic, and by failing to grasp the difference between the two totalitarianisms – and thus seeing the genocide of the Jews as the same as the Stalinist gulag – Stéphane Courtois, a former 'anarcho-Maoist' who became a disciple of Nolte and then of Furet, ended up seeing the blindness of the communists to Stalin's crimes as a form of Holocaust denial (*Le Monde*, 26 December 1995). This idea was repeated and then criticized in Stéphane Courtois et al., *The black book of communism*,

trans. Jonathan Murphy and Mark Kramer (Cambridge, MA, and London: Harvard University Press, 1999).

80 See Alain Besançon, *A century of horrors: communism, Nazism and the uniqueness of the Shoah*, trans. Ralph C. Hancock and Nathaniel H. Hancock (Wilmington, DE: ISI Books, 2007).

81 Articles 17 and 18 of the Charter of the Palestine Liberation Organization, 2 June 1964:

> Article 17. The Partitioning of Palestine in 1947 and the establishment of Israel are illegal and false regardless of the loss of time, because they were contrary to the wish of the Palestine people and its natural right to its homeland, and in violation of the basic principles embodied in the charter of the United Nations, foremost among which is the right to self-determination.
>
> Article 18. The Balfour Declaration, the Mandate system and all that has been based upon them are considered fraud. The claims of historic and spiritual ties, ties between Jews and Palestine are not in agreement with the facts of history or with the true basis of sound statehood. Judaism because it is a divine religion is not a nationality with independent existence. Furthermore the Jews are not one people with an independent personality because they are citizens of the countries to which they belong. (www.jewishvirtuallibrary.org/jsource/Peace/cove1.html; accessed 5 November 2012)

As I have already emphasized, this Charter was declared 'null and void' by Yasser Arafat in 1989.

82 On 5 June 1967, feeling threatened, the Israeli government, dominated by the right, decided to attack the coalition formed between Egypt, Syria, Iraq, and Jordan. Under the leadership of General Moshe Dayan, the Israeli Army (Tzahal) overran Sinai, the Golan Heights, Transjordan, Gaza, and East Jerusalem in six days.

83 In 1975, on the initiative of the Arab and African countries and the Soviet bloc, the General Assembly of the UN adopted a resolution that considered Zionism to be a form of racism and discrimination. This was annulled in 1991, but the denunciations continued and were repeated by an NGO at the first Durban Conference in South Africa, on the eve of the attacks of 11 September 2001.

84 This is how Pierre Vidal-Naquet puts it in *Assassins of Memory*, p. 131. See also Amnon Kapeliouk, *Sabra et Chatila: enquête sur un massacre* (Paris: Seuil, 1982).

Chapter 6   A Great and Destructive Madness

1 Adolphe Crémieux (1796–1880): lawyer, president of the Consistoire of the Alliance israélite universelle. He was the author of a decree which, in 1870, granted French citizenship to the Jews of Algeria: it was abolished by the Vichy regime.

2   Jacques Derrida, letter of August 1952, Institut mémoires de l'édition contemporaine (IMEC). Thanks to Benoît Peeters for drawing my attention to this, and see his *Derrida*, trans. Andrew Brown (Cambridge: Polity, 2012), p. 56. See also Jacques Derrida and Élisabeth Roudinesco, *For what tomorrow: a dialogue*, trans. Jeff Fort (Stanford, CA: Stanford University Press, 2004), chapter on anti-Semitism. Note that Derrida here points to the link between anti-Semitism and stupidity.

3   A survey by the Institut français d'opinion publique, 'Les Français et le problème juif' ['The French and the Jewish problem'], quoted in *Le Nouvel Adam*, December 1966. See also Valérie Igounet, *Histoire du négationnisme en France* (Paris: Seuil, 2000), p. 116.

4   The play had just been put on at the Odéon-Théâtre de France in April 1966, directed by Roger Blin: the performance caused a scandal. See Jean Genet, *Théâtre complet*, ed. Michel Corvin and Albert Dichy (Paris: Gallimard, 2002). On the scandal provoked by the former supporters of French Algeria and the courageous decision of André Malraux, then minister of culture, to ban performances, see Edmund White, *Genet* (London: Picador in association with Chatto & Windus, 1994), pp. 561–9.

5   Maurienne, *Le déserteur* (Paris: Minuit, 1960).

6   Teaching generally stopped at the end of June.

7   My father wrote a book on the subject and possessed an almost complete library on anti-Semitism and the Jewish question, which I inherited. See my *Généalogies* (Paris: Fayard, 1994).

8   See Catherine Simon, *Algérie: les années pieds rouges* (Paris: La Découverte, 2009).

9   Pierre Vidal-Naquet emphasizes this in his *The Jews: history, memory, and the present*, trans. David Ames Curtis (New York and Chichester: Columbia University Press, 1996).

10 Aimé Césaire, *Discourse on colonialism*, trans. Joan Pinkham (New York: Monthly Review Press, 2000), p. 36. And his celebrated words: 'Hitler? Rosenberg? No, Renan.'

11 The idea of a new anti-Semitism has won support in France from Jacques Givet, *La gauche contre Israël? Essai sur le néo-antisémitisme* (Paris: Pauvert, 1968). It was then taken up by Pierre-André Taguieff and others, keen either to revise history and turn the Enlightenment into the antechamber to Auschwitz or to uncover anti-Semitism where there is actually none. I will return to this in chapter 7. In the United States, the debate became extremely violent and was focused on the review *Commentary*, which also explains Noam Chomsky's attitude, as we shall see.

12 See Alain Dieckhoff (ed.), *L'État d'Israël* (Paris: Fayard, 2008), p. 10.

13 The successive charters of the PLO are available online. I will be returning to the question of the Jewish state in chapter 7.

14 Henry Rousso coined the French term *'négationnisme'* in 1987: it denotes Holocaust denial and replaces the inadequate term

'revisionism'. See his *The Vichy syndrome: history and memory in France since 1944*, trans. Arthur Goldhammer (Cambridge, MA, and London: Harvard University Press, 1991). Holocaust denial is not a revision of history, as its proponents would claim, but a pathological discourse that consists in denying the existence of the genocide of the Jews and more precisely the existence of the gas chambers. We should also note that Holocaust deniers are not interested in the extermination of the mentally ill, the gypsies, or the Jehovah's Witnesses, which clearly shows that their denial is essentially a form of anti-Semitism.

15   This is the term used by Yosef Hayim Yerushalmi and taken up by Pierre Vidal-Naquet.

16   Maurice Bardèche, *Nuremberg ou la terre promise* (Paris: Les Sept Couleurs, 1948).

17   Paul Rassinier, *Le mensonge d'Ulysse: regard sur la littérature concentrationnaire* (Paris: La Vieille Taupe, 1979; first published 1950).

18   Pierre Vidal-Naquet, in *Assassins of memory: essays on the denial of the Holocaust*, trans. and with a foreword by Jeffrey Mehlman (New York: Columbia University Press, 1992), has listed in seven points the methods used by Holocaust deniers. See also Igounet, *Histoire du négationnisme*.

19   Vidal-Naquet, *Assassins of memory*, p. 118.

20   According to Vidal-Naquet, ibid.

21   He drew inspiration from a famous phrase of Hegel's, repeated by Marx, describing the French Revolution: the words are strangely reminiscent of the story of Jacob's struggle with the Angel: 'Spirit often seems to have forgotten and lost itself, but inwardly opposed to itself, it is inwardly working ever forward (as when Hamlet says of the ghost of his father, "Well said, old mole! canst work i' the ground so fast?")'.

22   On Serge Thion's previous relations with Pierre Vidal-Naquet, Edgar Morin, and Nadine Fresco, see Igounet, *Histoire du négationnisme*, p. 258.

23   He left the ranks of Holocaust deniers in 1981, stating that he strongly disapproved of Faurisson's views.

24   Holocaust denial exists in several countries, but the Faurisson case really is a 'French exception', as it is bound up with the history of the literary avant-gardes and the teaching given in the seraglio of the *khâgnes* [highly selective classes for post-baccalaureate students – Trans.] – in other words, where future students of the École normale supérieure are trained. I shall come back to this in chapter 7.

25   François Dosse, *History of structuralism*, vol. 2: *Sign sets, 1967–present*, trans. Deborah Glassman (Minneapolis and London: University of Minnesota Press, 1997), p. 11; Noam Chomsky, *Syntactic structures*, 2nd edn (Berlin and Hawthorne, NY: Mouton de Gruyter, 2002); Chomsky, *Language and thought* (Wakefield, RI, and London: Moyer Bell, 1993). On the impact of Chomsky's ideas on

psychoanalysis, see Roudinesco, *Jacques Lacan & Co.: a history of psychoanalysis in France, 1925–1985*, trans. Jeffrey Mehlman (London: Free Association, 1990). On the cognitivist revolution in psychiatry, see Roudinesco, *Why psychoanalysis?*, trans. Rachel Bowlby (New York and Chichester: Columbia University Press, 2001). I was trained as a linguist and, about the time I was taking my Masters with Todorov, personally witnessed the corruption of a whole generation of young linguists who had gone over to Chomskyism and were not interested in anything except the description of phrases such as: 'It is the cat's milk that the dog is drinking, the cat's milk is being drunk by the dog, the cat's milk that the dog is drinking is warm, the cat does not like the dog drinking its milk and chased the dog who was drinking it', etc. Following the Chomskyan 'revolution', Jean-Claude Milner ended his own career as a linguist.

26　Chomsky's name for the capitalist imperialism composed of 'gigantic immortal persons' (transcontinental companies in finance, industry, and commerce which share out the planet's wealth between themselves) is TINA ('There Is No Alternative'). He contrasts them with 'people of flesh and blood'. See Noam Chomsky, 'Taking control of our lives: freedom, sovereignty, and other endangered species' (talk given at Santa Fe, New Mexico, 26 February 2000), available at: www.ratical.org/co-globalize/NC022600.html.

27　A novel in three volumes by Alexander Solzhenitsyn, published in English translation in 1974–8 and in French in 1974–6.

28　Noam Chomsky and Edward S. Herman, *Bains de sang constructifs: dans les faits et la propagande*, together with Jean-Pierre Faye, *L'Archipel Bloodbath*, trans. Marie-Odile and Jean-Pierre Faye (Paris: Seghers/Laffont, 1974). *Bains de sang* is a translation of *Counter-revolutionary violence: bloodbaths in fact and propaganda*. See also *Change*, 24, October 1975, for Chomsky's letters to Jean-Pierre Faye.

29　Noam Chomsky, 'Les raisons de mon engagement politique', in *Noam Chomsky*, ed. Jean Bricmont and Julie Franck (Paris: Éditions de l'Herne, 2007), p. 308.

30　Robert Faurisson, *Mémoire en défense contre ceux qui m'accusent de falsifier l'histoire: la question des chambres à gaz* (Paris: La Vieille Taupe, 1980), with a preface by Noam Chomsky. (Arno Mayer, who tried in vain to stop him writing this preface, confirmed to me that Chomsky had not read the book.) See also Serge Thion, *Vérité historique, ou Vérité politique? Le dossier de l'affaire Faurisson, la question des chambres à gaz* (Paris: La Vieille Taupe, 1980).

31　Rudolf Höss, *Commandant of Auschwitz: the autobiography of Rudolf Höss*, trans. Constantine FitzGibbon, with an introduction by Primo Levi, trans. Joachim Neugroschel (London: Phoenix, 2000); Saul Friedländer, *Counterfeit Nazi: the ambiguity of good*, trans. Charles Fullman (London: Weidenfeld & Nicolson, 1969).

32　*Le Monde*, 5 July 1980, p. 23.

33 William Shakespeare, *The Merchant of Venice*, Act III, scene 1. Shakespeare had been inspired partly by the Marrano Jewish doctor Rodrigo Lopez, who had been hanged, drawn, and quartered after being (wrongly) accused by Robert Devereux, earl of Essex (1566–1601), the queen's favourite, of having plotted to poison her. Devereux was beheaded in turn.

34 In reference to the Naqba. Ur Shlonsky emphasizes this in 'Israël et le sionisme', in Bricmont and Franck (eds), *Noam Chomsky*, p. 330. See also Noam Chomsky, 'Réponses à mes détracteurs parisiens . . .', ibid., pp. 219–27.

35 Robert F. Barsky: *Noam Chomsky: a life of dissent* (Cambridge, MA, and London: MIT Press, 1997), pp. 11–12.

36 Noam Chomsky: 'French intellectual life has, in my opinion, been turned into something cheap and meretricious by the "star" system. It is something like Hollywood. Thus we go from one absurdity to another – Stalinism, existentialism, structuralism, Lacan, Derrida – some of them obscene (Stalinism), some simply infantile and ridiculous (Lacan and Derrida). What is striking, however, is the pomposity and self-importance, at each stage.' See Bricmont and Franck (eds), *Noam Chomsky*, p. 213.

37 Barsky, *Noam Chomsky*, p. 197.

38 Vidal-Naquet, *Assassins of memory*, p. 70.

39 This did not stop him claiming later on that his country was the only one in which he could express himself freely.

40 Noam Chomsky: 'Some elementary comments on the rights of freedom of expression', available at www.chomsky.info/articles/19801011.htm. At that date, the inadequate term 'revisionism' was used to refer to Holocaust denial.

41 Alan Sokal and Jean Bricmont, *Intellectual impostures: postmodern philosophers' abuse of science*, 2nd edn (London: Profile, 1999). The 'imposters' include Henri Bergson, Gilles Deleuze, Michel Foucault, Paul Virilio, Jean Baudrillard, Jacques Derrida, Régis Debray, Jacques Lacan, etc. I have replied to this book in 'Sokal et Bricmont sont-ils des imposteurs?', *L'Infini*, 562, summer 1998.

42 Jean Bricmont, 'Chomsky, Faurisson et Vidal-Naquet', in Bricmont and Franck (eds), *Noam Chomsky*, p. 276.

43 Norman Finkelstein, *The Holocaust industry: reflections on the exploitation of Jewish suffering*, with a new foreword and new postscript (London and New York: Verso, 2001). For the severe criticism with which this book was met, see Dominique Vidal, 'Ambiguïtés', *Le Monde diplomatique*, 565, April 2001.

44 See Françoise S. Ouzan, *Histoire des Américains juifs* (Paris: André Versaille, 2008).

45 See 'On the future of Israel and Palestine', Ilan Pappé and Noam Chomsky interviewed by Frank Barat, 6 June 2008, in *Counterpunch*: available at www.chomsky.info/interviews/20080606.htm. See also Noam Chomsky, *What we say goes: conversations on U.S. power in*

a changing world: interviews with David Barsamian (New York: Metropolitan Books, 2007).

46 'The legitimacy of violence as a political act?', debate between Noam Chomsky, Hannah Arendt, and Susan Sontag, 15 December 1967, available at www.chomsky.info/debates/19671215.htm.

47 Yitzak Rabin (1922–1995): prime minister of Israel between 1974 and 1977 and again between 1992 and 1995; assassinated by a fundamentalist Israeli Jew, Ygal Amir, hostile to the Oslo Accords. Arafat and Rabin famously shook hands in the presence of Bill Clinton in Washington on 13 September 1993.

48 See Charles Enderlin, *Le grand aveuglement: Israël et l'irrésistible ascension de l'islam radical* (Paris: Albin Michel, 2009).

49 In Egypt, Iran, Lebanon, etc.

50 Roger Garaudy, *The mythical foundations of Israeli policy* (London: Studies Forum International, 1997); available at: https://ia700308.us. archive.org/19/items/TheFoundingMythsOfIsraeliPolitics/RGfounding .pdf, p. 5 (translation modified). For an analysis of Garaudy as a Holocaust denier, see Michaël Prazan and Adrien Minard, *Roger Garaudy: itinéraire d'une négation* (Paris: Calmann-Lévy, 2007). Despite several significant errors, this is an interesting work.

51 At the European elections in June 2009, they formed a list of candidates described as 'anti-Zionist for a Europe freed from censorship, communitarianism, speculators, and NATO' – a way of designating the Jews, yet again, as responsible for all the misfortunes in the world.

52 This was actually article 9 of law no. 90-615 of 13 July 1990, inserting an article 24 into the law of 1881 on press freedom: 'Those who have contested by one of the means described in article 23 the existence of one or more crimes against humanity as defined in article 6 of the statute of the International Military Tribunal annexed to the London Agreement of 8 August, committed either by members of an organization declared criminal in application of article 9 of the said statute, or by a person declared to be guilty of such crimes by a French or international jurisdiction, will be sentenced to the punishments laid down in the 6th line of article 24.'

53 'Any deed committed by a man who causes damage to another obliges the person by whom the damage occurred to repair it.'

54 'La loi menace-t-elle les historiens?', interview with Françoise Chandernagor, *L'Histoire*, 306, February 2006.

55 As was the case during the Tehran conference on the Holocaust in December 2006.

56 In Austria and Germany, as I have said, the laws are even stricter than in France. It is worth noting that one should not confuse the ban on teaching, which, in the case of Holocaust denial, racism, anti-Semitism, etc., is a salutary measure, with the ban on publishing. David Irving was given a severe sentence in the United States after a trial he had brought against Deborah Lipstadt, who was herself

opposed to any law banning the right to expression of Holocaust deniers. On this, see Derrida and Roudinesco, *For what tomorrow.*

57 Four dead and twenty-six wounded.

58 Declaration on radio station TF1, 3 October 1980.

59 It should be pointed out that the English word 'lobby' [used by Barre himself in this exchange – Trans.], referring to an enclosure for animals, a corridor, a hall, or a pressure group, does not have the negative connotations it does in France.

60 A full transcription of the interview is available on the Internet.

61 Raphaël Enthoven has confirmed to me that his interlocutor was quite unaware of the real significance of his remarks. See also Claude Lanzmann, 'Raymond Barre, un "Français innocent" ', *Les Temps modernes*, 642, February–March 2007.

62 Renaud Camus, *La campagne de France* (Paris: Fayard, 2002).

63 A programme, since discontinued, in which publications in the human sciences, philosophy, and literature were discussed in a very lively way.

64 Camus, *La campagne de France*, pp. 48 and 55.

65 I was closely involved in this affair, as it was Olivier Bétourné, then vice-president of the Arthème Fayard bookshop, who was behind the book being withdrawn from sale. It was later put back into circulation, with anything that obviously tended to incite violence having been cut. Jacques Derrida and I discussed this affair at some length in *For what tomorrow.*

66 Renaud was a very frequent guest of American universities.

67 This adjective was, it is true, exaggerated and inappropriate.

68 *Le Monde*, 25 May 2000.

69 Pierre-André Taguieff, *Rising from the muck: the new anti-Semitism in Europe*, trans. Patrick Camiller (Chicago: Ivan R. Dee, 2004); and Taguieff, *La judéophobie des modernes: des Lumières au Jihad mondial* (Paris: Odile Jacob, 2008).

70 Alain Finkielkraut, *L'imparfait du présent: pièces brèves* (Paris: Gallimard, 2002), p. 54.

71 Marc-Édouard Nabe, *Au régal des vermines* (Paris: Le Dilettante, 2006; first published 1985).

72 Morgan Sportès and Gérard Miller were courageous enough to attack Nabe directly during two television programmes, one on *Apostrophes* on 15 February 1985, the other on Laurent Ruquier's programme in 2006.

73 Marc-Édouard Nabe, *Non* (Monaco: Éditions du Rocher, 1999), p. 26. In anti-Semitic and Holocaust-denying discourse, Hiroshima is always used against the Shoah. The same is true of the Stalinist Gulag.

74 Statement made on 20 January 2009, available on the Internet. These remarks need to be compared with those made on 20 January 2009 to Lorraine Millot, the correspondent of the daily *Libération*, in Moscow, on the occasion of Barack Obama's election as president of the United States. Noting the extent to which a majority of Russians were racist, sometimes without even realizing it, she quotes a researcher

at the Academy of Sciences who was not surprised by this situation: 'Racism has become stronger recently in Russia, and we even hear comments of the kind, "If they have a negro as president in America today, then tomorrow we'll have a Jew in Russia."' Obviously, this is a racist remark, but, lurking in the shadows, we can make out the decisive element in these words: racism always springs from anti-Semitism.

75 I have here quoted the work of several of them, including Idith Zertal.

76 'Un historien dans la cité', a homage paid at the Bibliothèque nationale de France on 10 November 2006.

77 See Régine Azria, 'L'État d'Israël et la diaspora, une relation complexe', in Dieckhoff (ed.), *L'État d'Israël*, pp. 333–49.

78 *Controverses*, 4, 'Les alterjuifs', February 2007. I am not citing the names mentioned on this list, precisely because it claims to pillory exclusively Jews, which comes down to applying methods worthy of anti-Semites. Tariq Ramadan used the same method when he attempted to draw up, in a highly critical article, a 'list' of so-called communitarian Jews in which, of course, at least one non-Jew appeared. See his 'Critique des nouveaux intellectuels communautaires', 3 October 2003, an article turned down by *Le Monde* and *Libération*. How is a Jew to be distinguished from a non-Jew? This is the main question raised by anti-Semites, and we have seen what a nightmare the State of Israel became embroiled in when it had to define who was a Jew without resorting to 'stigmas' of body or name.

79 Edgar Morin, Sami Naïr, and Danielle Sallenave, 'Israël–Palestine: le cancer', *Le Monde*, 3 June 2002.

80 A neologism invented by the author to define a so-called science of research aimed at laying bare impostures.

81 For instance, that between Carla Bruni and Nicolas Sarkozy.

82 Paul Éric Blanrue, *Le monde contre soi: anthologie des propos contre les Juifs, le judaïsme et le sionisme*, with a preface by Yann Moix (Paris: Éditions Blanche, 2007); later renamed *Dictionnaire de l'antisémitisme*.

83 Ibid., p. 7.

84 Thierry Meyssan, *L'effroyable imposture* (Paris: Carnot, 2002). Under the title *Nicolas Sarkozy, Israël et les Juifs*, Blanrue's book, which was issued by a Belgian publisher in 2009, was not put on sale in bookshops, which enabled the author to claim, in an interview with Meyssan on 27 May 2009 (Voltaire network, online) that he was now a victim of Zionists, having been hailed by the B'nai Brith for his denunciation of anti-Semites.

85 John J. Mearheimer and Stephen Walt, *The Israel lobby and US foreign policy* (London: Penguin, 2008); Noam Chomsky, 'The Israel lobby?', 30 March 2006, available at: www.chomsky.info/articles/20060328.htm.

86 Jean-Paul Sartre, *Anti-Semite and Jew*, trans. George J. Becker (New York: Schocken Books, 1976, pp. 17 and 47.

Chapter 7 Inquisitorial Figures

1 Traces of this can be found, as I have pointed out, even in the founding charter of Hamas quoted above.

2 To this was added the theme of the Jesuit plot – Jesuits, especially in the Enlightenment, being often compared with Jews.

3 Fernand Braudel, *The Identity of France*, trans. Siân Reynolds, 3 vols (London: Collins, 1988–90).

4 Élisabeth Roudinesco, *Jacques Lacan & Co.: a history of psychoanalysis in France, 1925–1985*, trans. Jeffrey Mehlman (London: Free Association, 1990). On the resurgence of anti-Semitism in the history of the French psychoanalytical movement, see especially the section 'Heritages'. See also Roudinesco, *Why psychoanalysis?*, trans. Rachel Bowlby (New York and Chichester: Columbia University Press, 2001).

5 Bela Grunberger and Janine Chasseguet-Smirgel, *L'univers contestationnaire* (1969), new edn (Paris: In Press, 2004), p. 53, with a new foreword and without the subtitle referring to Christians.

6 Ibid., p. 51.

7 On 3 May, in *L'Humanité*, Georges Marchais, the secretary general of the French Communist Party, wrote some words that would become famous in which he called Cohn-Bendit a 'German anarchist', thereby branding him simultaneously as the enemy of communism and the enemy of France. On 21 May, the government issued a warrant for the expulsion of the young man: this triggered one of the most amazing demonstrations of the period, since it took as its slogan 'We are all German Jews'.

8 And not, as they claimed, to 'protect their patients'.

9 Anne-Lise Stern, *Le savoir déporté: camps, histoire, psychanalyse*, with a foreword, *Une vie à l'oeuvre*, by Nadine Fresco and Martine Leibovici (Paris: Seuil, 2004), p. 223. I recounted this whole affair in *Jacques Lacan & Co.*

10 *Le Nouvel Observateur*, 3 May 1969.

11 Thus, Paul Yonnet thinks that those who took part in the events of 1968 under the slogan 'We are all German Jews' bear a heavy responsibility for the hatred that subsequently developed in France against the nation. See Yonnet, *Voyage au centre du malaise français* (Paris: Gallimard, 1993). For the study of these aggressive discourses, see Serge Audier, *La pensée anti-68: essai sur les origines d'une restauration intellectuelle* (Paris: La Découverte, 2008). Furthermore, I have to say that I do not agree with Jean-Claude Milner's subtle analysis, which concludes that, in the slogan, the signifier 'German' serves to disguise the signifier 'Jewish' and that the demonstrators could simply have said 'We are all Jews': 'In comparison with the emergence of the name "Jewish", the formula is playing a very specific role. It is its task to make up for the risk of the subjective break which the name

"Jewish" still brings with it.' See *L'arrogance du présent: regards sur une décennie 1965–1975* (Paris: Grasset, 2009), pp. 174–5. Of course, this honest, intelligent, and personal analysis should in no way be confused with that of those who vehementhy voiced their support for *L'univers contestationnaire*.

12 Founded in 1970 by Georges Liebert, an anti-Marxist and supporter of French Algeria, and Patrick Devedjian, who had come from the far right and the Occident group, the review *Contrepoint* gave birth in 1978 to the review *Commentaire*, edited by Jean-Claude Casanova, and modelled on the neo-conservative American review *Commentary*.

13 Pierre-André Taguieff, *Les contre-réactionnaires: le progressisme entre illusion et imposture* (Paris: Denoël, 2007).

14 In the same vein, Chasseguet-Smirgel denounced male homosexuals with unprecedented violence, stating that perversion had now been brought to its peak by the dominant culture. In fact, she identified homosexuality with sodomy, drawing on the vocabulary of the mediaeval period and condemning as 'against nature', and thus 'anal', any attempt to legalize homosexual couples. See 'Entretiens avec J. Chasseguet-Smirgel', *Revue française de psychanalyse*, 54 (1990), pp. 187–8.

15 Grunberger and Chasseguet-Smirgel, *L'univers contestationnaire*, p. 36. It is hardly common practice in enlightened circles to use words like this to refer to such a historian.

16 I studied this question in my *Jacques Lacan & Co.*

17 This happened on 5 May 1986, at a meeting organized by Alain de Mijolla: I had been invited with a view to holding a conference on psychoanalysts during the Second World War. A few months later, I published the second volume of my *Jacques Lacan and Co.*, and in it I revealed for the first time the names of the two authors of *L'univers contestationnaire*, as well as the part played by German psychoanalysts in the so-called salvaging operation and the affair of the failed collaboration of René Laforgue. René Major had given me considerable support in this affair, criticizing the attitude of the SPP, of which he was a member. My renewed thanks go to him. The conference in question was held on 3 May 1987, under the aegis of the Association internationale d'histoire de la psychanalyse, ten days before Klaus Barbie's trial opened. The question of Ernest Jones's collaboration with the Nazis was not discussed directly. See my 'Au temps des psychanazistes', *Libération*, 16–17 May 1987.

18 Louis-Ferdinand Céline, *Journey to the end of the night* and *Death on the instalment plan* (first published in French in 1932 and 1936 respectively). Céline's novels have been published by Gallimard, in the prestigious 'Bibliothèque de la Pléiade'.

19 Louis-Ferdinand Céline, *Féerie pour une autre fois* (Paris: Gallimard, 1952), p. 60.

20 Albert Cohen, *Ô vous frères humains* (Paris: Gallimard, 1972), pp. 172–5.

21 Hannah Arendt, Jean-Paul Sartre, Primo Levi, and many others had attempted this, as I have already shown on the basis of the work of Enzo Traverso.

22 Georges Stevens and Samuel Fuller, who accompanied the American Army, were the first directors to film the liberation of the camps. See Antoine de Baecque, *Camera historica: the century in cinema*, trans. Ninon Vinsonneau and Jonathan Magidof (New York: Columbia University Press, 2012).

23 I am here using the concept of the 'real' in the Lacanian sense: that which is foreclosed and heterogeneous and returns in reality.

24 It is, by the way, ridiculous to accuse Alain Resnais and Jean Cayrol of having disguised the specific nature of the genocide of the Jews. Likewise, it is incongruous to accuse Sartre, as some people have, of disguising the extermination in favour of a reflection on Drumont's anti-Semitism. Claude Lanzmann has sprung to the defence of Alain Resnais, and rightly so, in his *The Patagonian Hare: a memoir*, trans. Frank Wynne (London: Atlantic, 2012), p. 512.

25 Alain Resnais' film *Night and Fog* (1955) was commissioned by Anatole Dauman and the Committee for the History of the Second World War, to commemorate the tenth anniversary of the liberation of the camps. This was the first film dedicated to the memory of those who died in the deportation.

26 Antoine de Baecque, *La cinéphilie: invention d'un regard, histoire d'une culture, 1944–1968* (Paris: Fayard, 2003), p. 206.

27 Jacques Rivette, 'De l'abjection', in *Les Cahiers du cinéma*, June 1961. Gillo Pontecorvo (1919–2006) was an Italian film director: Emmanuelle Riva starred in the title role of his film *Kapo* (1959).

28 As Antoine de Baecque points out, in *Camera historica*, Jean-Luc Godard was the first director who sought to define an ethics of the representation of the Shoah.

29 Martin Heidegger, *Being and Time* (Oxford: Blackwell, 1978); first published in German in 1927.

30 I have discussed all these debates in my *Jacques Lacan & Co.* But various works on the subject have shed significant light: Denis Hollier (ed.), *A New history of French literature* (Cambridge, MA, and London: Harvard University Press, 1994); Gisèle Sapiro, *La guerre des écrivains, 1940–1953* (Paris: Fayard, 1999); Dominique Janicaud, *Heidegger en France*, vol. 1: *Récit* (Paris: Albin Michel, 2001), vol. 2, *Entretiens* – interviews with, among others, Kostas Axelos, Michel Deguy, Jacques Derrida, Gérard Granel, Jean-Pierre Faye, Edgar Morin, Jean-Luc Marion, Jean-Luc Nancy and Philippe Lacoue-Labarthe (Paris: Albin Michel, 2001).

31 Jean-Paul Sartre, 'A propos de l'existentialisme: mise au point', *Action*, 29 December 1944; Michel Contat and Michel Rybalka, *Les écrits de Sartre* (Paris: Gallimard, 1970), p. 654; Hugo Ott, *Martin Heidegger: a political life*, trans. Allan Blunden (London: HarperCollins, 1993).

32 This would be the position adopted by Maurice Blanchot, *Les intellectuels en question* (Paris: Fourbis, 1996), and of Philippe Lacoue-Labarthe, *La fiction du politique* (Paris: Christian Bourgois, 1988).

33 Quoted by Emmanuel Faye, *Introduction du nazisme dans la philosophie* (Paris: Albin Michel, 2005), pp. 490 and 492.

34 When he was interviewed in 1963, Adorno replied: 'Anyone who surveys the continuity of my work should not be allowed to compare me with Heidegger, whose philosophy is fascistic right down to its most intimate components'; see Theodor Adorno, *The Jargon of Authenticity*, trans. Knut Tarnowski and Frederic Will (London and New York: Routledge, 1973).

35 I have detailed the career of Jean Beaufret (1907–1982), who was analysed by Lacan, in Roudinesco, *Jacques Lacan & Co.*, pp. 298–9. On the introduction of Heidegger's thought into France, the main work is Janicaud, *Heidegger en France*. Beaufret was so eager to deny that Heidegger was a Nazi that, in two letters, of 1978 and 1979, he encouraged his former student, Robert Faurisson, to doubt the existence of the gas chambers. See Michel Kajman, 'Heidegger et le fil invisible', *Le Monde*, 22 January 1988.

36 He merely said 'I made a stupid mistake'.

37 Victor Farías, *Heidegger et le nazisme* (Lagrasse: Verdier, 1987), with a preface by Christian Jambet; Eng. trans., as *Heidegger and Nazism*, ed. Joseph Margolis and Tom Rockmore, trans. Paul Burrell et al. (Philadelphia: Temple University Press, 1989). The book, written in Spanish and German, was initially published in French, which confirms that the controversy over Heidegger's Nazism involved mainly France.

38 At this date, Hugo Ott's book had not yet been translated into French, and it was generally considered that Heidegger's Nazism was limited to his period as rector [of Freiburg University] and did not imbue the rest of his work.

39 Farías, *Heidegger and Nazism*, pp. 12–13 and p. 39.

40 The history of the proletarian left and its philosophical founders, some of them Sartreans (Benny Lévy), others Lacanians or Althusserians (Christian Jambet, Jean-Claude Milner, Robert Linhart), remains to be written. I referred to this question in a chapter of my *Jacques Lacan* (New York: Columbia University Press, 1997). See also Milner, *L'arrogance du présent*; Benny Lévy, *Le nom de l'homme: dialogue avec Sartre* (Lagrasse: Verdier, 1991); Lévy, *L'espoir maintenant: les entretiens de 1980* (Lagrasse: Verdier, 1991); Alain Finkielkraut and Benny Lévy, *Le livre des livres: entretiens sur la laïcité* (Lagrasse: Verdier, 2006); and Virginie Linhart, *Le jour où mon père s'est tu* (Paris: Seuil, 2008).

41 This preface is not included in the English translation: see Victor Farías, *Heidegger et le nazisme* (Lagrasse: Verdier, 1987), p. 9.

42 Lacoue-Labarthe, *La fiction du politique*, p. 59.

43 On 13 November 1987, I wrote a letter to Jacques Derrida on Farías's work, pointing out that it was intellectually weak, but that it included information of which I was unaware. I pointed out the obvious divergence between the book and its preface (Archives de l'Institut mémoires de l'édition contemporaine [IMEC]). At that time, I had not yet analysed the relation between Lacan and Heidegger. But I never had any liking for Heidegger as a person, nor had I taken any particular interest in his philosophy. I explained all this to Derrida, whom I had criticized on this point.

44 Derrida, *Of spirit: Heidegger and the question*, trans. Geoffrey Bennington and Rachel Bowlby (Chicago: University of Chicago Press, 1989).

45 This term, first used by Derrida in 1967 in his *Of grammatology*, refers to an activity of unconscious thought ('It [*ça*] deconstructs itself') which consists in undoing without destroying a hegemonic or dominant system of thought. To deconstruct, as it were, is to resist the tyranny of the One, the *logos*, (Western) metaphysics in the very language in which it is expressed, with the same raw materials that one is shifting, moving around so as to produce moving and ever unsettled reconstructions. Derrida always said that he had used this term to mark his distance from the Heideggerian concepts of *Destruktion* and *Abbau* (destruction, demolition).

46 Derrida 'Circumfession', in Derrida and Geoffrey Bennington, *Jacques Derrida* (Chicago and London: University of Chicago Press, 1993), pp. 58 and 303.

47 His first text on Mandela was published in *Psyche*, the same year as *Of spirit*: see 'The laws of reflection: Nelson Mandela in admiration', in *Psyche: inventions of the other*, ed. Peggy Kamuf and Elizabeth Rottenberg (Stanford, CA: Stanford University Press, 2007).

48 In an unpublished nine-page letter to Claude Lanzmann on 30 January 2002, Derrida explained that, as a Jew, he was in a position to judge more severely than others the policies of the State of Israel (Archives de l'IMEC). See Benoît Peeters, *Derrida*, trans. Andrew Brown (Cambridge: Polity, 2012), p. 510.

49 Jacques Derrida, lecture given on 8 May 2004, at a meeting organized by *Le Monde diplomatique*, and published in the same journal in November 2004.

50 Derrida travelled to Jerusalem on several occasions to meet Israeli and Palestinian intellectuals.

51 Derrida and Roudinesco, *For what tomorrow: a dialogue*, trans. Jeff Fort (Stanford, CA: Stanford University Press, 2004), p. 195.

52 Derrida, 'Heidegger, l'enfer des philosophes', an interview with Didier Eribon, was first published in *Le Nouvel observateur* (6–12 November 1987); Eng. trans. as 'Heidegger, the philosophers' hell', in *Points: interviews, 1974–1994*, ed. Elisabeth Weber, trans. Peggy Kamuf et al. (Stanford, CA: Stanford University Press, 1995), pp. 181–90.

53 Luc Ferry and Alain Renaut, *French philosophy of the sixties*, trans. Mary Schnackenberg Cattani (Amherst: University of Massachusetts Press, 1990).

54 See Roudinesco, *Jacques Lacan and Co.*, p. xv.

55 On the career of Henri (Hendrik) de Man, see Zeev Sternhell, *Ni droite, ni gauche: l'idéologie fasciste en France*, 4th edn (Paris: Gallimard, 2012).

56 Published in *Le Soir*, 4 March 1941, and quoted in Paul de Man, 'The Jews and contemporary literature', in Martin McQuillan, *Paul de Man* (London: Routledge, 2001), pp. 127–9, at p. 129.

57 Quoted by David Lehman, 'Deconstructing de Man's life', *Newsweek*, 15 February 1988, p. 63. See also David Lehman, *Signs of the times: deconstruction and the fall of Paul de Man* (New York: Poseidon Press, 1991), pp. 24 and 79; Jeffrey Mehlman, *Genealogy of the text: literature, psychoanalysis and politics in modern France* (Cambridge: Cambridge University Press, 1995).

58 Interview with Hassan Arfaoui, 25 September 2003; available online.

59 Jacques Derrida, 'Biodegradables: seven diary fragments', *Critical Inquiry*, 15, Summer 1989; *Memoires for Paul de Man*; 'Réponse à Élisabeth de Fontenay', papers of the Collège international de philosophie, session of 10 March 1990. The whole affair is discussed in Peeters, *Derrida*.

60 Emmanuel Faye, *Heidegger: the introduction of Nazism into philosophy in light of the unpublished seminars of 1933–1935*, trans. Michael B. Smith (New Haven, CT, and London: Yale University Press, 2009), p. 320.

61 Victor Farías, *Allende, la face cachée: antisémitisme et eugénisme* (Paris: Granchet, 2006). All this information, as well as Allende's thesis, is available on the website of the President Allende Foundation. In 2006, this foundation took Farias to court for defaming the memory of a dead man. See also Élisabeth Roudinesco, 'La mémoire salie d'Allende', *Libération*, 12 July 2005.

62 Jeffrey Mehlman, 'Blanchot philosémite', conference on 'The Jewish face of contemporary thought', Alliance israélite universelle, 18 May 2008.

63 Jeffrey Mehlman, *Legacies of anti-Semitism in France* (Minneapolis: Minnesota University Press, 1983). His article on Maurice Blanchot was published in the review *Tel Quel* in 1982 in a poor (in his view) translation, and thus incomprehensible. It was, nonetheless, hailed as a path-breaking revelation of some old French demons by many journalists. Jeffrey Mehlman's reply appeared in the French review *L'Infini*, 1, Winter 1983, p. 123.

64 In 2005, Régis Debray compared Mehlman to the great historian Robert Paxton, the author of the first essential book on Vichy: *Vichy France: old guard and new order, 1940–1944* (London: Barrie & Jenkins, 1972). 'What Paxton was to our history, Jeffrey Mehlman is to our literary history [. . .] and lo and behold, caught in the act':

preface to Jeffrey Mehlman, *Émigrés à New York: les intellectuels français à Manhattan, 1940–1944* (Paris: Albin Michel, 2005), p. 10. (This is the French translation of Jeffrey Mehlman, *Émigré New York: French intellectuals in wartime Manhattan, 1940–1944* (Baltimore and London: Johns Hopkins University Press, 2000)).

65 Jean Giraudoux, *Pleins pouvoirs* (Paris: Gallimard, 1939), p. 66.

66 Ibid., p. 26.

67 Lacan, *The four fundamental concepts of psycho-analysis*, ed. Jacques-Alain Milner, trans. Alan Sheridan (London: Vintage, 1998), p. 189.

68 Mehlman, *Legacies of anti-Semitism in France*.

69 Mehlman, 'Blanchot philosémite'.

70 Christophe Bident had devoted 500 pages to this question, and, when you read his description of all the horrors that were poured over Blanchot, the man, and his work after the publication of Mehlman's book, you are dumbstruck. See Bident, *Maurice Blanchot, partenaire invisible: essai biographique* (Seyssel: Champ Vallon, 1998).

71 Salomon Malka, 'Maurice Blanchot et le judaïsme', *L'Arche*, 373, May 1988, and *Lévinas, la vie et sa trace* (Paris: Jean-Claude Lattès, 2002).

72 Emmanuel Lévinas, 'Reflections on the philosophy of Hitlerism', trans. Seán Hand, *Critical Inquiry*, 17/1 (1990), pp. 63–71. It should be pointed out that, even at the period when Blanchot was writing such controversial texts, Lévinas did not in the slightest view him as an anti-Semite: 'He experienced Blanchot's monarchism as a curiosity that was barely compatible with the rest of his personality, though this incompatibility was itself thinkable': Bident, *Maurice Blanchot*, p. 41.

73 Harry E. Stewart and Rob Roy McGregor, 'Jean Genet's "Mentalité douteuse"', *Romance Quarterly*, 39 (1992), pp. 299–310; and *Jean Genet: from fascism to nihilism* (New York: Peter Lang, 1994). The two authors rely on cognitive-behaviourist psychiatry and make Genet into not just an anti-Semite, but a deviant with a troubled mind: a psychopathic personality, a sociopath, anti-social, disturbed, and weak.

74 Jean-Paul Sartre, *Saint Genet, actor and martyr* (New York: New American Library, 1964).

75 There are in fact several articles gathered in two works by Éric Marty: *Bref séjour à Jérusalem* (Paris: Gallimard, 2003) and *Jean Genet, post-scriptum* (Lagrasse: Verdier, 2006).

76 Marty, *Bref séjour*, pp. 57, 73, and 165.

77 In the new edition of *L'univers concentrationnaire*, p. 21, Janine Chasseguet-Smirgel hailed the courage shown by Éric Marty in his denunciation of Genet's anti-Semitism without actually realizing that she was dealing with a Lacanian who (quite unlike Mehlman) exonerated Lacan of any anti-Semitism, but forgot to mention that Lacan had been one of the commentators on Genet's dramatic works, especially *The Balcony*: see Jacques Lacan, *Le Séminaire*, V: *Les formations de l'inconscient* (Paris: Seuil, 1998), pp. 262–8.

78 The best works to consult include Edmund White, *Genet* (London: Picador in association with Chatto & Windus, 1994), with a chronology by Albert Dichy; and Hadrien Laroche, *Le dernier Genet* (Paris: Seuil, 1997). See also Michelle Perrot, *Histoire de chambres* (Paris: Seuil, 2009), with its fine portrait of Genet, which brings out how, throughout his life and right up to his death, the hotel room was the only place he could live in – a symbol of his wandering existence.

79 Ivan Jablonka, *Les vérités inavouables de Jean Genet* (Paris: Seuil, 2004).

80 Especially by Albert Dichy, 'La part d'ombre de Genet', *Le Monde*, 20 January 2005; Dichy, 'Il faut avoir le courage de lire Genet sans défaillir', and Hadrien Laroche, 'Une interrogation radicale', *Magazine littéraire*, 436, 1 December 2006.

81 Abel Barbin, *Herculine Barbin, dite Alexina B.*, ed. Michel Foucault (Paris: Gallimard, 1978).

82 As Derrida – another philosopher who devotes a sumptuous text to Genet – emphasizes. He calls him a great deconstructor of absolute knowledge and makes him 'marry' Hegel in accordance with a rite of funereal writing based closely on Talmudic exegesis: see *Glas*, trans. John P. Leavey, Jr., and Richard Rand (Lincoln: University of Nebraska Press, 1986).

83 On the fate of children placed, abandoned, and separated, and the role of Georges Heuyer (1884–1977), see the book by my mother for which I wrote a foreword: Jenny Aubry, *Psychanalyse des enfants séparés: études cliniques, 1952–1986* (Paris: Denoël, 2003).

84 Henri Claude (1869–1945): French psychiatrist, a specialist in schizophrenia, the master of the first generation of French psychoanalysts, and the proponent of a 'Latinized' psychoanalysis.

85 White, *Genet*, p. 254.

86 Jean Genet, *Our Lady of the Flowers*, trans. Bernard Frechtman (London: Faber & Faber, 1990); first published in French in 1943.

87 To rebuke Genet, a man among other men, for having evaded deportation, as a prisoner of common law, at the very same time as millions of Jews were being exterminated, flies in the face of all Jewish thought before and after the Shoah. And yet this is just what his detractors do, convinced that, by brandishing the figure of the inquisitorial Jew, they are avenging the Jews. But 'Jewish vengeance' is a notion foreign to the tradition of Jewish humanism.

88 Jean Genet, *Funeral Rites*, trans. Bernard Frechtman (London: Faber & Faber, 1990).

89 Ibid.

90 We should point out that Emmanuel Lévinas had even seen Nazism as the greatest trial that Judaism had needed to face, insofar as affront and outrage had 'added a poignant savour of despair to humiliation': see *Lévinas*, ed. Catherine Chalier and Miguel Abensour (Paris: Éditions de l'Herne, 1991), p. 144.

91   Jean Genet, *L'enfant criminel*, first published in 1949; in *Oeuvres complètes*, vol. 5 (Paris: Gallimard, 1979), p. 389.

92   The Rote Armee Fraktion was a far-left terrorist group that, after 1968, supported urban guerrilla warfare and the murder of hostages so as to fight 'American imperialism' and its allies in the Federal Republic (whom they also reproached for their Nazi pasts). Its two main leaders, Andreas Baader and Ulrike Meinhof, were gaoled in 1972 in the top-security section of Stammheim prison in Stuttgart. They died in 1976, probably by their own hands, but the conditions of their death have never been completely cleared up. They were supported by Michel Foucault and Jean-Paul Sartre, who both disapproved of their political line but denounced the conditions in which they had been imprisoned. The Black Panther Party was a revolutionary African-American movement, founded in 1966 by Bobby Seale and Huey P. Newton: it faded away in 1982 as a result of internal rivalries, which Genet witnessed in difficult conditions. See White, *Genet*.

93   Jean Genet, 'Violence and brutality', first published in *Le Monde*, 2 September 1977; in Genet, *The declared enemy: texts and interviews*, ed. Albert Dichy, trans. Jeff Fort (Stanford, CA: Stanford University Press, 2004), pp. 171–7.

94   Genet, 'The tenacity of American blacks' (1977), ibid., pp. 159–63; 'Violence and brutality' (1977); 'Four hours in Chatila' (1982), ibid., pp. 208–28.

95   Genet, 'Interview with Hubert Fichte', first published in *Die Zeit*, 13 February 1976; in Genet, *The declared enemy*, pp. 118–51.

96   Jean Genet, *Prisoner of Love*, trans. Barbara Bray (New York: New York Review of Books, 2003).

97   Edward Said, 'Reflections on twenty years of Palestinian history', *Journal of Palestine Studies*, 20/4 (1991), pp. 12 and 15.

98   Tom Seguev, *Le septième million: les Israéliens et le génocide* (Paris: Liana Lévi, 1993), p. 218; see also Laroche, *Le dernier Genet*, p. 201.

99   Genet, *Prisoner of Love*, p. 271.

100 Ibid., p. 184.

101 Sartre, *Saint Genet, actor and martyr*, p. 203, note. When Derrida was violently attacked by Marty for denying the so-called anti-Semitism of Genet and also for supporting the Palestinian cause, he replied with a scathing quotation from Lévinas: 'To cite "the Holocaust" in order to say God is with us in all circumstances is as hateful as the *Gott mit uns* that appeared on the belts of the killers': *Magazine littéraire*, 419, April 2003, p. 34; remarks quoted by Alain David.

102 Hadrien Laroche noted this.

103 Sartre, *Saint Genet, actor and martyr*.

104 Aharon Appelfeld: an Israeli writer, born in 1932 in Romania. A left-wing Zionist, the author of some forty books, and a pupil of Gershom Scholem, he emigrated to Palestine in 1946. Roth makes him one of the heroes of the novel, another double of himself.

105 Philip Roth, *Operation Shylock: a confession* (London: Jonathan Cape, 1993).
106 Meir David Kahane (1932–1990): an Israeli-American rabbi and politician, the founder of the Jewish Defence League and then Kach, a far-right political party, exluded from the Knesset in 1984 for racism. He was assassinated by an extremist after exhorting American Jews to emigrate to Israel.
107 Yoram Hazony, *The Jewish State: the struggle for Israel's soul* (New York: Basic Books, 2000). The Second Intifida was triggered in September 2000, after Ariel Sharon's visit to the compound of the al-Aqsa mosque/Temple Mount. This visit was felt to be a provocation by the Palestinians, while on the day before Yasser Arafat had asked the Israeli prime minister, Ehud Barak, to ban it. At this date, Arafat faced the rise of Hamas, which was in fact favoured by successive Israeli governments, and the policies – disastrous as far as the peace process was concerned – of George Bush, the neo-conservative president who was driven by the idea that his country should lead a global crusade against the forces of evil.
108 This is similar to the denunciation in France of '*alterjuifs*'.

Index